I0812692

IMAGES
of America

AGAWAM AND FEEDING HILLS REVISITED

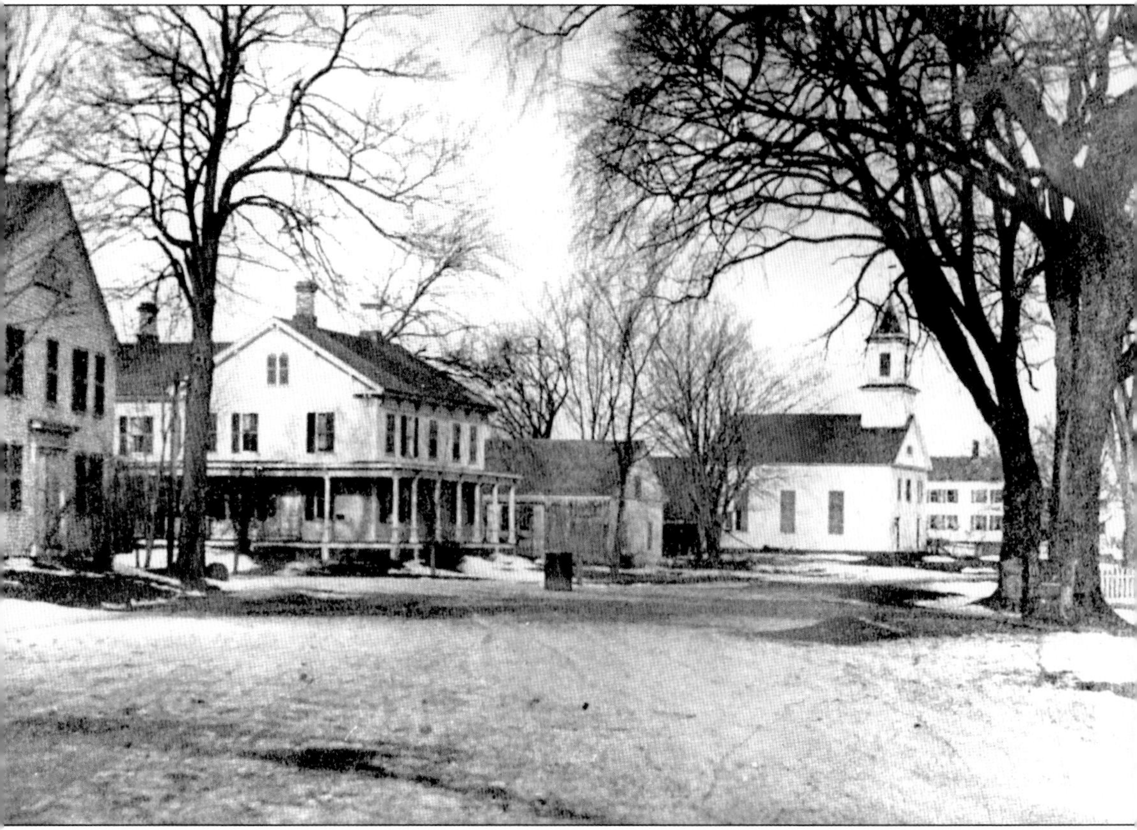

The Feeding Hills Center of more than a century ago was quintessential small-town New England. Although the 21st century has made its presence evident throughout Agawam, the Charles Wright House (center), Feeding Hills Congregational Church, and the house just beyond all still remain. The Hamilton House (far left) was demolished in the 1970s. (Author's collection.)

IMAGES
of America

AGAWAM AND FEEDING HILLS REVISITED

David Cecchi
for the Agawam Historical Association

ARCADIA
PUBLISHING

ISBN 978-0-7385-3754-2

Published by Arcadia Publishing
Charleston, South Carolina

Printed in the United States of America

Library of Congress Catalog Card Number: 2004115788

For all general information, contact Arcadia Publishing:
Telephone 843-853-2070
Fax 843-853-0044
E-mail sales@arcadiapublishing.com
For customer service and orders:
Toll-free 1-888-313-2665

Visit us on the Internet at www.arcadiapublishing.com

In honor of my grandfathers, "Nono," Erminio Cecchi (1912–1978), and "Grampa," Ted Dynia (1918–1995), who instilled in me the importance of hard work and community service.

On the cover: A group poses *c.* 1891 at the Porter farm homestead. On the front cover are, from left to right, the following: (first row) William H. Porter, Frank Jackson, John W. Jackson, and Harry P. Jackson; (second row) Matilda Porter, H. S. Porter, and Sadie Jackson (holding the baby). On the back cover are Carrie Porter and George Porter. (Courtesy Mr. and Mrs. John Porter.)

Contents

ACKNOWLEDGMENTS

Since *Agawam and Feeding Hills* (2000) was published, I have received calls and letters from as far away as Florida and Ireland. It seems people could not get enough of seeing what Agawam used to be. It is no wonder. Until the publication of *Agawam and Feeding Hills*, images of Agawam's past simply were not readily available to the public. I am glad to have had a hand in changing that. I believe history is to be shared, and I sincerely thank everyone who has shared their family stories with me and loaned the photographs within this book.

I have learned much in the past five years, and I want to thank the following for helping me along the way: Anita Rising, Dick Chapman, Marilyn Curry, Detective (ret.) Joe Dymon, Ken Grady, Mr. and Mrs. Russell Jenks, Jarl Johnson, Ray Pond, Jeffrey Reynolds, Norman Roberts, Shirley Harrison (great newspaper clippings), my fellow trustees at the Leonard House, the late Ben Bassani, and the late Esther Reynolds. I also want to thank my wife, Laurie; my family; and the board of directors of the Agawam Historical Association for their support. And I especially want to thank Paul Toelken. A former Agawam resident whose family's roots in this town are deep, Paul had only recently learned of *Agawam and Feeding Hills* when he called me last fall from his home in Prescott Valley, Arizona, to find out how he could obtain a copy. I told him I could send him one, and, oh, by the way, I was currently working on a follow-up. Within a matter of days, he had sent me a box of nearly 50 photographs dating back to the 1890s, with accompanying notes, many of which appear in this book. Do I believe in serendipity? You bet. Enjoy.

—David Cecchi
Agawam, Massachusetts
January 12, 2005

INTRODUCTION

When *Agawam and Feeding Hills* was published in 2000, most people's reaction was "When is the next one coming out?" That the book was well received is an understatement. The book went through two printings, and the Agawam Historical Association continues to sell them. The association received over $10,000 in profits from that volume, which was used to help fund renovations to the old Elm Street Fire Station, which was opened by the association as the Agawam Historical & Fire House Museum in May 2002.

Where that first book focused heavily on place, this volume focuses on the people of Agawam and Feeding Hills—at work, at play, at home, in school, and on the go. The 1993 town report *Coming Together for Consensus* stated, "From Agawam's rural past we've retained a sense of being a small town where friendly people with a wide range of incomes know each other and participate in civic activities, school affairs and sports events. This is a good place to raise a family." After reading *Agawam and Feeding Hills Revisited*, you will see it always has been.

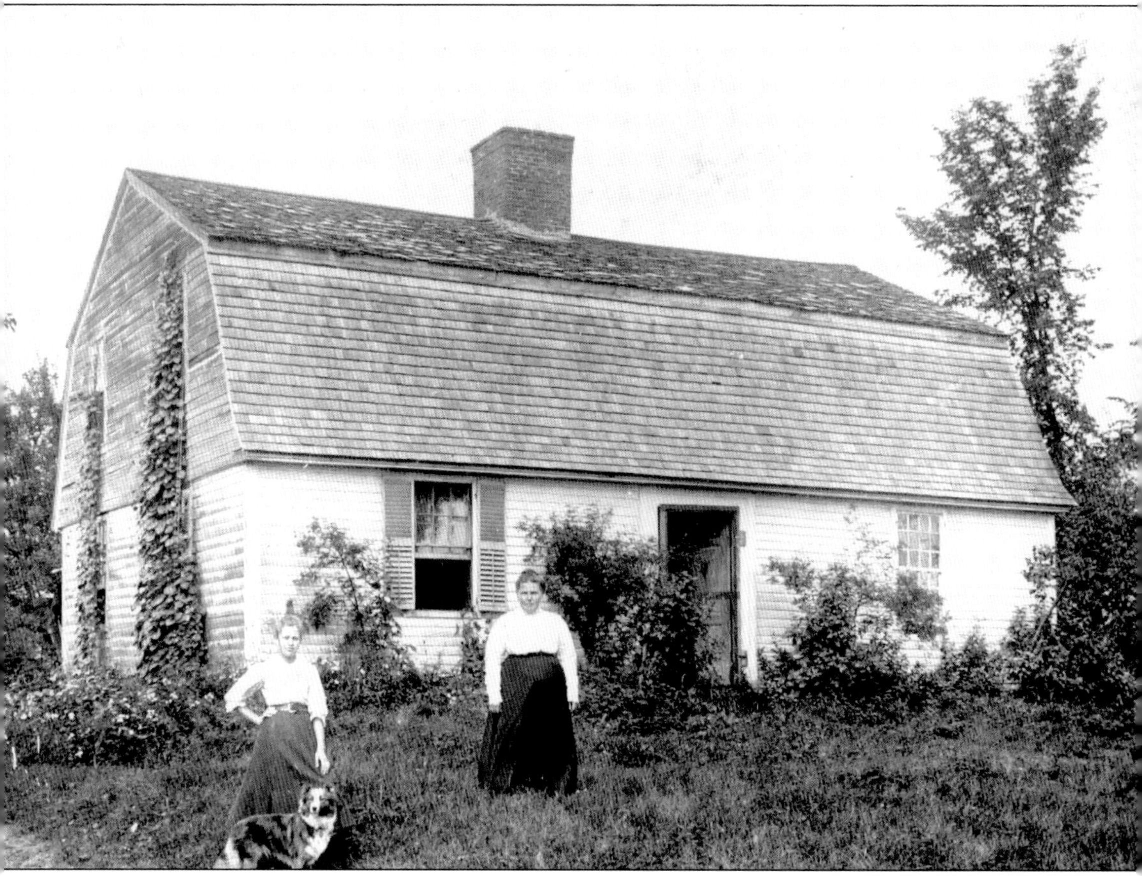

The Thomas Smith House (formerly known as the Mathew Noble House), at 251 North West Street in Feeding Hills, was purchased by the Agawam Historical Association in June 2002. Proceeds from the sale of this book will be used toward the preservation of the property, which dates from the mid-18th century and remains largely in original condition (page 127). (Courtesy the collection of the late John Rosenberg.)

One

Dear Hearts

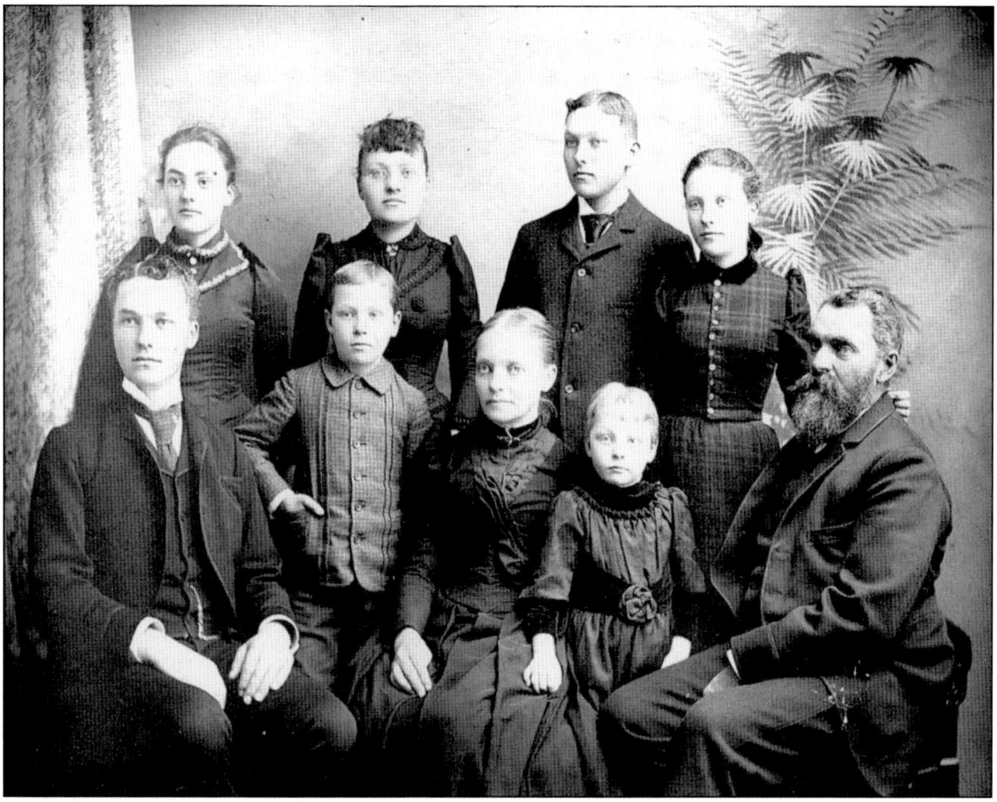

The Daniel W. Brown family is pictured in 1892. The family members are, from left to right, as follows: (first row) Walter, Sam, unidentified, Miriam, and Daniel; (second row) Alice, Grace, Charles, and Edith (later Granger). The Brown family lived on South West Street in Feeding Hills. (Courtesy Paul Toelken.)

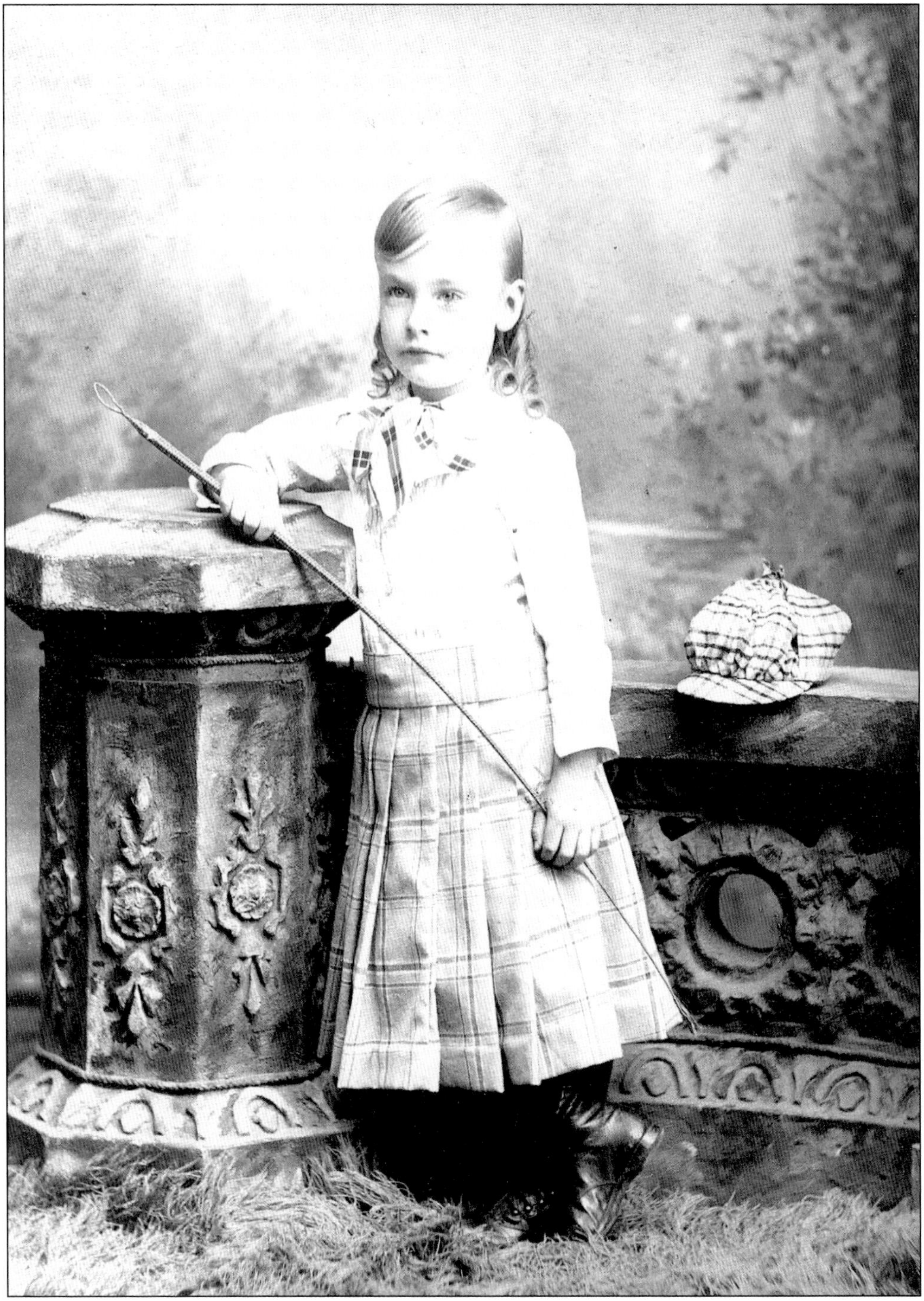

This 1891 portrait shows six-year-old George W. Porter in the curls and dress of the fashionable Victorian boy. Porter went on to become a farmer and writer. He served as a state legislator from 1940 until 1966. This photograph was taken by Goldsmith of 374 Main Street in Springfield. The studio was advertised as the "largest and finest studio in New England." (Courtesy Mr. and Mrs. John Porter.)

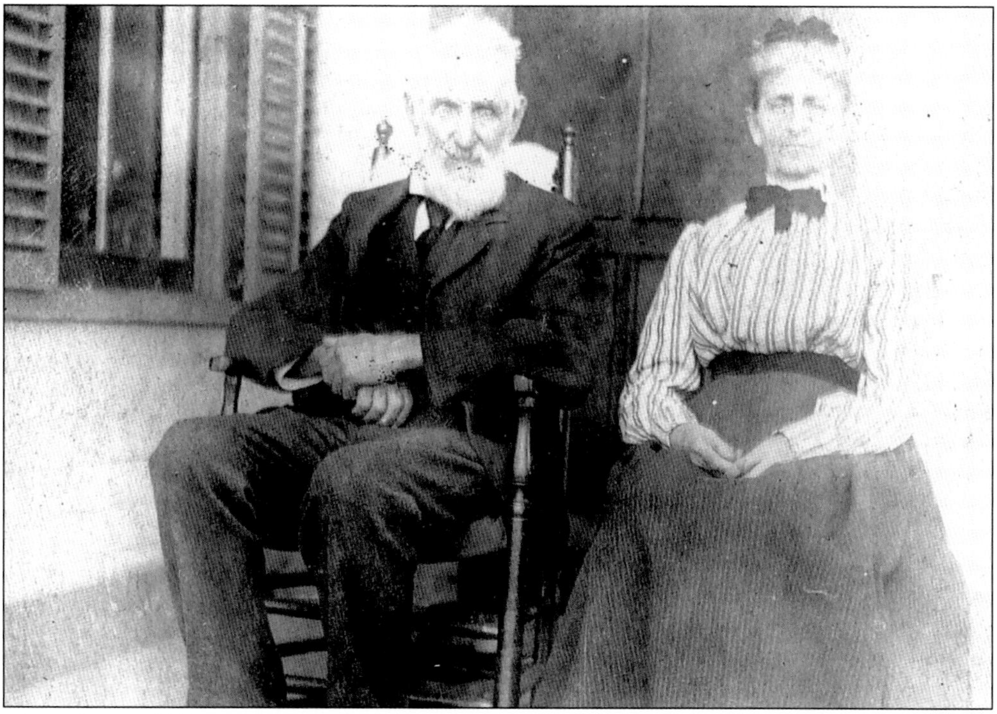

Mr. and Mrs. William Hastings are pictured on the porch of their son Charles W. Hastings's home at 684 Main Street. In his book *Chowder without Tomato* (1966), grandson Harry W. Hastings wrote, "Grandfather had abundant, silky white hair and beard and boasted that his face had never been touched by a razor." (Courtesy Henry C. Hastings.)

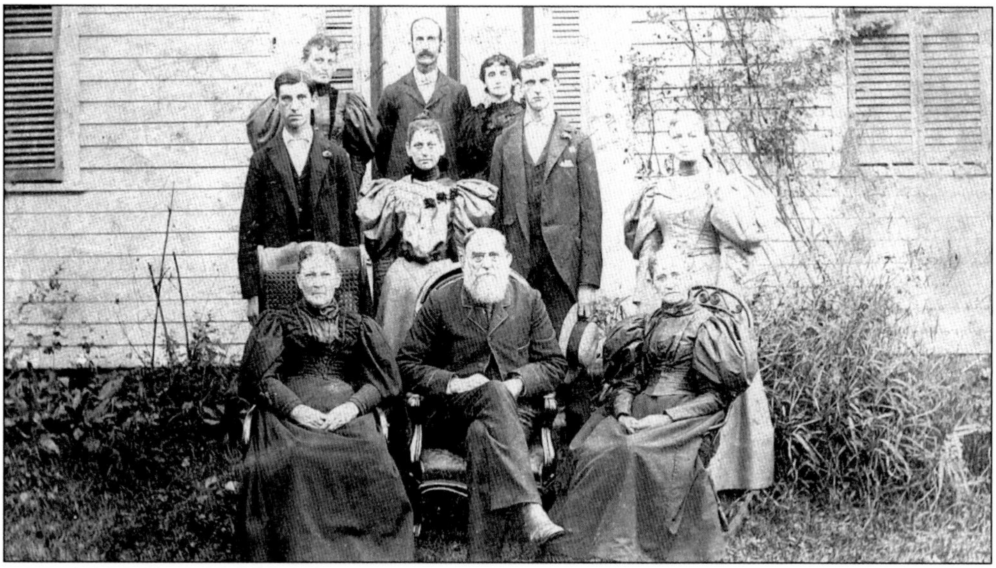

Edward Bodurtha is surrounded by family in front of the Bodurtha home at 41 Elm Street in 1895. His son Henry (back row, center) served as town clerk for over 30 years. Harry Hastings described Edward as "one of the prominent old men of my village . . . voted Democratic in a Republican town, generally knew what was going on or had a part in it." (Courtesy Jack Bodurtha.)

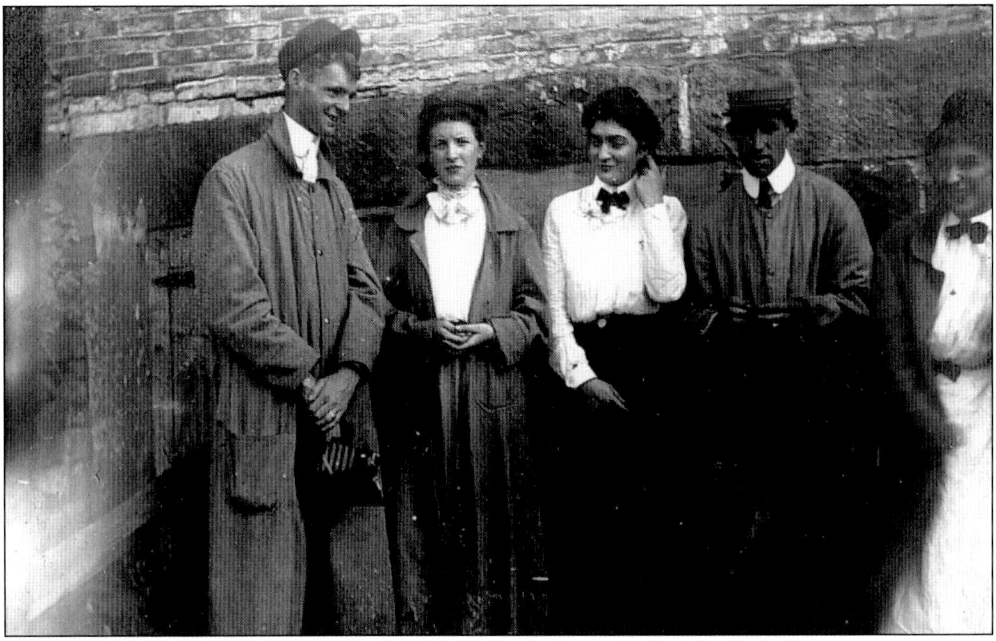

Harry W. Hastings (left) stands outside Old Newgate Prison in Granby, Connecticut, *c.* 1903. Hastings was the son of longtime Agawam postmaster Charles W. Hastings and later wrote *Chowder without Tomato*, about his hometown of Agawam. (Courtesy Henry C. Hastings.)

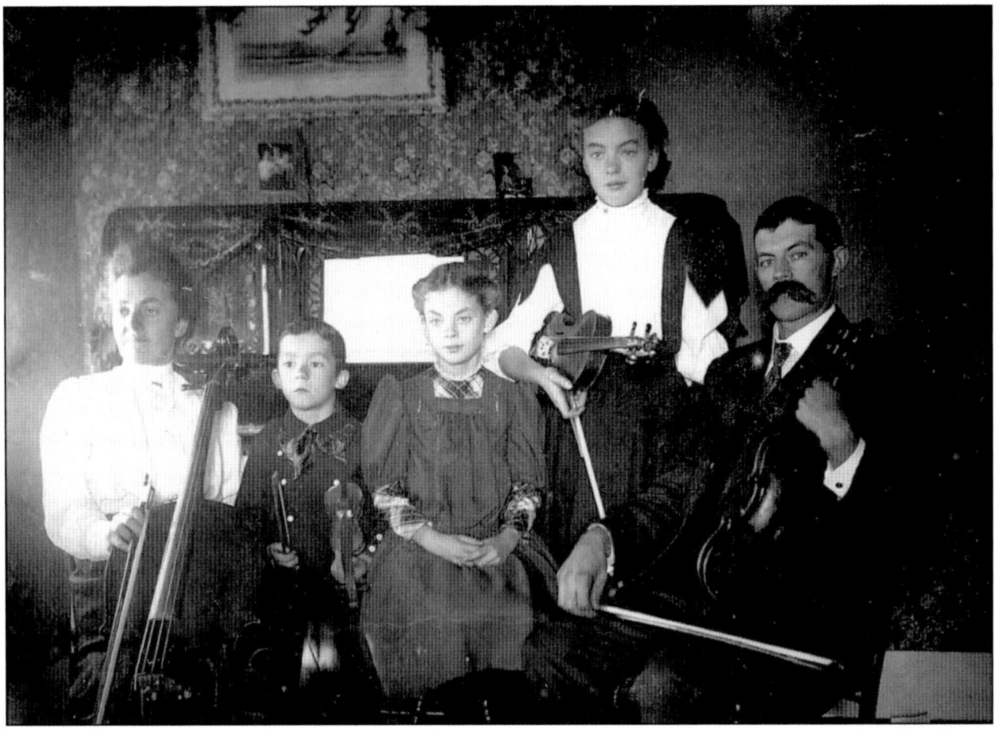

The Granger family gathers for a Christmas Day concert in the front room of their home at 160 North Westfield Street in 1908. Family members are, from left to right, Alice (Brown), Sydney, Phyllis, Edith, and Clarence H. (Courtesy Paul Toelken.)

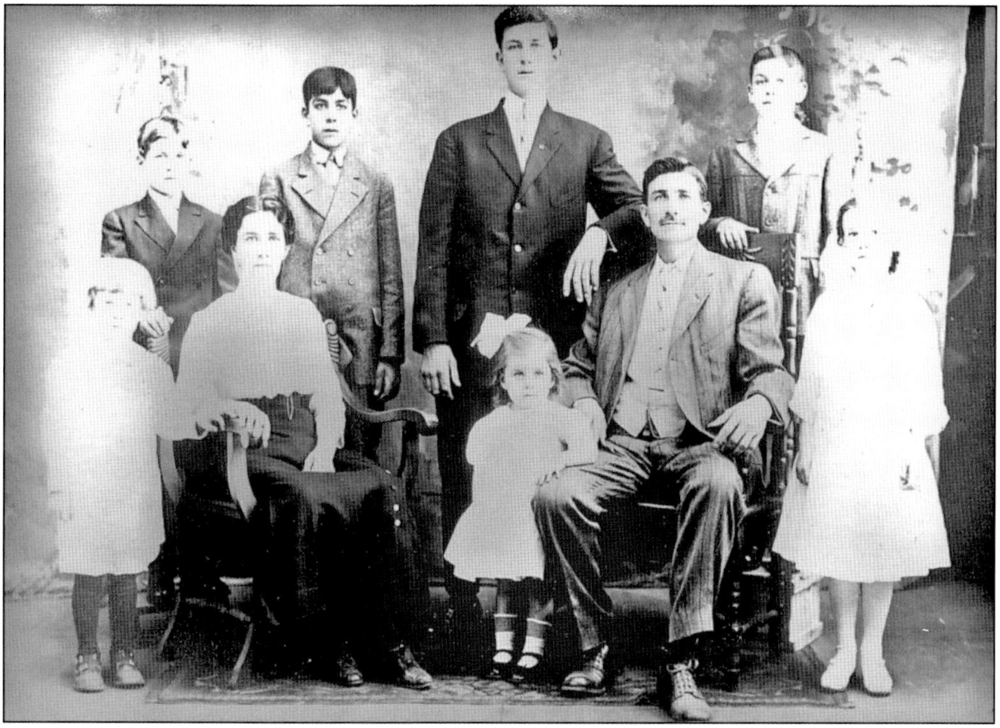

The Edouard Letendre family is pictured *c.* 1910. From left to right are the following: (first row) Albert, Louise, Annette, Edouard, and Blanche; (second row) Joseph, Adelard, Adam, and Sylvio. Edouard moved here from Canada and settled in the Letendre Avenue and North Street area, where many of his descendants built their own homes and still reside. (Courtesy Theresa Letendre.)

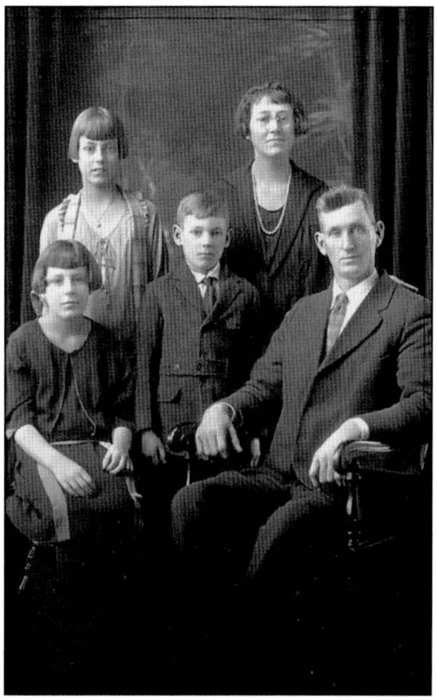

Herbert and Mattie Briggs are pictured with their three children, Hilda, Hazel, and Herbert Jr. The Briggs family lived at 901 Main Street, where they raised chickens to provide eggs for the Springfield market. Briggs also built many homes in Agawam. A 1928 town directory lists Herbert as "Teamster, Puffer Coal Co." Puffer Coal was located at Feeding Hills Center. (Courtesy Bob and Cindy Briggs.)

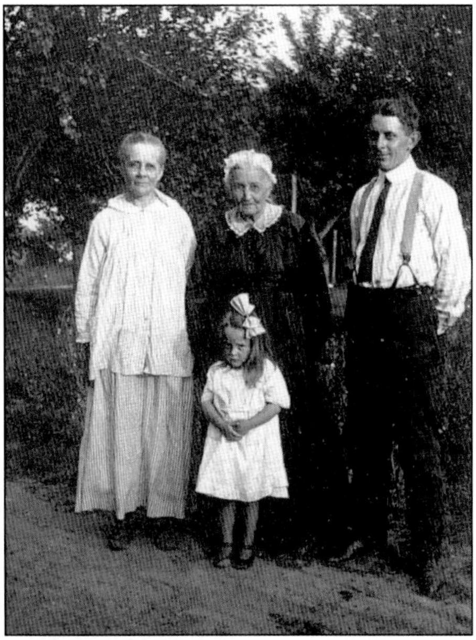

Four generations of the Chisholm-Cesan family are shown in this photograph from the second decade of the 20th century. Family members are, from left to right, as follows: daughter Louisa Cesan, "Great Grandma" Julia Chisholm, her grandson Daniel O. Cesan, and great-granddaughter Anita (Cesan) Rising. (Courtesy Anita [Cesan] Rising.)

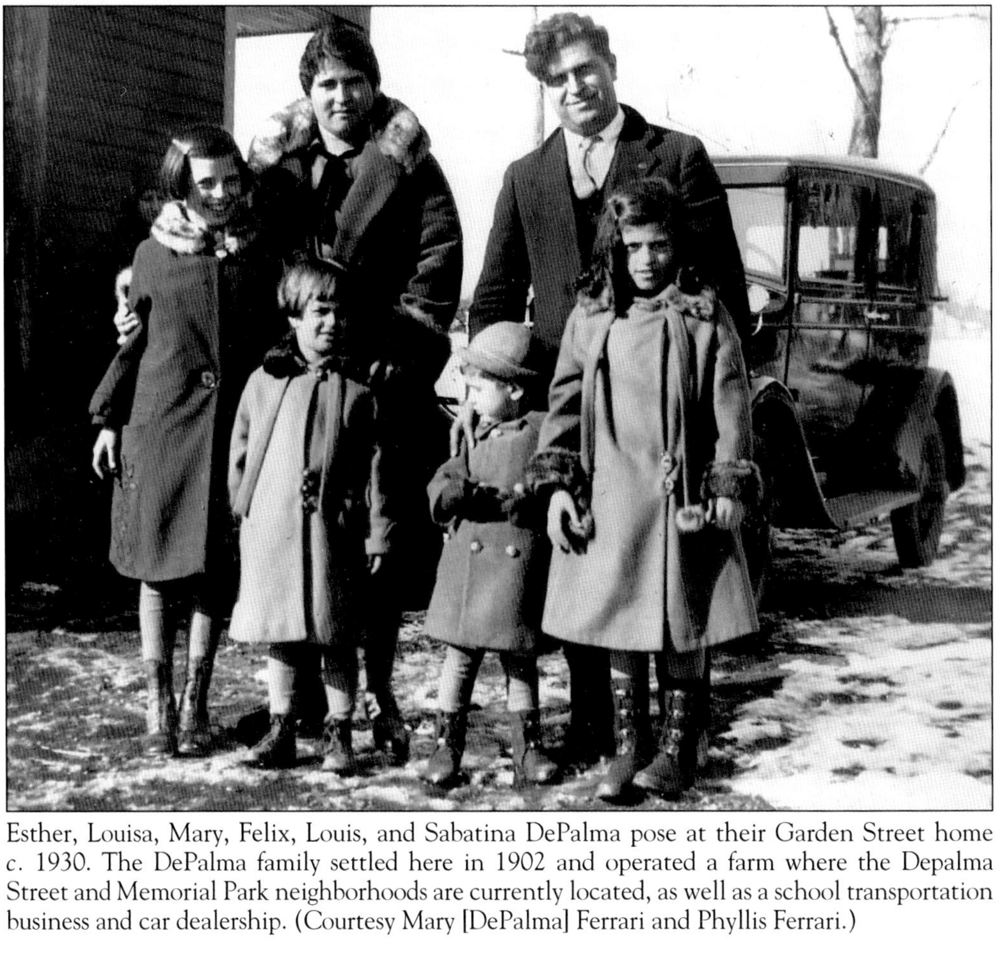

Esther, Louisa, Mary, Felix, Louis, and Sabatina DePalma pose at their Garden Street home c. 1930. The DePalma family settled here in 1902 and operated a farm where the Depalma Street and Memorial Park neighborhoods are currently located, as well as a school transportation business and car dealership. (Courtesy Mary [DePalma] Ferrari and Phyllis Ferrari.)

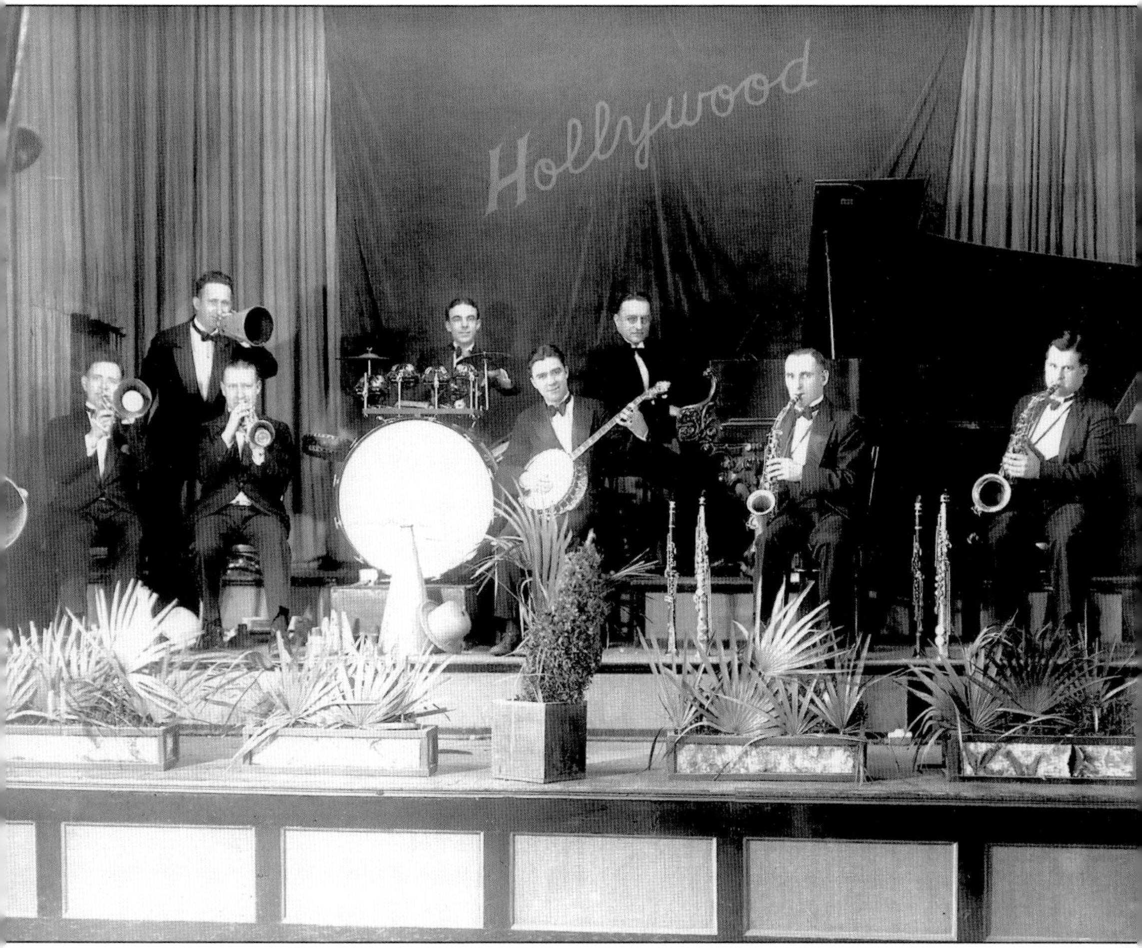

The Hollywood Orchestra, managed by Robert M. Schilling, was a popular attraction at Riverside Park's Butterfly Ballroom during the 1920s and 1930s. Orchestra members are, from left to right, Frank Cizek, trombone; Thomas Coughlin, caller; William Cizek, trumpet; Charles Tricker, drums; Eddie Beston, banjo; Robert Schilling, piano; Frank Shannhan, saxophone; and unidentified, saxophone. Musical numbers from August 1926 included "Show that Fellow the Door," "When the Red, Red, Robins Come Bob, Bob, Bobbing Along," "Louise You Tease," "She's a Corn Fed Indiana Girl," "What no Spinach!" and "The Sympathy Waltz: Too Many Parties and Too Many Girls." (Courtesy Geraldine Schilling-Nordal.)

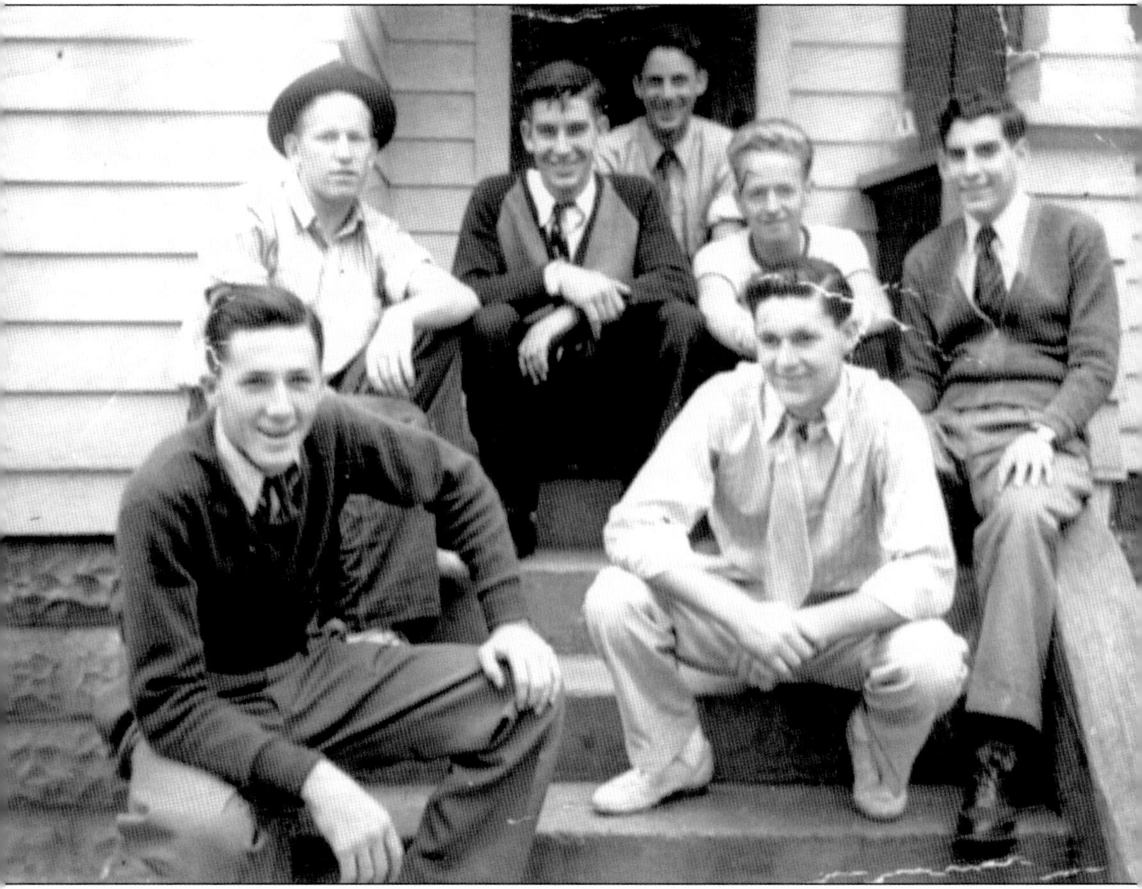

Members of the "Greatest Generation" are pictured on Letendre Avenue in 1938. Members are, from left to right, as follows: (first row) "Bobby" Letendre and Edmund Bouley; (second row) "Picky" Menard, George Beauchane, Donald Lamoreux, ? Blanchard, and Phil Bruso. They all served their country during World War II. Bruso was killed in England during the war. (Courtesy Ellen Janik.)

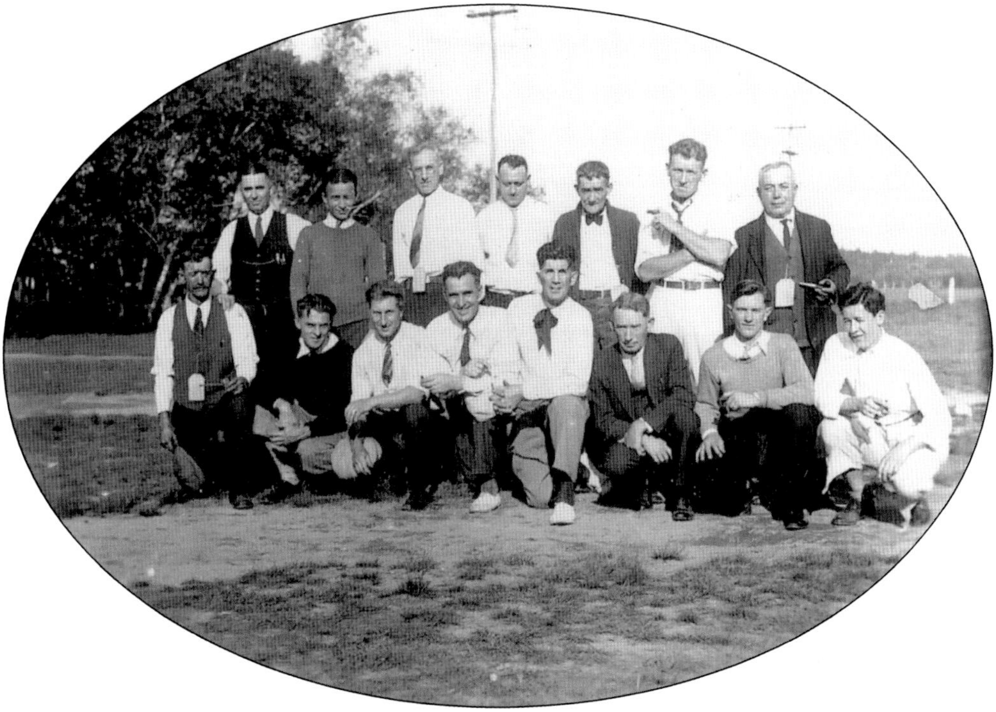

The West Agawam Community League met near Homer and Hall Streets during the 1920s and 1930s. The members shown here include Phil Jasmin, Roseare Couture, George Lepine, Edouard Letendre, "Toot" Murphy, Larry Bouley, Frank Russo, a Mr. Menard, and a Mr. Viens. (Courtesy Ellen Janik.)

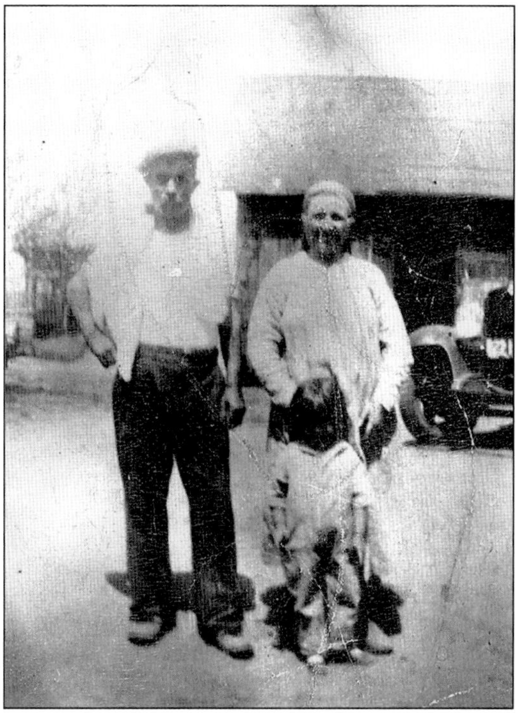

Pasquale "Patsy" Liquori, wife Maria, and granddaughter Mary "Totsie" Liquori pose in front of their barn at 712 Cooper Street *c.* 1932. The farm, purchased in 1909 and added on to in 1914, has been run by four generations of the Liquori family. Liquori's great-great-grandchildren still live on a small part of the farm. (Courtesy Patsy Liquori.)

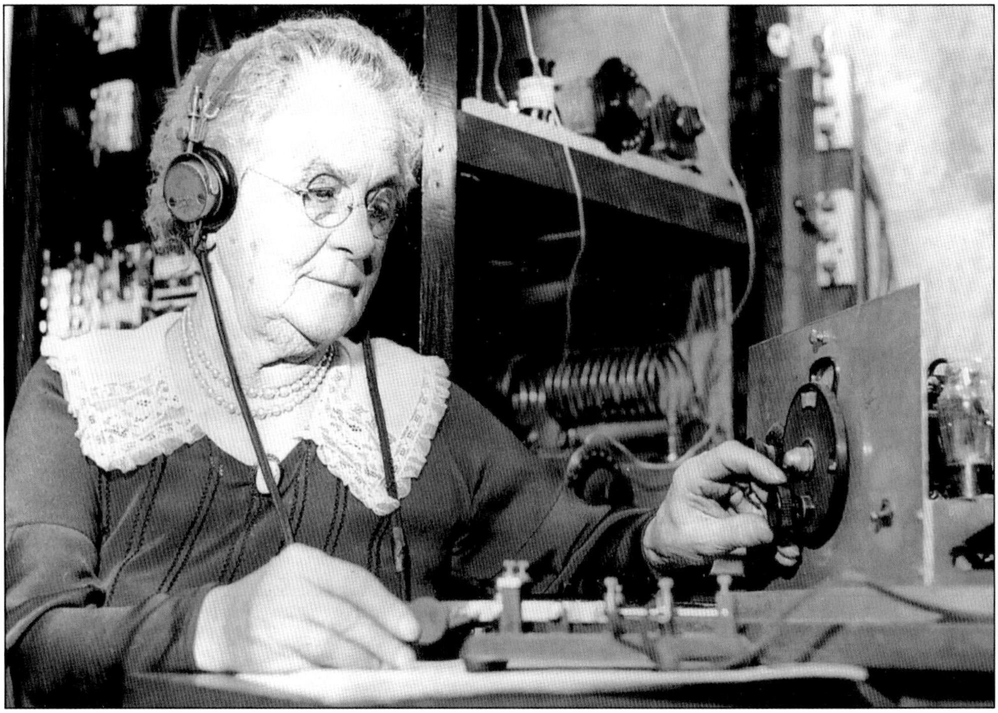

In this press photograph dated March 21, 1935, Feeding Hills resident Madeline Boeder, age 73, is shown transmitting Morse code to her son from her amateur broadcasting station. (Author's collection.)

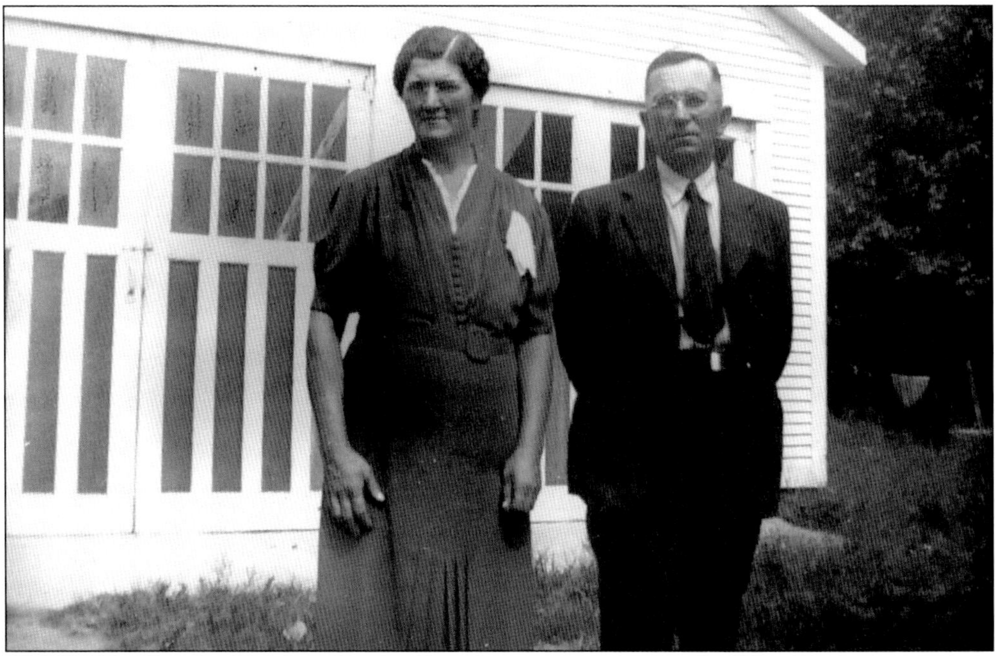

Mary and John Stepanik are pictured on Labor Day 1938. John Stepanik Farms began in 1925 with 15 acres of land on Twin Oaks Road. Over the years, parcels amounting to 74 acres were added on North West Street, Southwick Street, and Shoemaker Lane. (Courtesy Eleanor Stepanik.)

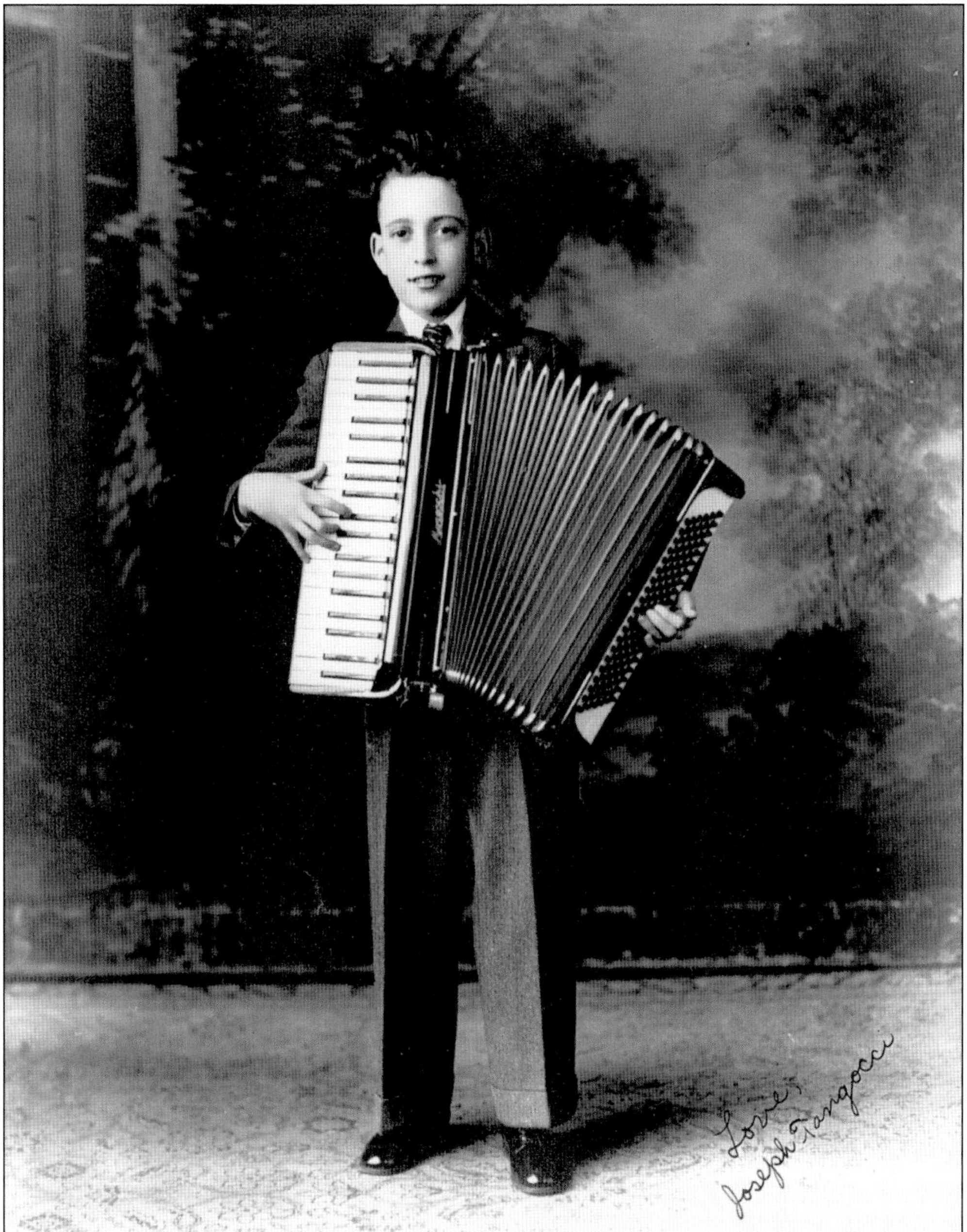

Growing up in North Agawam, Joe Tangocci had mastered the accordion well enough by the early 1940s to be part of Leone's Accordionaires. The trio consisted of Tangocci, Gus Aversa, and Freddie DiMauro. They played at local women's clubs and minstrel shows and appeared on local radio programs. They played for the 104th Infantry before the unit shipped out during World War II, and they tried out for *Major Bowes Original Amateur Hour*, where they "almost made it." (Courtesy Joe Tangocci.)

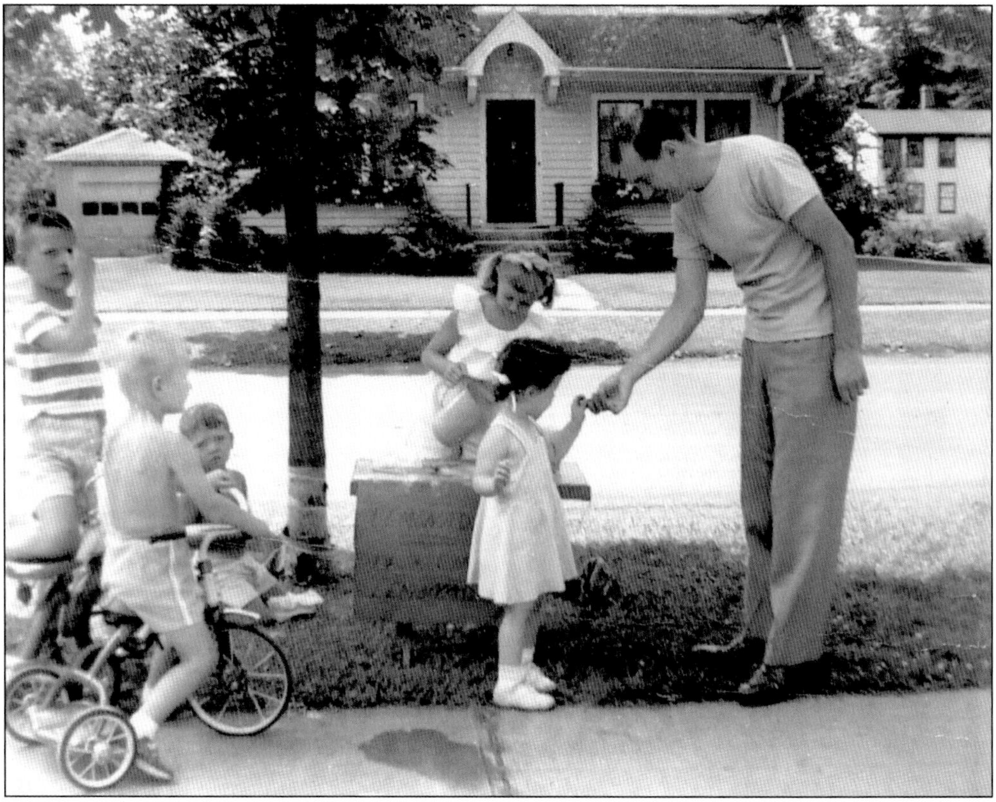

Joseph Della-Giustina purchases lemonade from daughters Marsha and Jo-Ann in front of their Albert Street residence. The house at 18 Albert Street, seen across the street, has been home to the Moriarty family for many years. To the right is the rear ell of the house that formerly stood on Main Street where Westfield Bank is today. (Courtesy Jennie and Joseph Della-Giustina.)

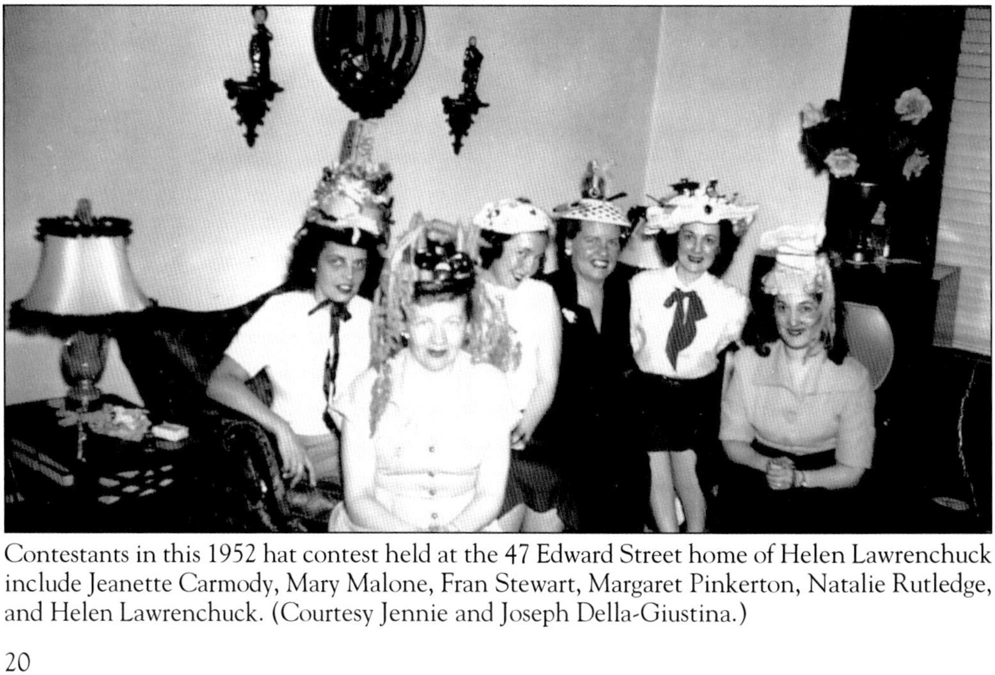

Contestants in this 1952 hat contest held at the 47 Edward Street home of Helen Lawrenchuck include Jeanette Carmody, Mary Malone, Fran Stewart, Margaret Pinkerton, Natalie Rutledge, and Helen Lawrenchuck. (Courtesy Jennie and Joseph Della-Giustina.)

Two

The Faith of Our Fathers

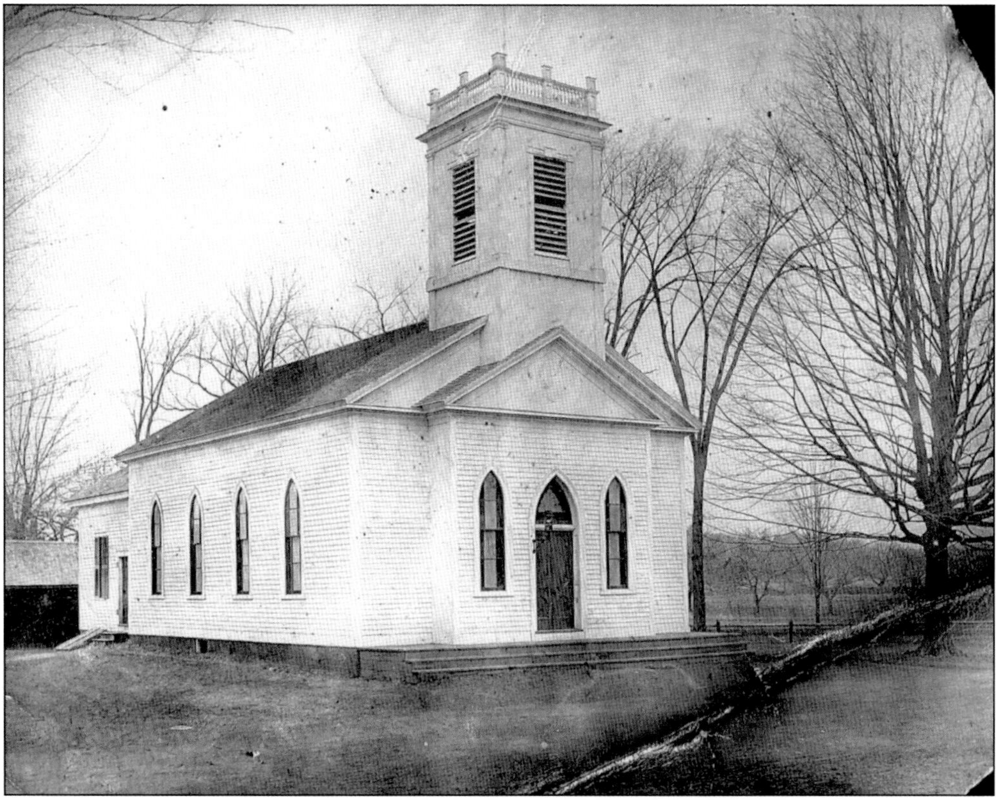

A landmark at Elm and Main Streets since it was built in 1830, the Agawam Baptist Church is seen here *c*. 1895. The church was founded in 1790, and its original 11 members were John and Mary Porter; Stephen Bodurtha; Johnathon, Margaret, and Martha Purchase; Earle and Roxanna Bancroft; Molly Worthington; Abigail Palmer; and Eleanor Bodurtha. The church was enlarged and remodeled in 1967. (Courtesy Henry C. Hastings.)

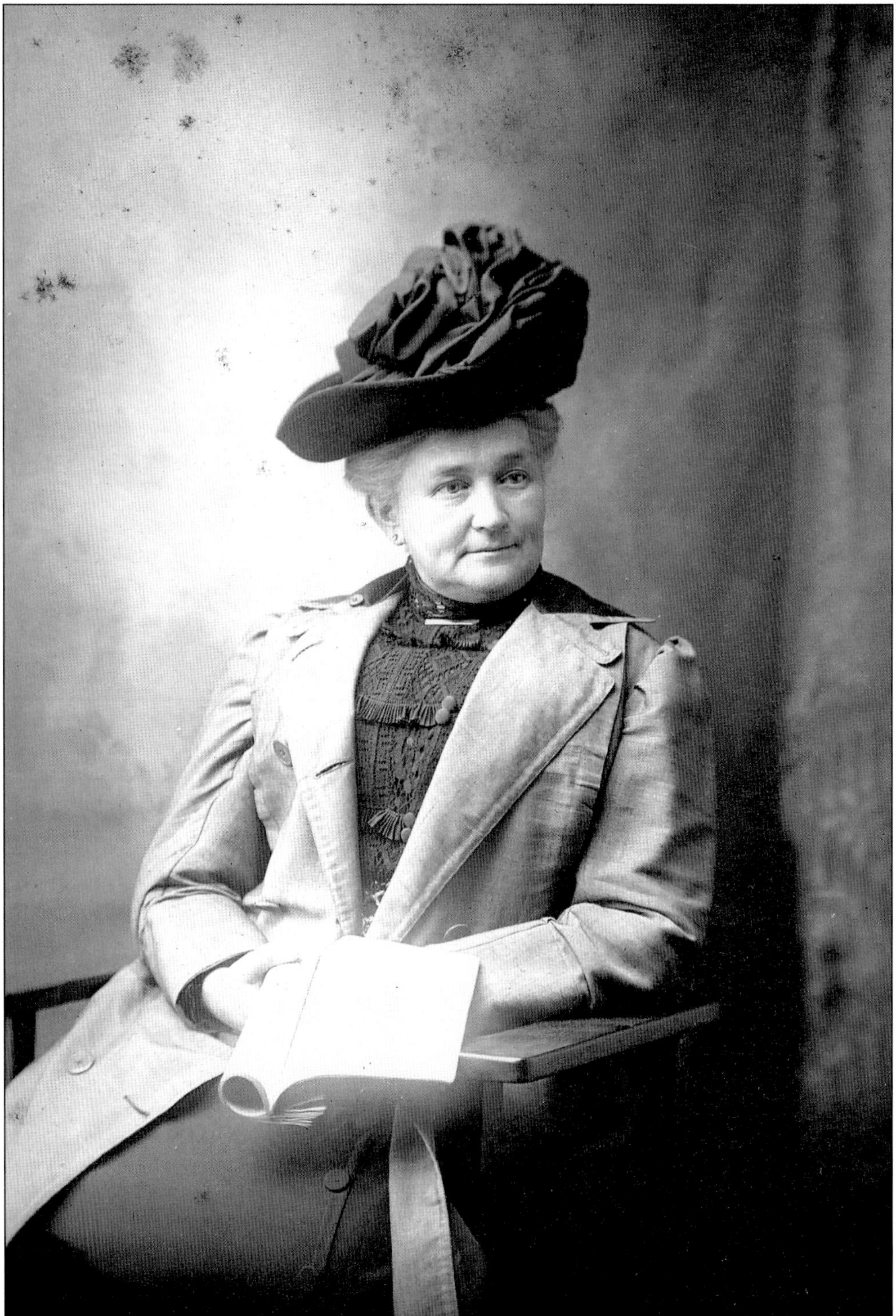

Mrs. F. A. Johnson is shown in December 1910. She was very well known in Feeding Hills at that time and was Edith (Brown) Granger's Sunday school teacher. (Courtesy Paul Toelken.)

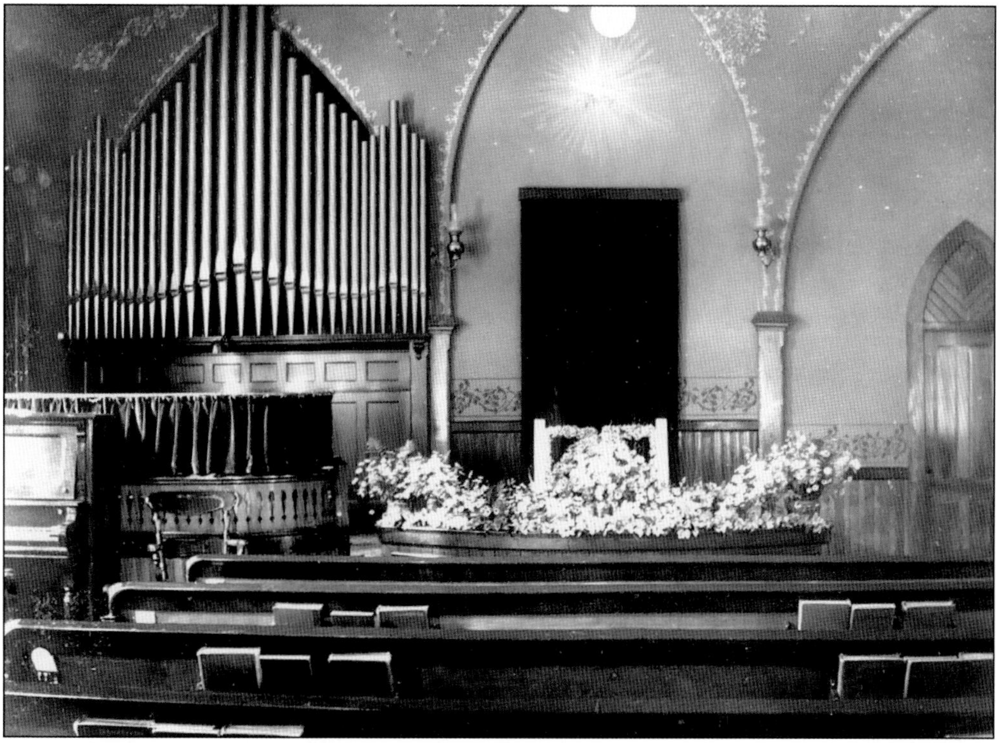

This photograph, taken on Children's Day in 1906, shows the interior of the Agawam Baptist Church and the new Esty pipe organ. Note how the interior finish mimics the Gothic-arch windows seen on page 21. (Courtesy Paul Toelken.)

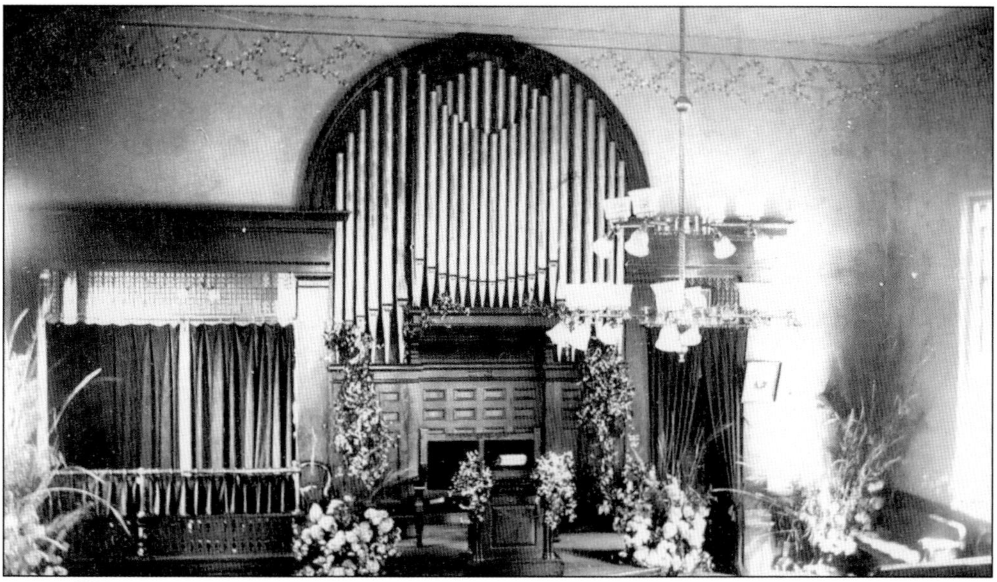

Relocated here from Suffield in 1815, the original Agawam Congregational Church was completely remodeled in 1905, when a new pipe organ was installed. The church was demolished in 1966, and the present edifice was completed and dedicated in 1967. (Agawam Historical Association collection.)

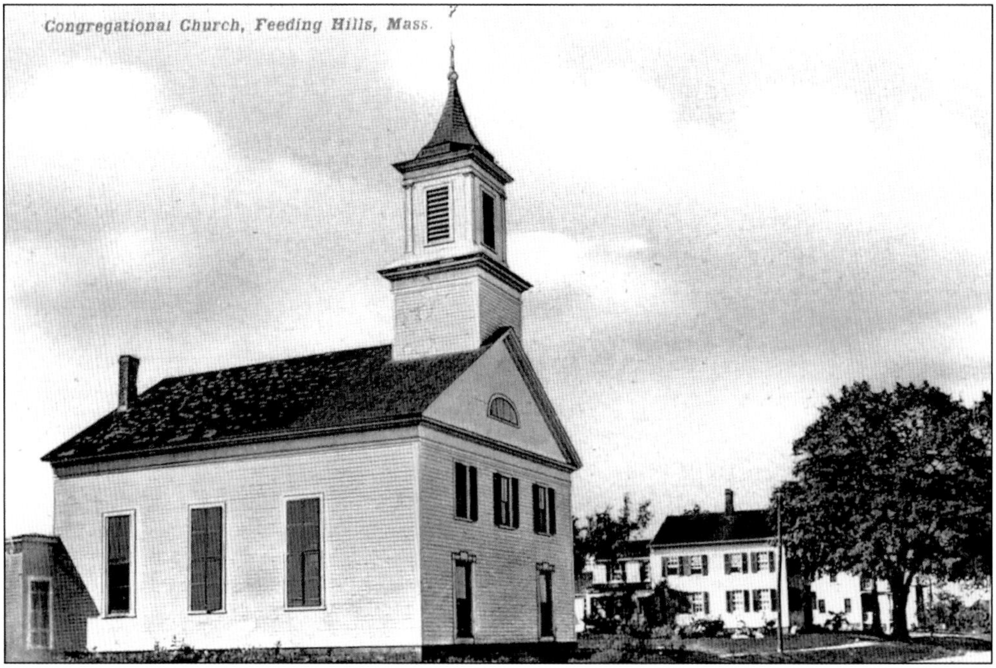

The Congregational church in Feeding Hills was organized on November 10, 1762. The present meetinghouse, seen here in the early 1900s, was built in 1834. Sylvanus Griswold, an early minister, served for 57 years. It is said that he knew the names of only children he had baptized. (Author's collection.)

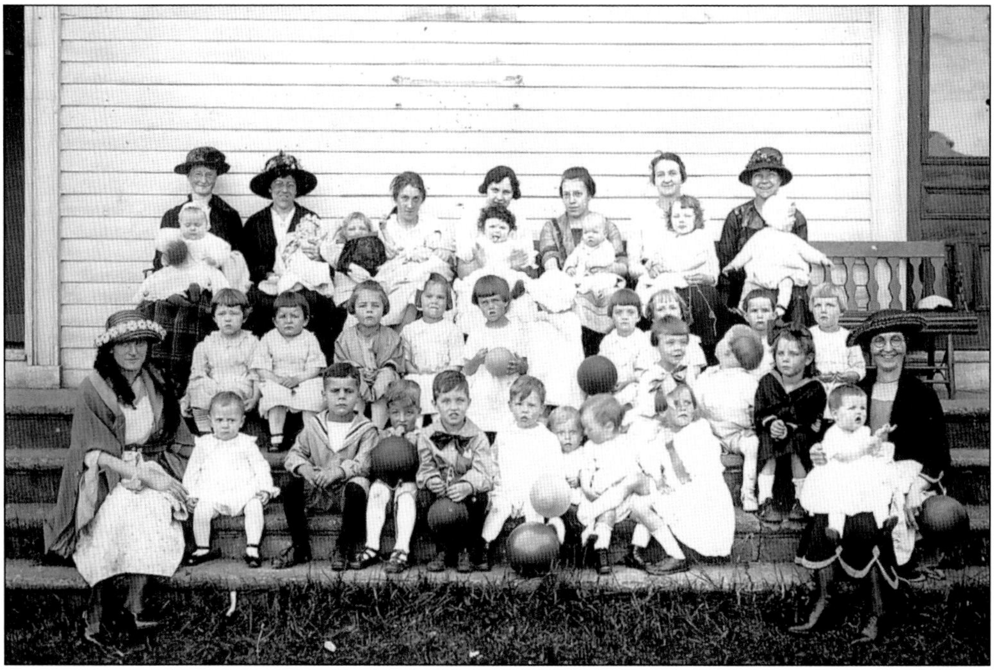

This group portrait (perhaps of Sunday school students) was taken on the steps of the Feeding Hills Congregational Church during the first decade of the 20th century. The adults here seem to be in much better spirits than the majority of their charges. (Courtesy Helen Light.)

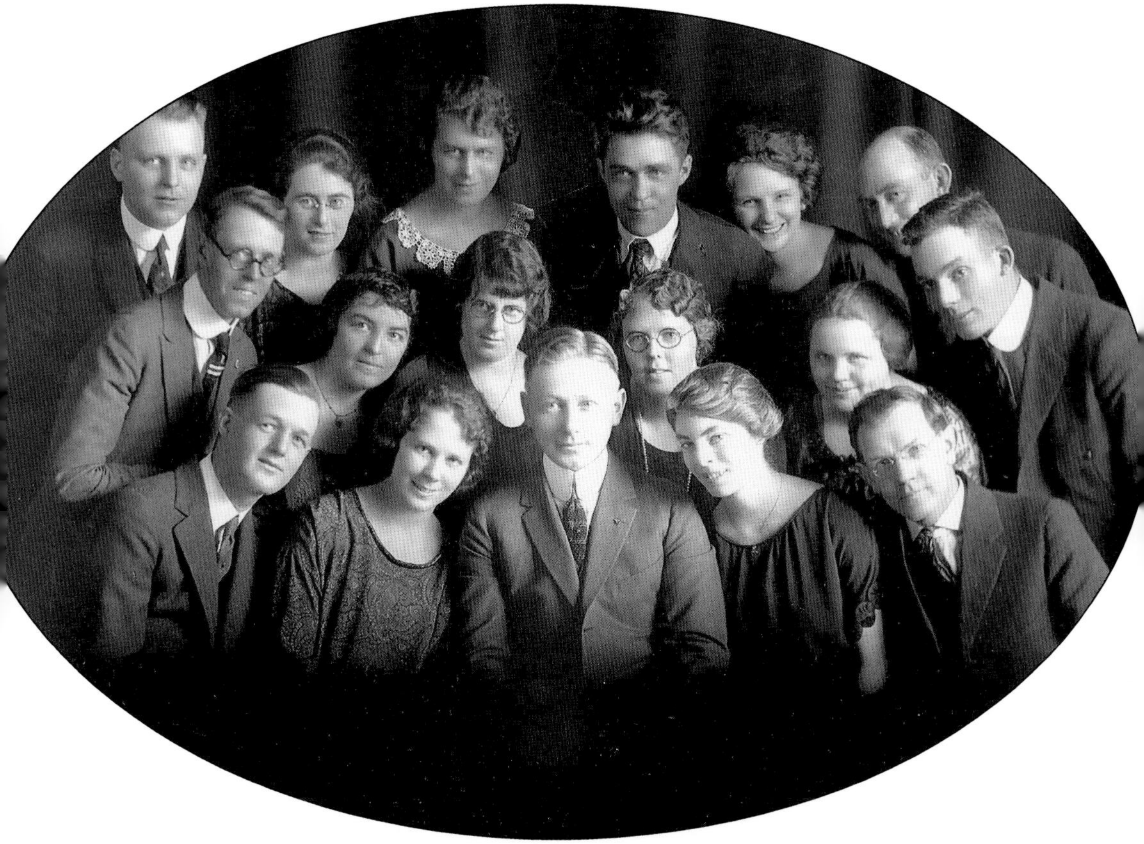

The choir of Agawam Congregational Church is pictured here in 1923. Harold Hudson served as director, and Phyllis (Granger) Hudson was organist. From left to right are the following: (first row) Donald Havens, Gladys (Pond) Havens, Harold Hudson, Phyllis (Granger) Hudson, and Robert Shields; (second row) James Atwater, K. Atwater, Doris Havens, Lillian (Young) Wells, Rebecca (Cesan) Granger, and Sydney Granger; (third row) Howard Pond, Anna (Crouss) Pond, Alice Shields, Charlie Wells, Bernice (Pond) Merrell, and Edwin Merrell. (Courtesy Paul Toelken.)

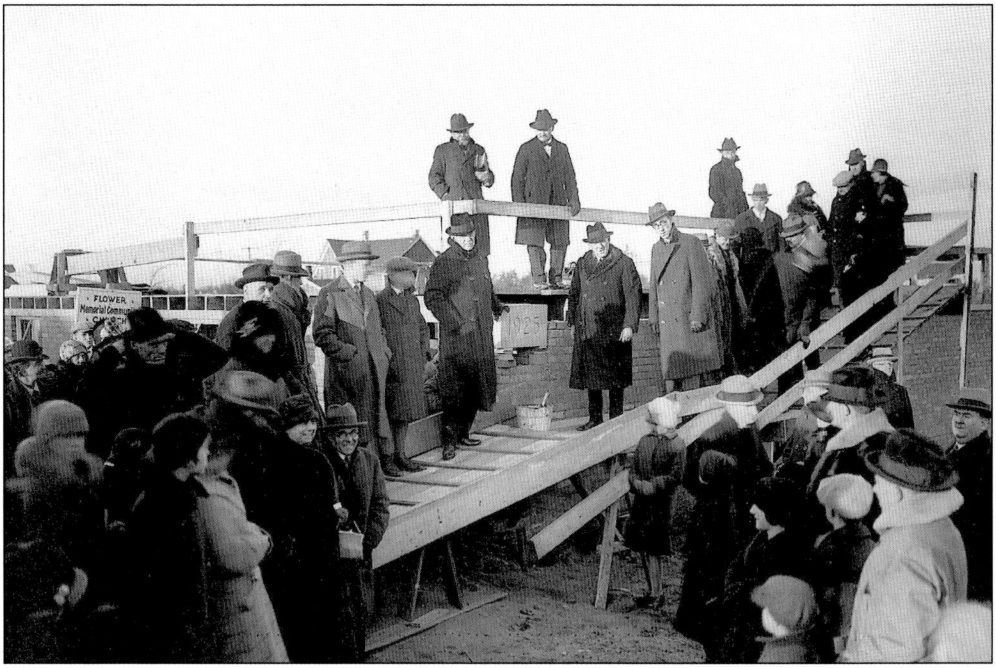

Rev. James J. Cesan (back left) holds books at the 1925 dedication of Flower Memorial Methodist Church, located at the corner of Hall and Springfield Streets. In 1950, the membership merged with the Lay Memorial Methodist Church in Feeding Hills. The building later served as a social hall for St. Anthony's Church. It is now home to a commercial enterprise. (Courtesy Anita [Cesan] Rising.)

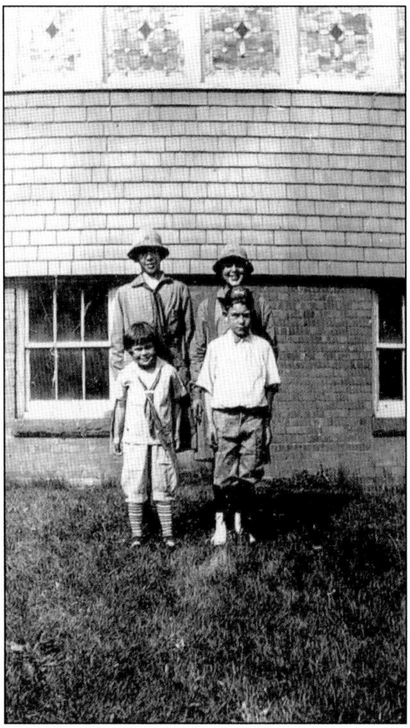

Girl Scouts Lorenza and Thelma Beauchane (back) pose with Verna and George Beauchane (front) outside Flower Memorial Methodist Church in the early 1930s. The church was named after Homer Flower, who donated land and money for its construction and furnishing. (Courtesy Ellen Janik.)

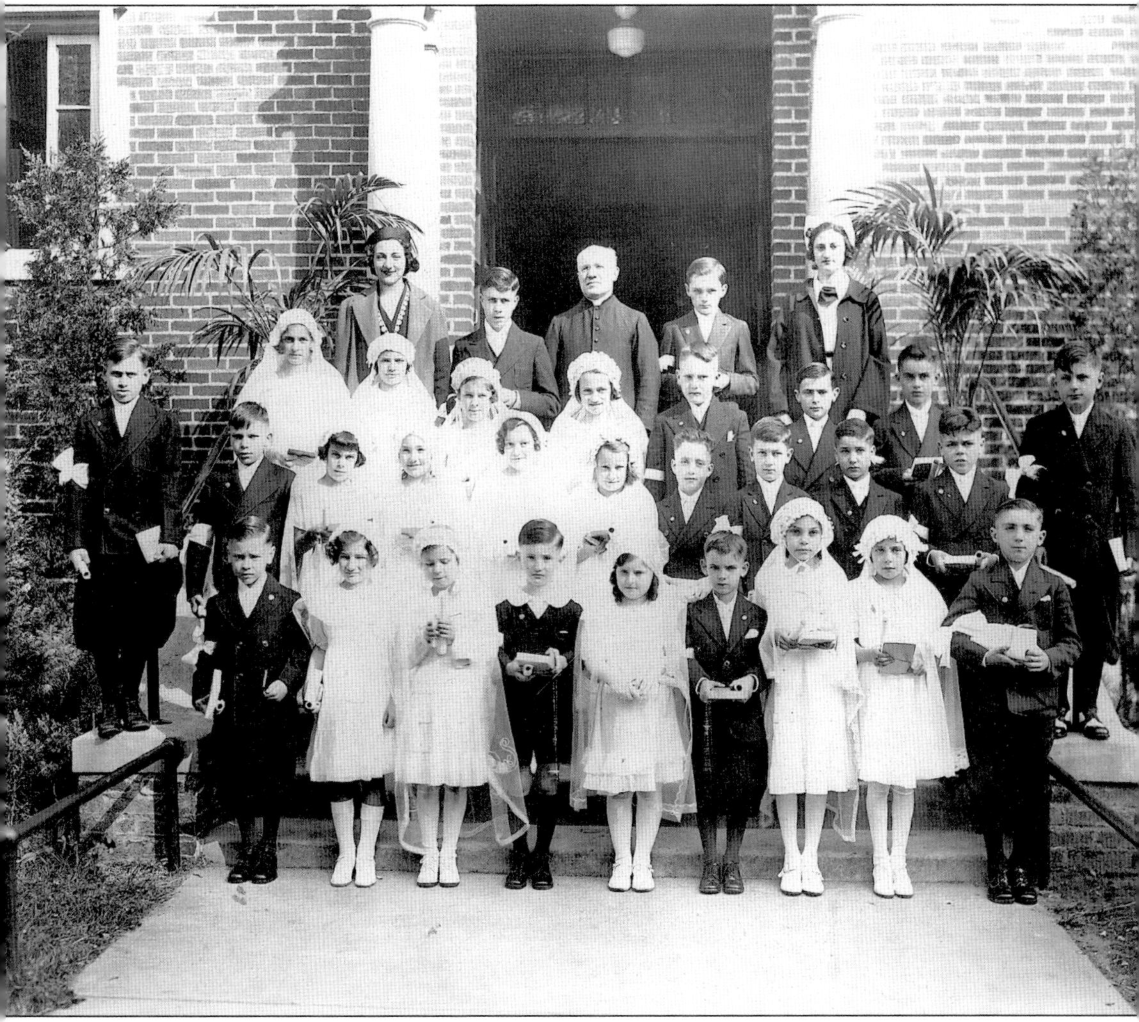

The first communion class of St. Anthony's Church poses on June 23, 1937. From left to right are the following: (first row) Paul Coppi, Louise Balboni, unidentified, Donald Loncrini, Ann Aloisi, Robert Castelli, two unidentified, and Albert Christopher; (second row) Frank Morassi, unidentified, Nina Mandirol, Amy Longo, Florida Tangocci, Venetia Penna, Joseph Tangocci, unidentified, Edward Gallerani, George Draghetti, and unidentified; (third row) four unidentified, Renzo Ceccarini, and Carlo Lavotti; (fourth row) Irene Montagna, unidentified, Fr. Henry Gabos, unidentified, and Rena Montagna. (Courtesy Joe Tangocci.)

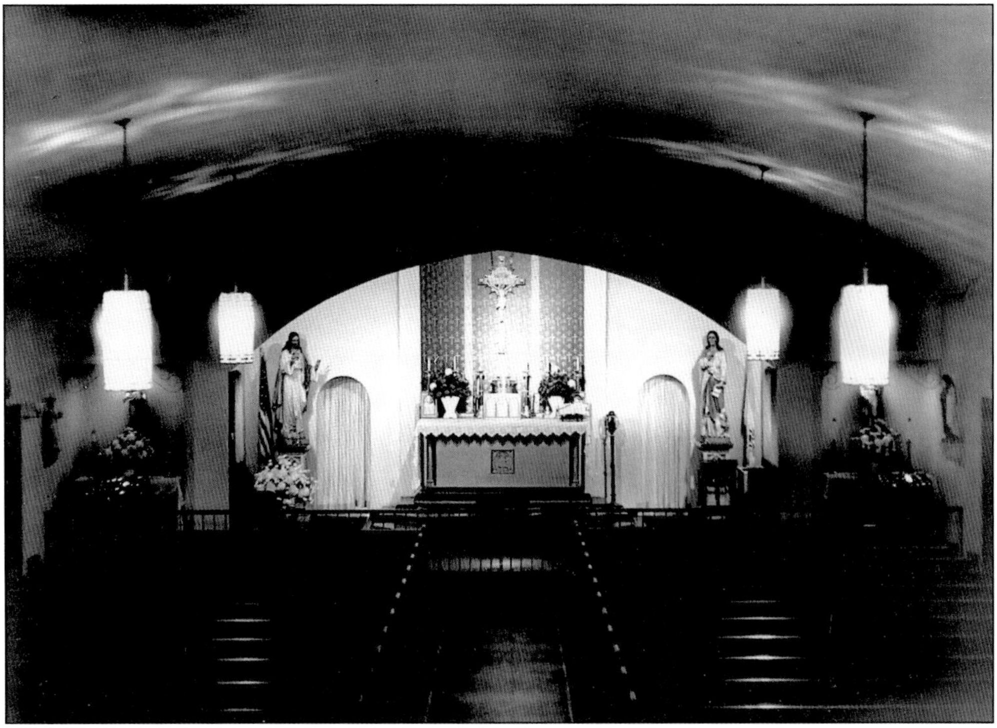

This interior view of St. John the Evangelist Church, at 833 Main Street, was taken in the late 1940s. The first Catholic church in Agawam Center, St. John's celebrated its first mass on Easter Sunday in 1946. Before that, mass was held briefly in the old town hall and later the Bowling Alley at Riverside Park. The church was enlarged and remodeled in 1987–1988. (Courtesy St. John the Evangelist Church.)

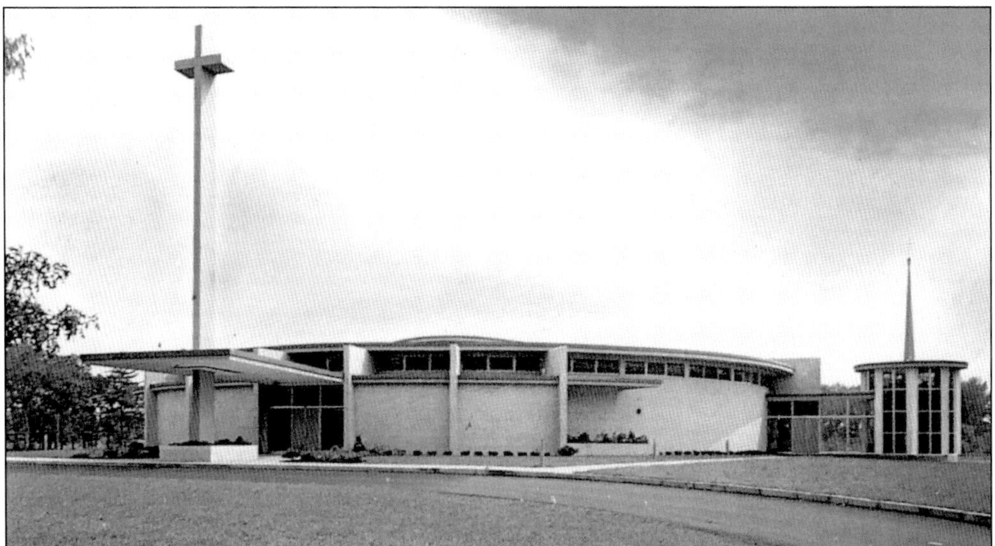

Originally a mission branch of St. Anthony's and located on William Street, Sacred Heart was created in 1946. The present building at the corner of Mill, Poplar, and Springfield Streets was constructed in 1959 on the former Homer Flower property. (Author's collection.)

Three

BACK TO SCHOOL

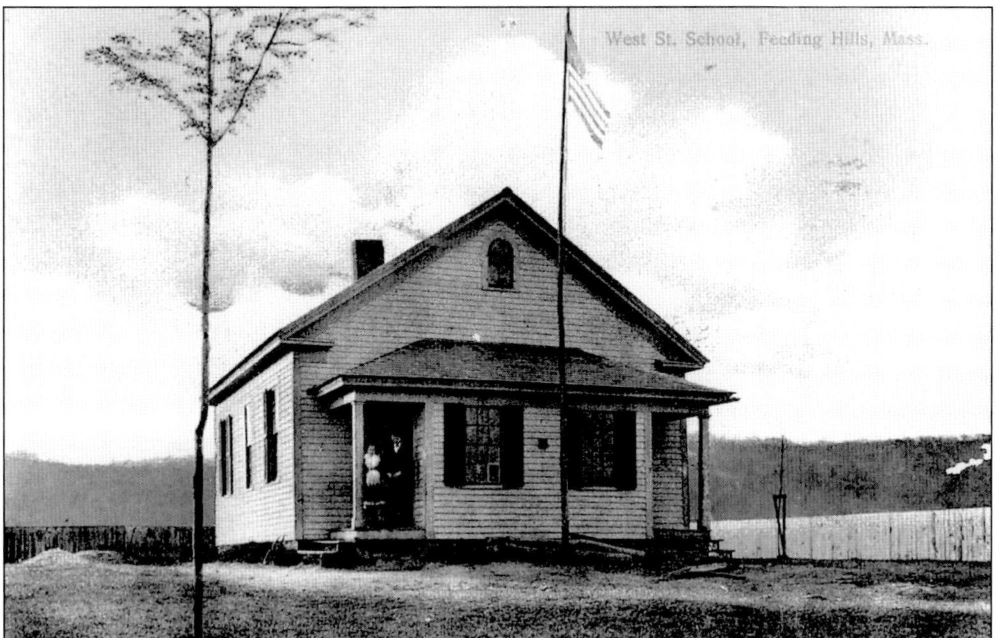

Built in 1872 to replace an earlier structure, the (North) West Street School is seen here in the early 1900s. In use as a schoolhouse until 1936–1937, since 1953 it has served as the Grange hall for Community Grange No. 382, where strawberry suppers are a springtime tradition. (Courtesy Joe Tangocci.)

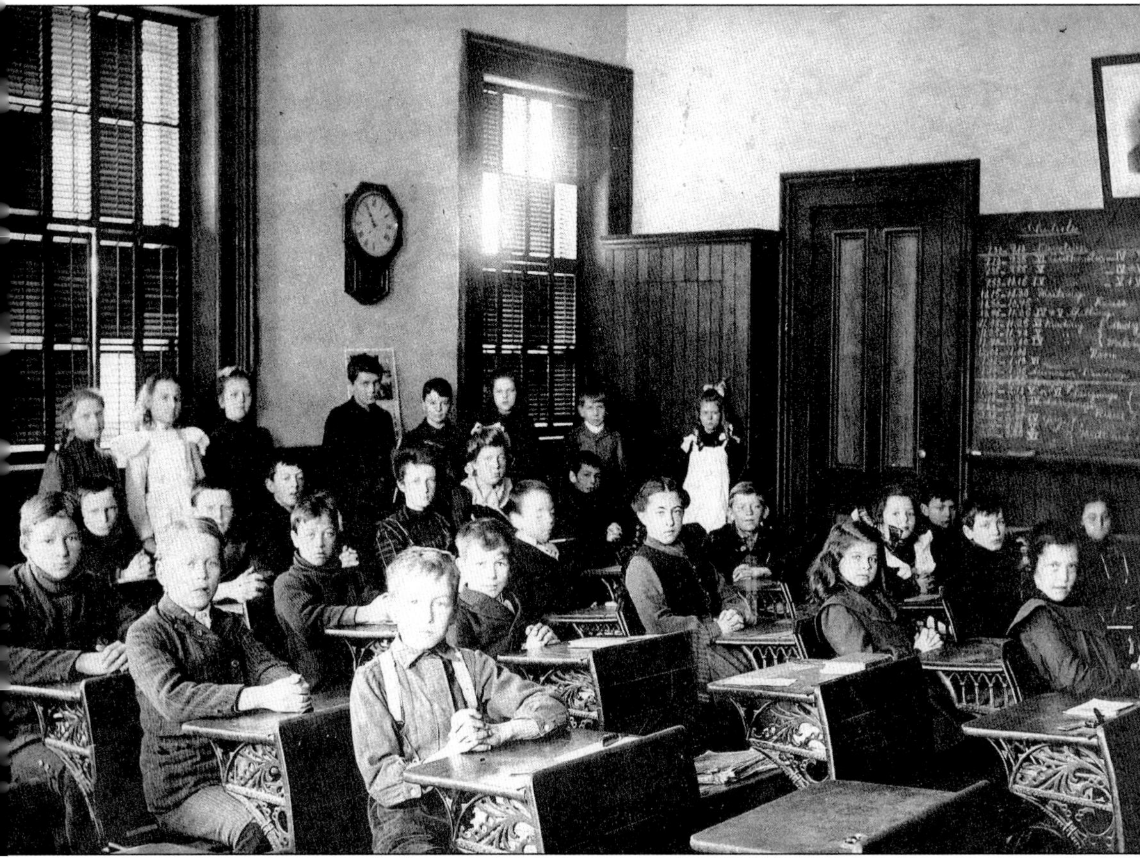

This classic schoolroom photograph was taken at the old Agawam Center School *c.* 1902. In the front row, third from left, is Richard E. Toelken (pages 69, 87, and 88). A schoolhouse clock identical to the one seen here was rescued during the demolition of the old Feeding Hills Center School by the late Walter T. Kerr and can be seen at the Agawam Historical & Fire House Museum. (Courtesy Paul Toelken.)

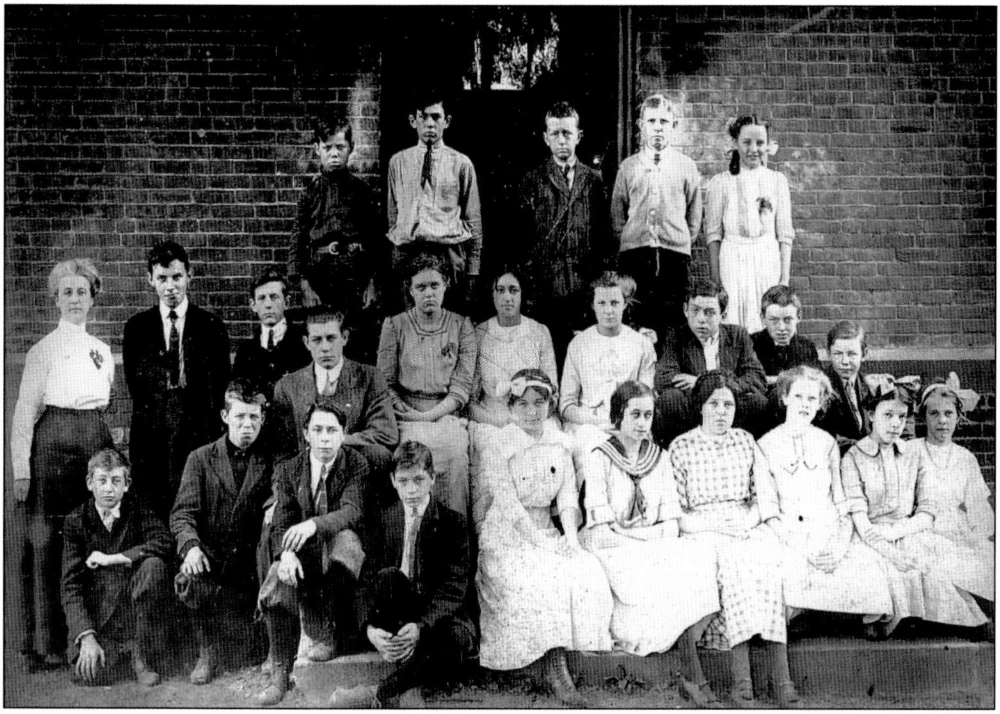

Two classes pose outside the old Feeding Hills Center School. The photograph below was taken in June 1910. Miss Richards is the teacher to the left in the photograph above. Classes for grades three through six were held in the brick building, which also served as town hall. Grades one and two were taught in a separate one-room schoolhouse on the property. An identical arrangement was in place at Agawam Center. (Courtesy Helen Light.)

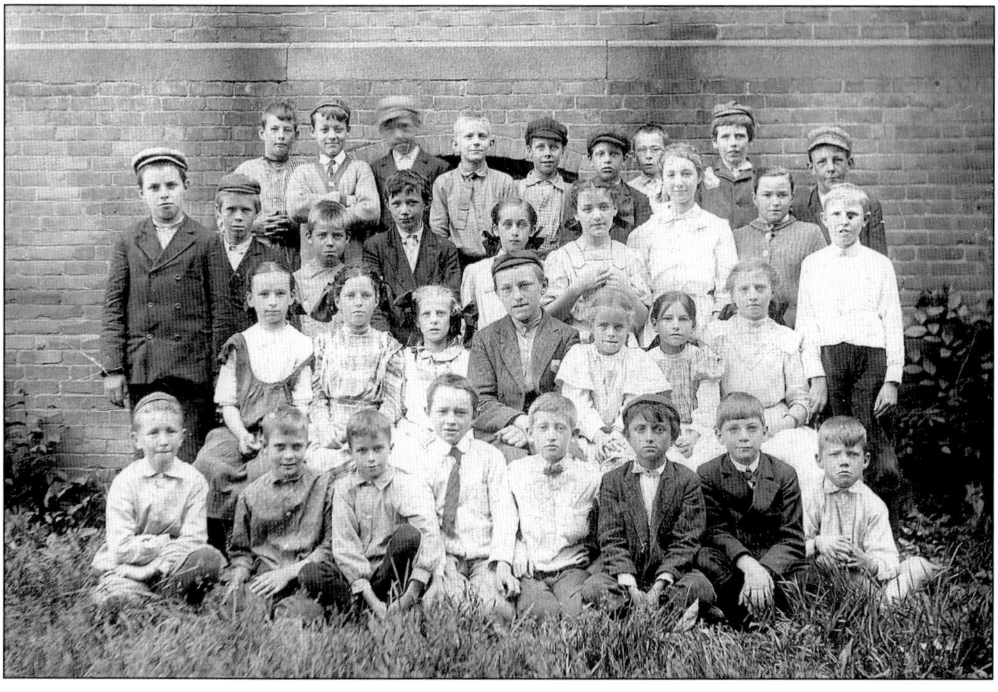

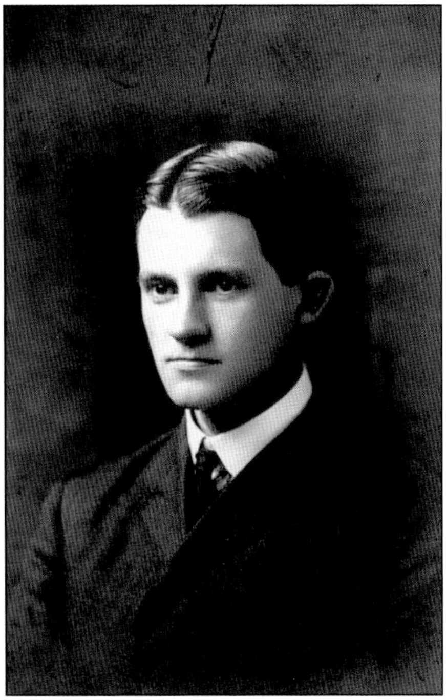

This photograph of Clifford M. Granger was most likely taken upon his graduation from Brown University *c.* 1902. Granger served as a member and chairman of the Agawam School Committee for 32 years. He was the younger brother of Clarence Granger. (Courtesy Paul Toelken.)

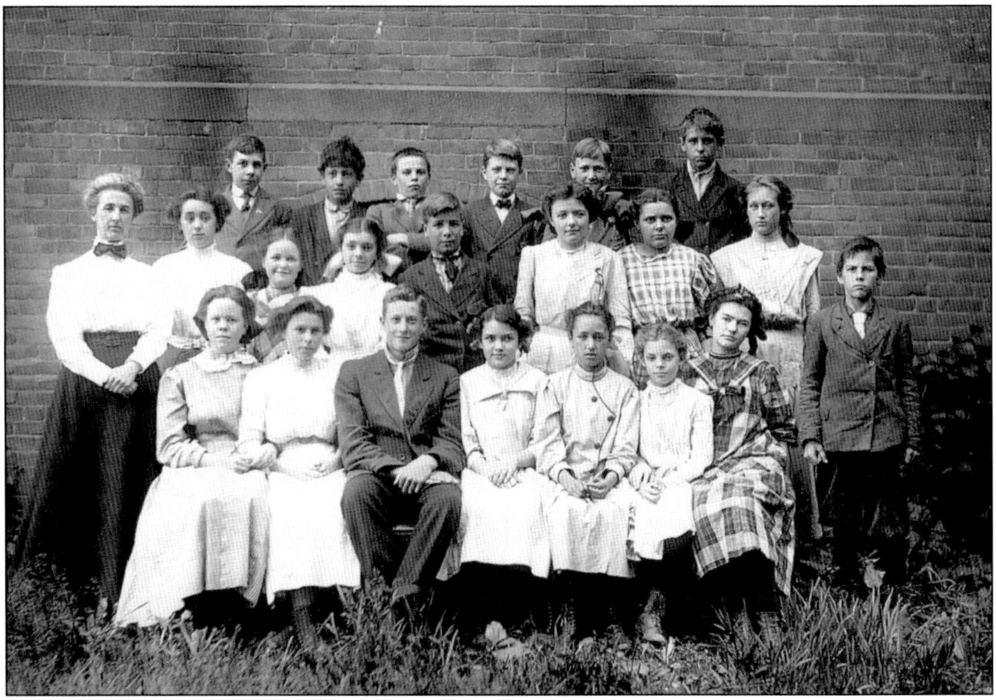

Miss Richards's class is pictured at the Feeding Hills Center School in June 1910. Included in the photograph are Clayton Roberts, Joseph Resigne, Harold Hillpold, Hermann Light, George Blackburn, Evelyn Cordes, Hazel Cooley, Edith Clark, Maude Light, Gilman Clark, Agnes Healy, Doris Meaum, Lena Fuller, Edward Schmantz, Gladys Steere, Robena Hillpold, Herbert Taylor, Laura Miner, Clara Fuller, Phyllis Granger, and Vivian Hastings. (Courtesy Paul Toelken.)

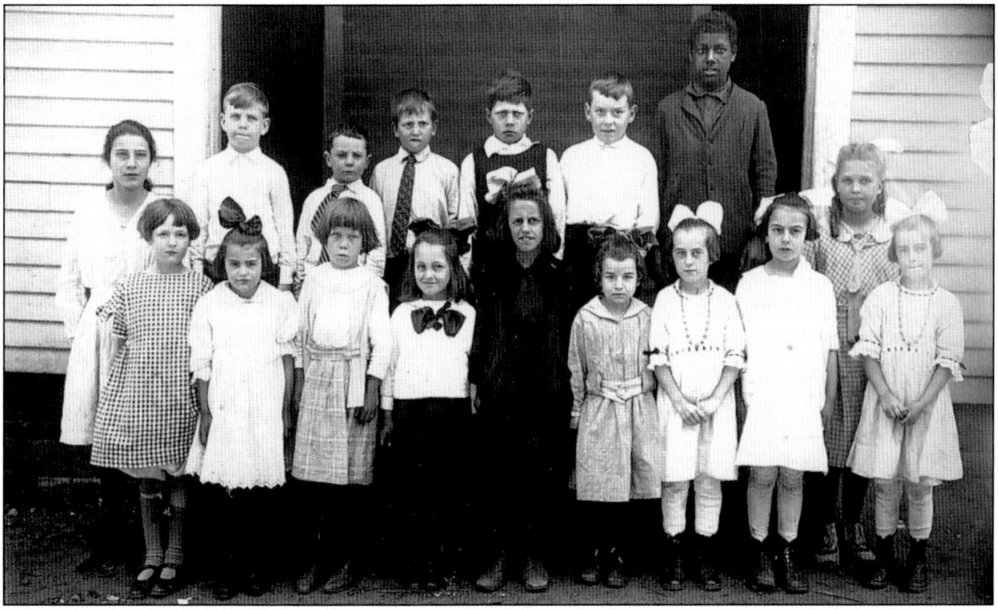

Students pose outside the one-room schoolhouse at Feeding Hills Center in May 1922. From left to right are the following: (first row) Claire Strong, Nina Arnold, ? Kaskaski, Anita Cesan (later Rising), Mary Christopher, Celestine Fournier, one of the Miller twins, Ethel Robinson, Lucy Smith, and the other Miller twin; (second row) Nancy Grimaldi, "Buster" Parent, Francis O'Connor, Francis Pilch, unidentified, Gerald Cleary, and Walter Gunn. (Courtesy Anita [Cesan] Rising.)

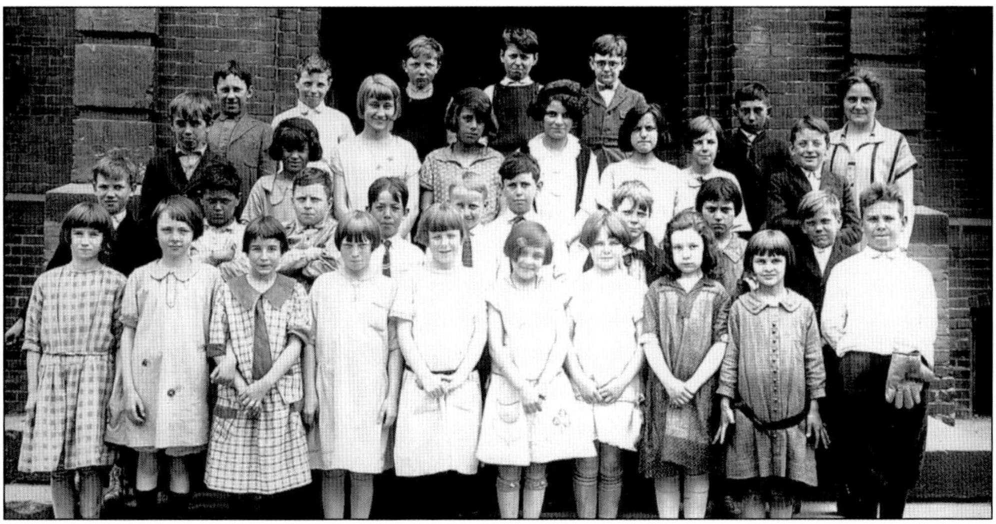

Students are shown outside the Feeding Hills Center School on May 19, 1925. From left to right are the following: (first row) Mary Drewnowski, unidentified, Celestine Fournier, ? Halloway, Barbara Halladay, Anita Cesan (later Rising), Ethel Renton, Mary Stalker, Sofie Drewnowski, and Buster Parent; (second row) two unidentified, Peter Demerski, Rudolph Zerra, Earl Cesan, Edmund Smith, Clarence Hawthorne, Pasqualina DiPinto, and Peter Kaskaski; (third row) Woodrow Humason, Lucy Graziano, ? August, ? Graziano, Nancy Grimaldi, Mary Christopher, Barbara Grout, ? Kopinski, and unidentified; (fourth row) two unidentified, ? Kopinski, unidentified, and Roderick White. (Courtesy Anita [Cesan] Rising.)

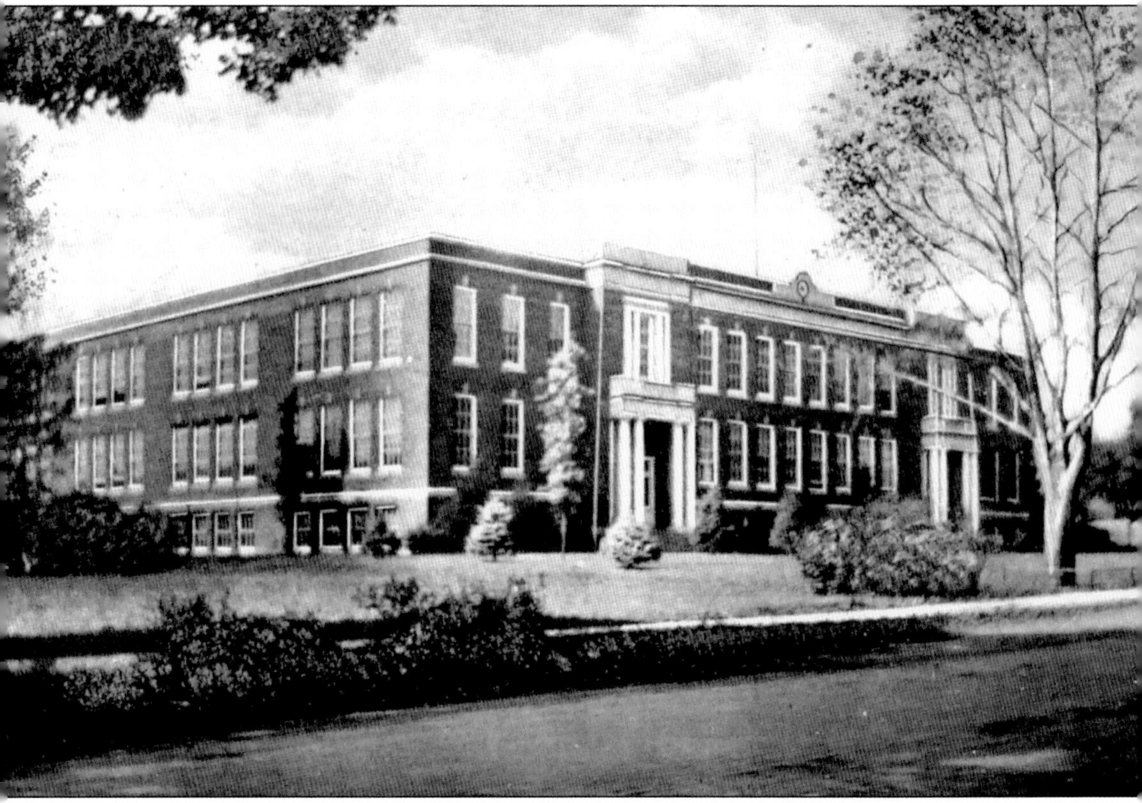

Prior to 1922, Agawam students attended and graduated high school in West Springfield. As early as 1895, the need for a town high school was recognized, although a motion "to build and equip a High School" at town meeting that year was voted down. It was not until 1920 that $250,000 was appropriated at town meeting to "purchase the Walter Barr lot and to erect a high school thereon." The new Agawam High School, located at 68 Main Street, was dedicated on December 8, 1922. The dedication exercises included musical selections from the school chorus and orchestra; remarks by town treasurer Henry Bodurtha and Massachusetts commissioner of secondary education Clarence D. Kingsley; the presentation of keys by building contractor W. W. Davis to John R. Lloyd, chairman of the building committee; and a dedication address by Massachusetts deputy commissioner of education Frank W. Wright. Lunch was served at 7:45 p.m., and there was dancing in the gymnasium from 10:30 p.m. to midnight. An addition was built in 1929, and a new cafeteria wing was added in 1963. The building currently serves grades five and six as the Agawam Middle School. (Author's collection.)

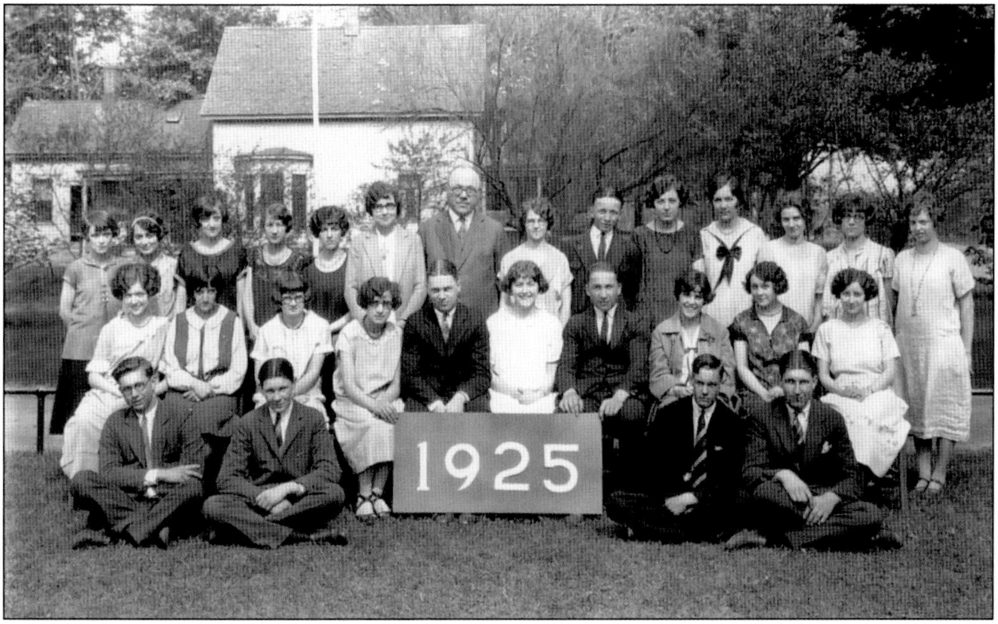

This portrait of the second class to graduate from Agawam High School was taken in front of the building, looking west. In addition to his role as high school principal, Benjamin J. Phelps (back row center, wearing glasses) was appointed superintendent of schools in 1922, a position he held until his death in 1946. (Agawam Historical Association collection.)

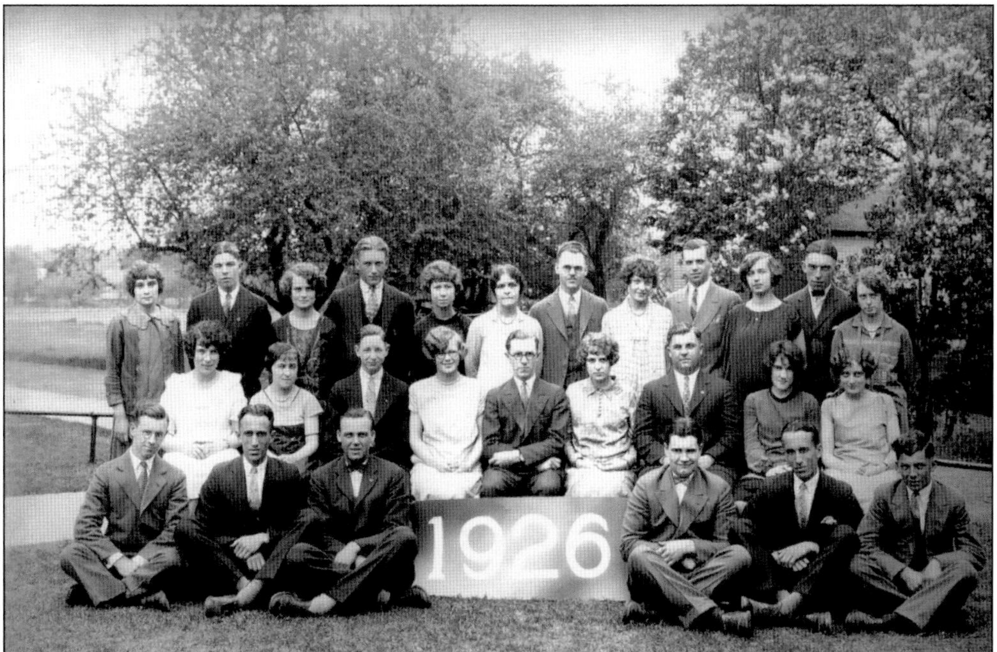

Pictured here is the Agawam High School class of 1926. Superintendent Benjamin J. Phelps said, "Agawam as the unit, not an Agawam of three villages [Agawam, Feeding Hills, and North Agawam or Mittineague] is what we want to develop, and that is the spirit our high school pupils are developing." (Agawam Historical Association collection.)

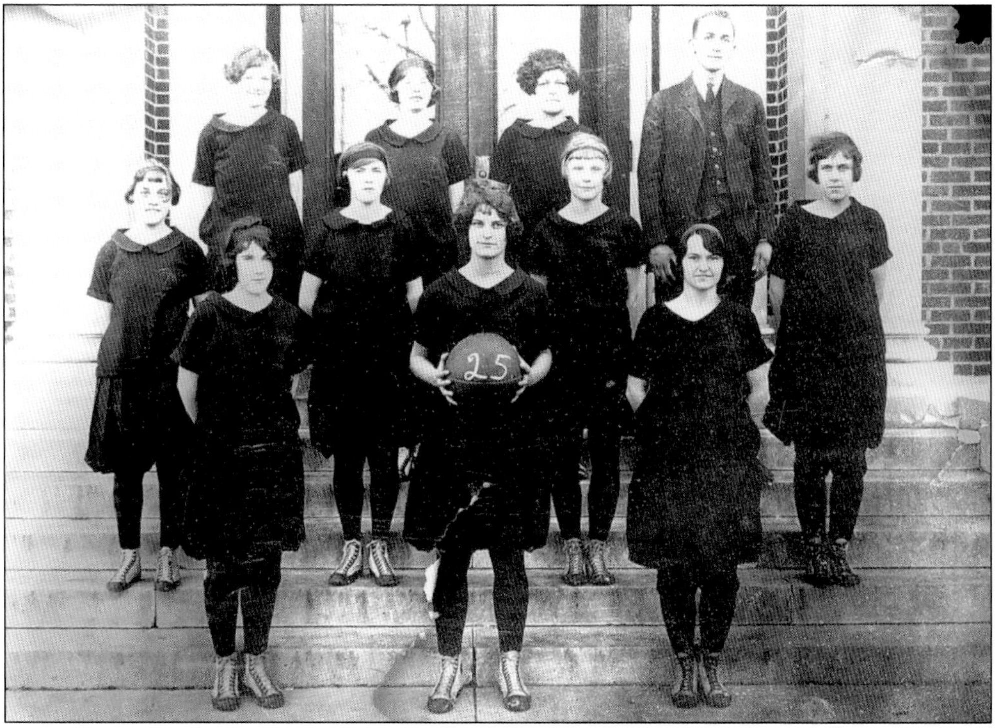

The Agawam High School girls basketball team poses in 1925. From left to right are the following: (first row) Meredith Reed, Grace Pond, and Audrey Phillips; (second row) Josey Novelli, Irene Costa, Esther Pond, and Esther Schwartz (later Reynolds); (third row) Dorothy Skinner, ? Rouillard, Eleanor "Soup" Campbell, and coach Harmon Smith. (Courtesy Everett Hodge.)

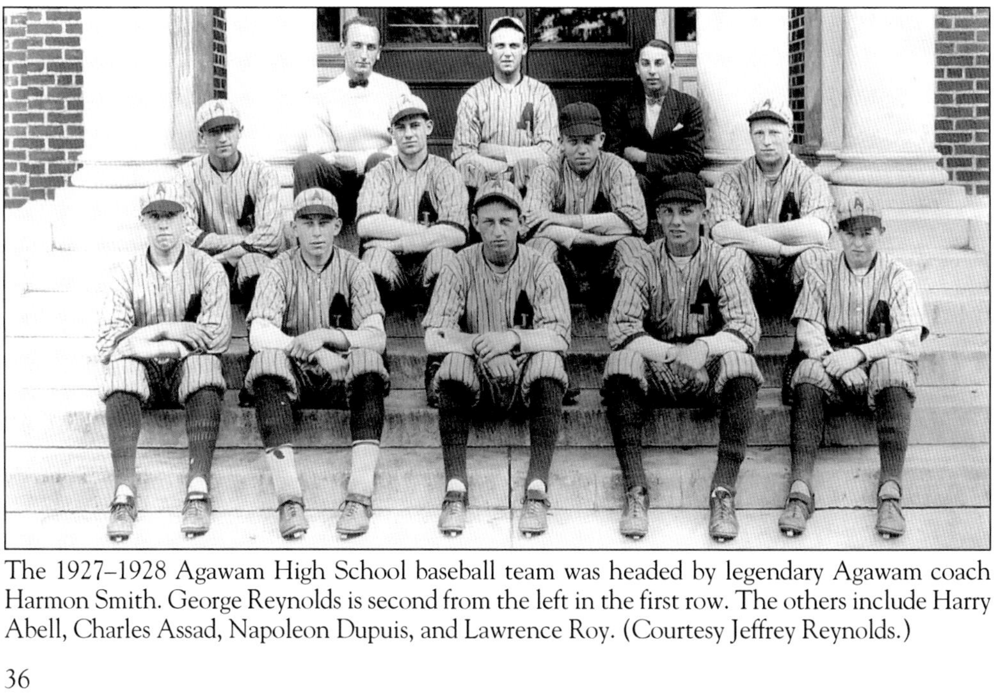

The 1927–1928 Agawam High School baseball team was headed by legendary Agawam coach Harmon Smith. George Reynolds is second from the left in the first row. The others include Harry Abell, Charles Assad, Napoleon Dupuis, and Lawrence Roy. (Courtesy Jeffrey Reynolds.)

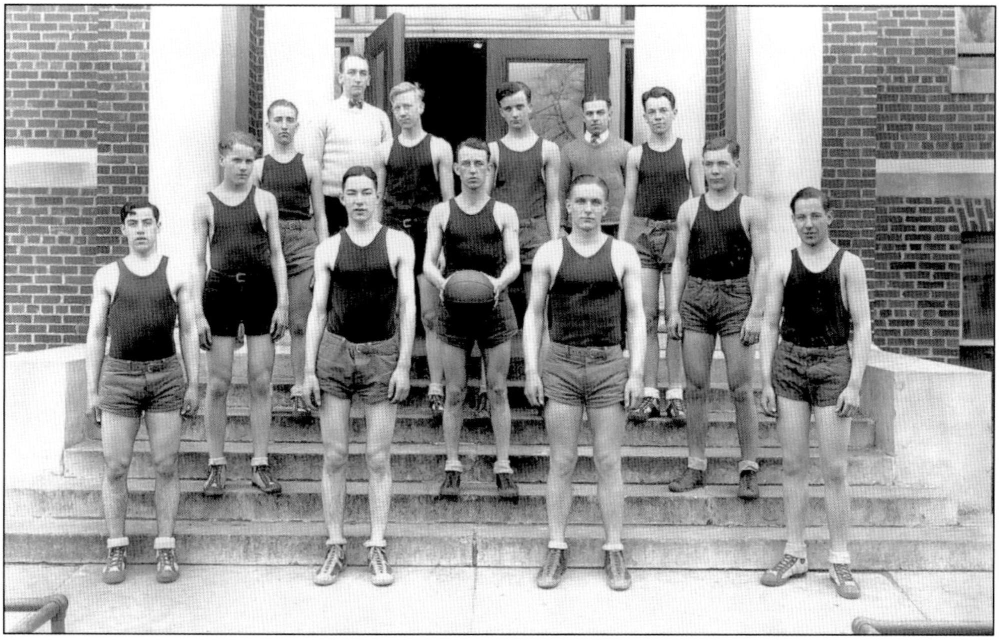

Pictured is the 1928–1929 Agawam High School boys basketball squad. Included in the photograph are Charles Assad, Walter Bodman, Raymond Fortini, Richard Kellogg, Richard Merrell, George Reynolds (first row, far right), Clifford Pond, Alfred Roy, Richard Wilson, captain Lawrence Roy (center, with ball), and manager Thomas Cascio (back row, at right, in sweater). Harmon Smith (wearing bowtie) was the coach. (Author's collection.)

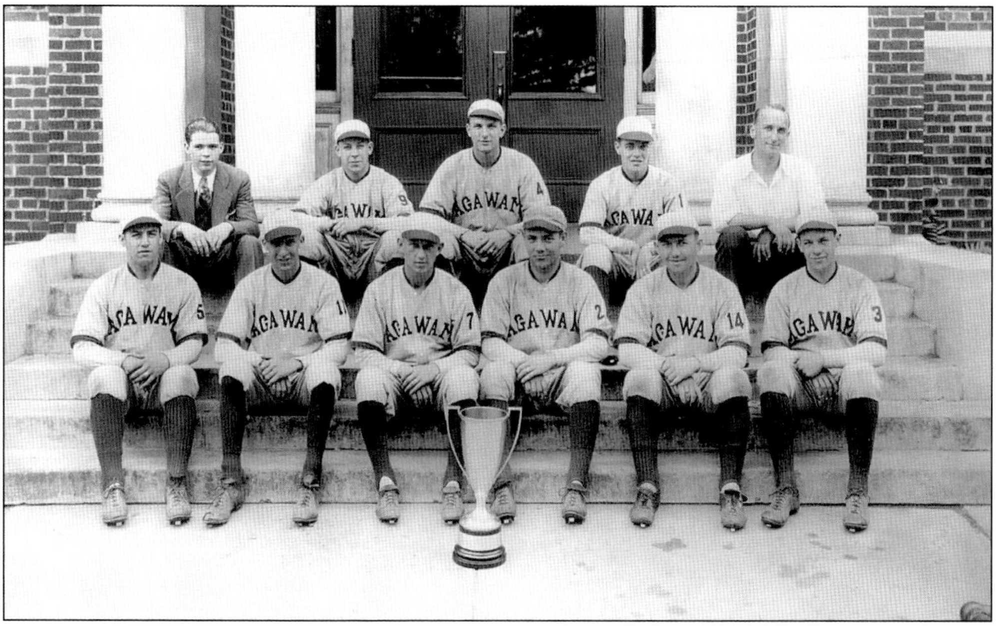

Seniors on coach Harmon Smith's 1929 Agawam High School baseball team include Harry Abell, Charles Assad, Richard Kellogg, Richard Merrell, Clifford Pond, and Lawrence Roy. (Author's collection.)

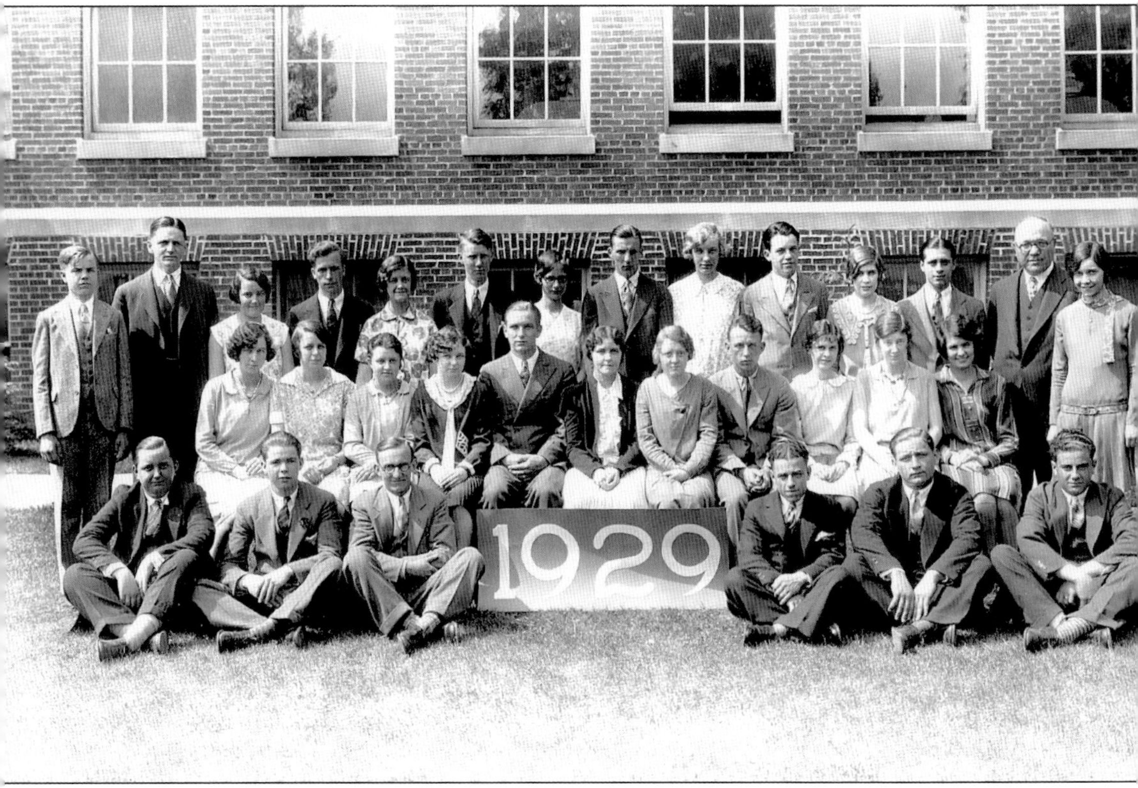

The Agawam High School class of 1929 is shown here. Their class motto was "Excelsior." Class members are Harry Abell, Henry Arnold, Charles Assad, Ruth Bitgood, Harris Blanchard, Marie Bozenhard, Catherine Burke, Thomas Cascio, Pauline Corriveau, Helen Mae Diamond, Napoleon Dupuis, Anna Fay (secretary), Alice Fickweiler, Hazel French, Thomas Holmes, Helen Humiston, Frank Keating, Richard Kellogg, Richard Merrell, Doris Parker, Harry Patterson, Clifford Pond (class president), Ruth Renton (vice president), Eva Richard, Doris Roberts, Helen Rudman, Lawrence Roy (treasurer), and Steven Sliech. High school principal and Agawam superintendent of schools Benjamin J. Phelps is in the back row, second from the right. (Agawam Historical Association collection.)

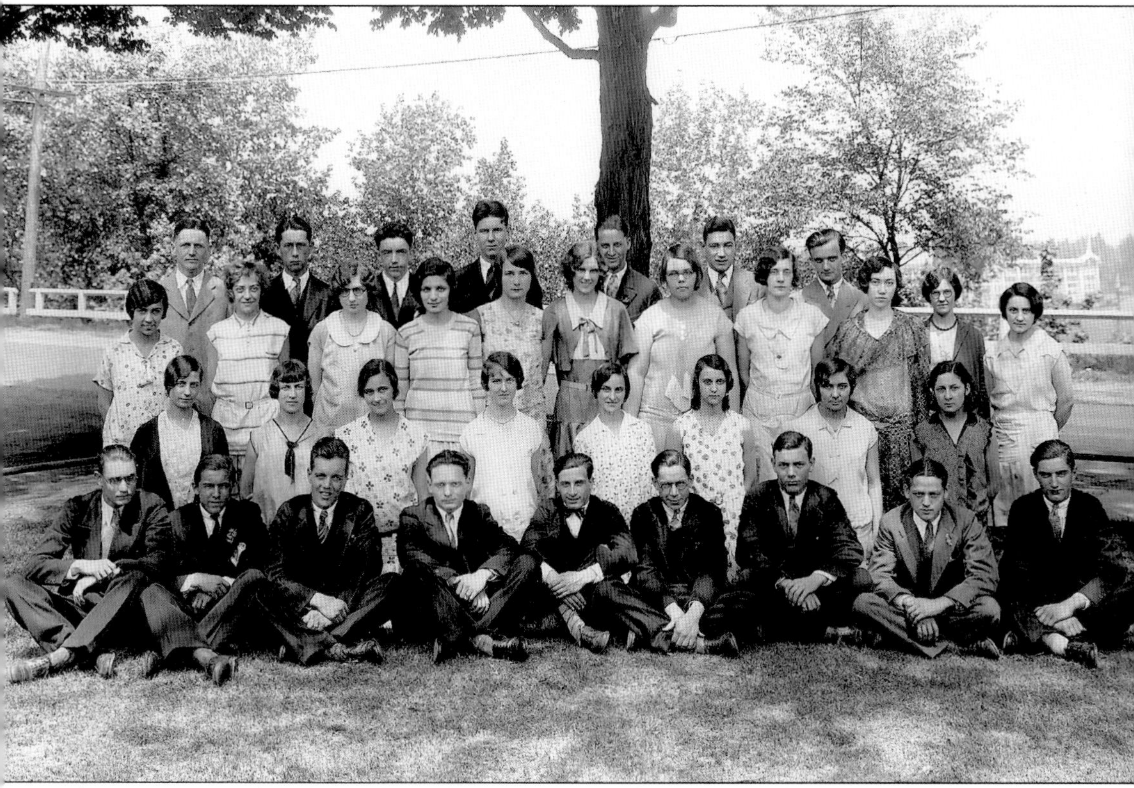

The Agawam High School class of 1930 is shown here. Their class motto was "Victoria patientiam coronat." Class members are Edwin Arnold, John Arnold, Walter Bodman, Grace Brady, Vera Brown, Ola Campbell, Robert Carroll, John Cirillo, Flory Costa (vice president), Marian Cowles, Mae Davis, Tina Fragomeni, Raymond Geoffrion (treasurer), Edward Grimes, Kathleen Grimes (secretary), Inez Lucardi, William Mabb, Constance Magovern, Grace Merrill, Angelina Novelli, Eileen Otto, Frances Pedulla, Lawrence Peterson, Ethel Pronk, James Reynolds, Maurice Rohan, George Roos (president), Alfred Roy, Corada Tinti, Rebelle Vancini, Lottie Voislow, Richard Wilson, and Jerry Zerra. The Hampden County Improvement League Building on the grounds of the Eastern States Exposition can be seen across the Agawam River at the upper right. (Agawam Historical Association collection.)

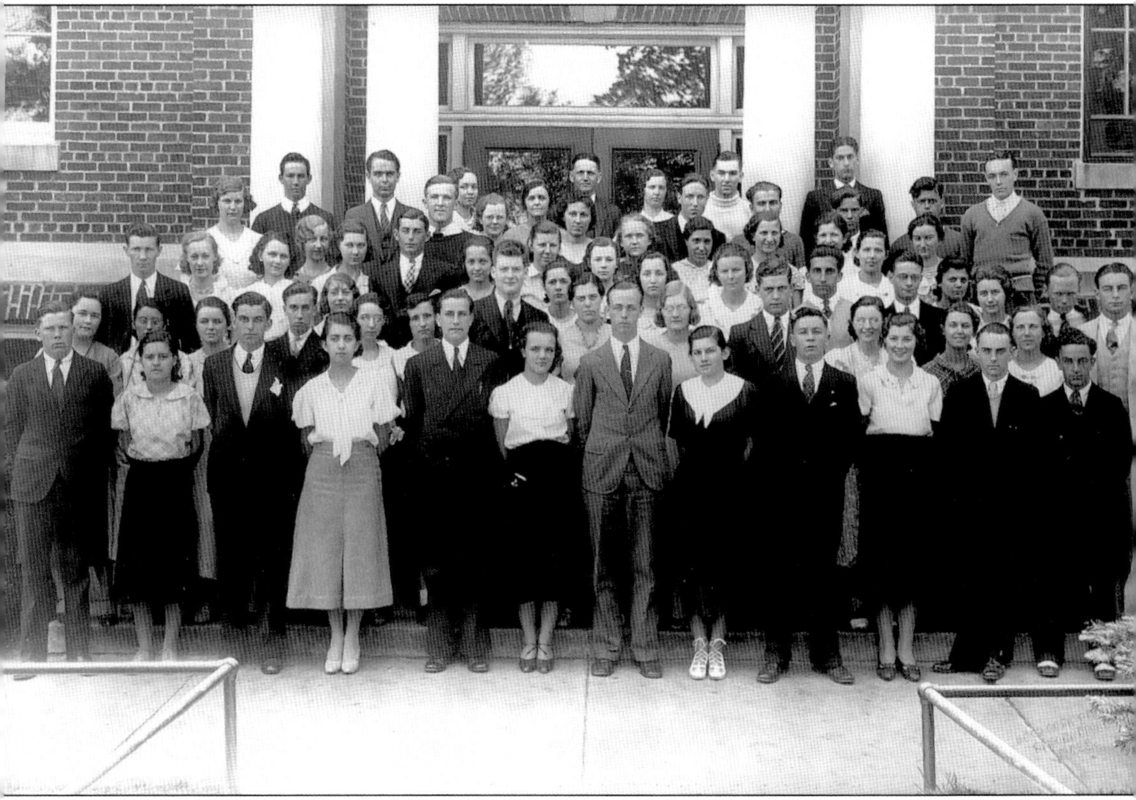

Agawam High School class of 1933 is shown here. Class members are Ruth Abbott, Valentina Agnoli, Charles Ardizoni, Nellie Mae Barden, Norma Best, Dorothy Brown, John Buckley, Martha Burnett, Elmer Cascio, Anita Cesan, Vincent Cirillo, Edward Connor, Blanche Couture, Paul D'Amato, Ralph D'Amato, Lucille Danforth, Alfred Davis, Perino Devecchi, Helen Donaldson, Patsy Ferrero, Dorothy Geoffrion, Roland Geoffrion, Frank Goss, Cecilia Grasso, Raymond Greenwood, Barbara Grout, Barbara Halladay, Charles Hamblen, Madeline Haynes, Justine Healy, Margrethe Jensen, Arthur Johnson, Elsie Johnson, Robert Johnston, Clark Jones, Mary Kalinowski, Peter Kaskaski, Donald Kenney, Clara Maley, Madalene Mencarelli, Catherine Moccio, Doris Morrison, Virginia Noble, Francis O'Connor, Rose Pedulla, Josephine Penna, Anna Piazzo, Rita Provost, Rena Raffinetti, Thomas Ramah, Robert Raymond, Ida Ricci, Marcel Rioux, Beulah Rivers, Norman Roberts, Edna Rust, Alyce Scherpa, Elsie Schultz, Malcolm Smith, Frederick Soden, Irma Soper, Marguerite Tatro, Mary Tatro, Thomas Voislow, Albert Wieland, Barbara Wright, and Eleanor Wright. (Courtesy Anita [Cesan] Rising.)

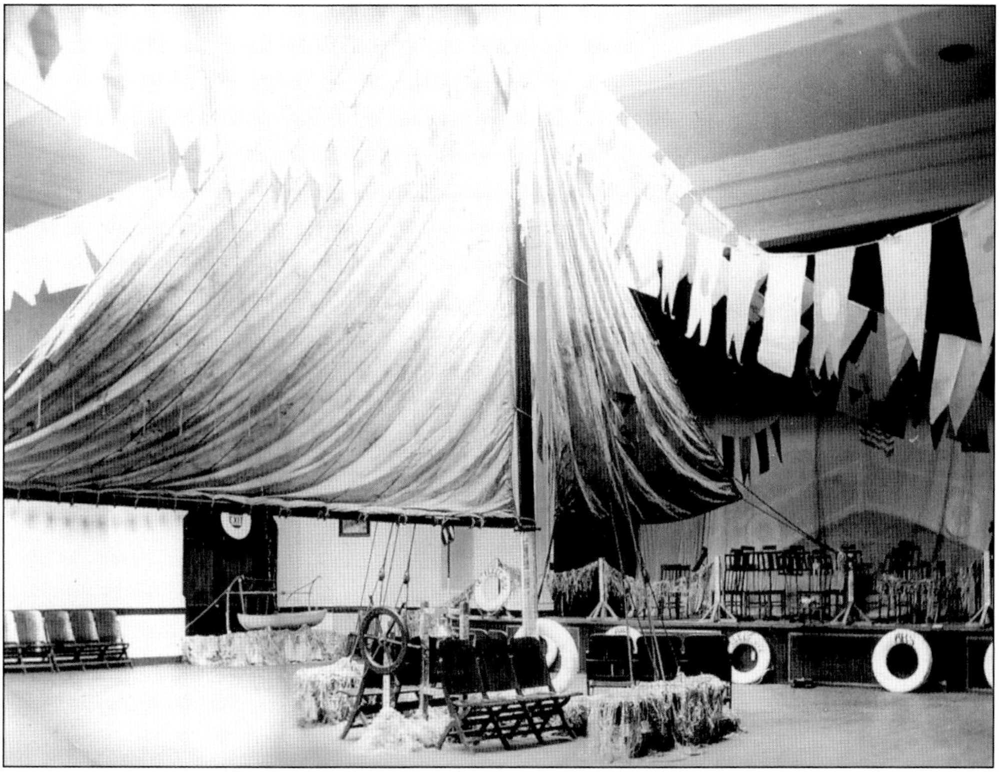

The Agawam High School junior prom was held in the school auditorium on May 19, 1933. The building now houses the middle school. (Courtesy Anita [Cesan] Rising.)

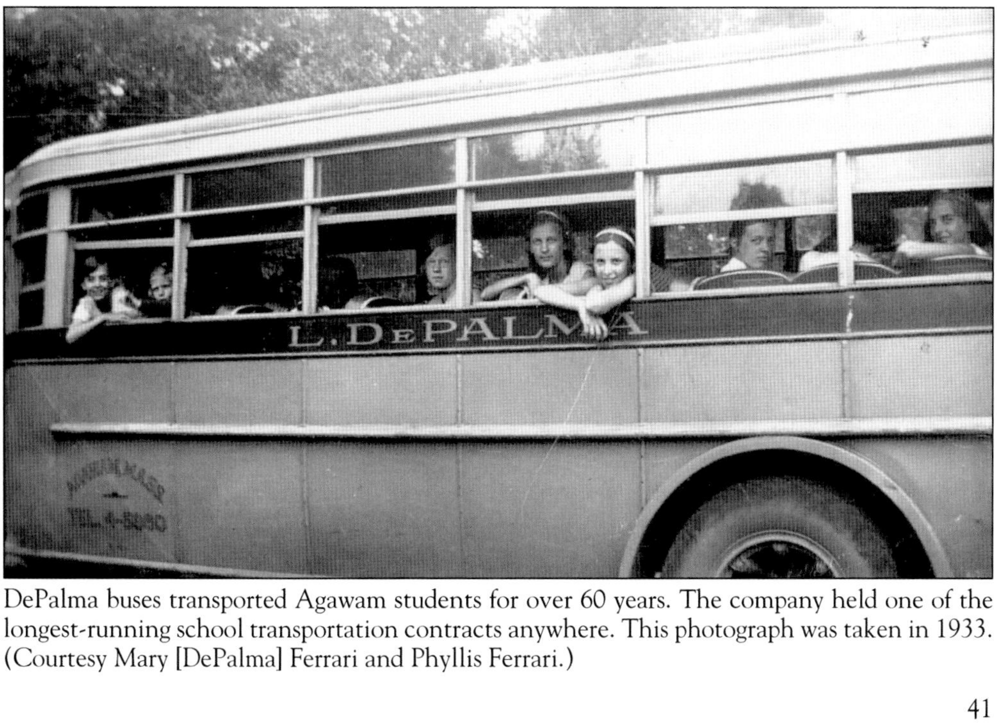

DePalma buses transported Agawam students for over 60 years. The company held one of the longest-running school transportation contracts anywhere. This photograph was taken in 1933. (Courtesy Mary [DePalma] Ferrari and Phyllis Ferrari.)

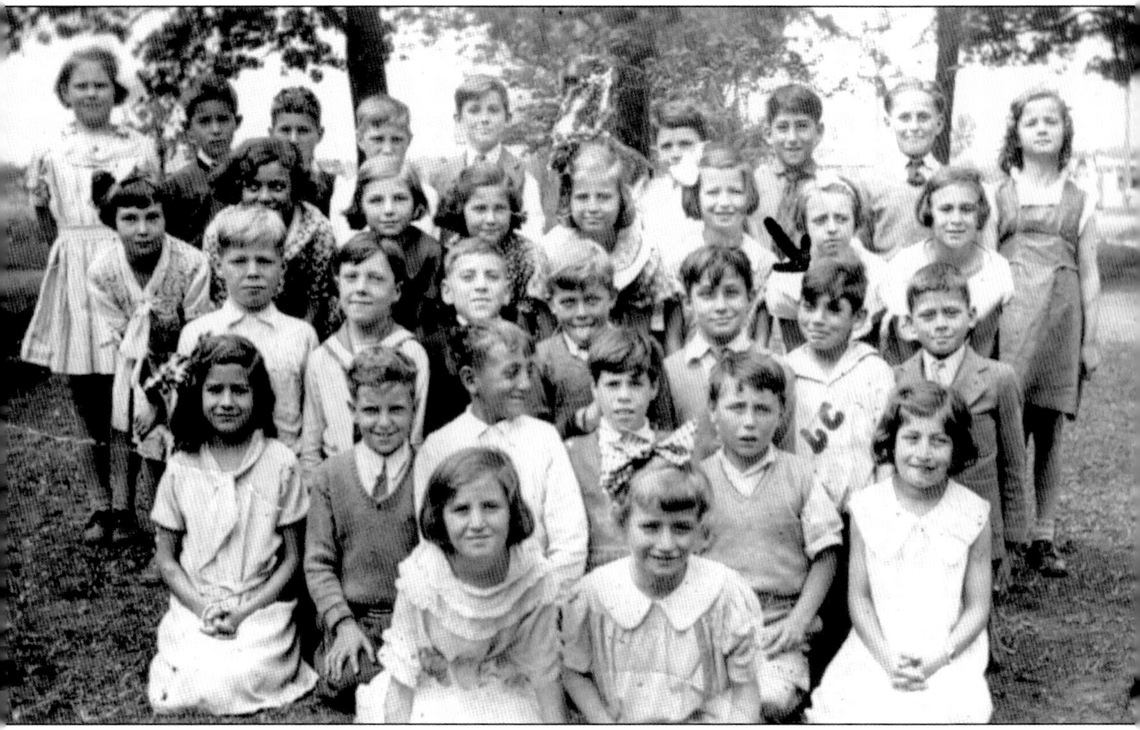

Lionel Cincotta (third row, second from the right) is shown with his fourth-grade classmates at the Springfield Street School in Feeding Hills in 1934–1935. The school was later named after Faolin Peirce, and it now serves as the Agawam Police Department headquarters. (Courtesy Felix Cincotta.)

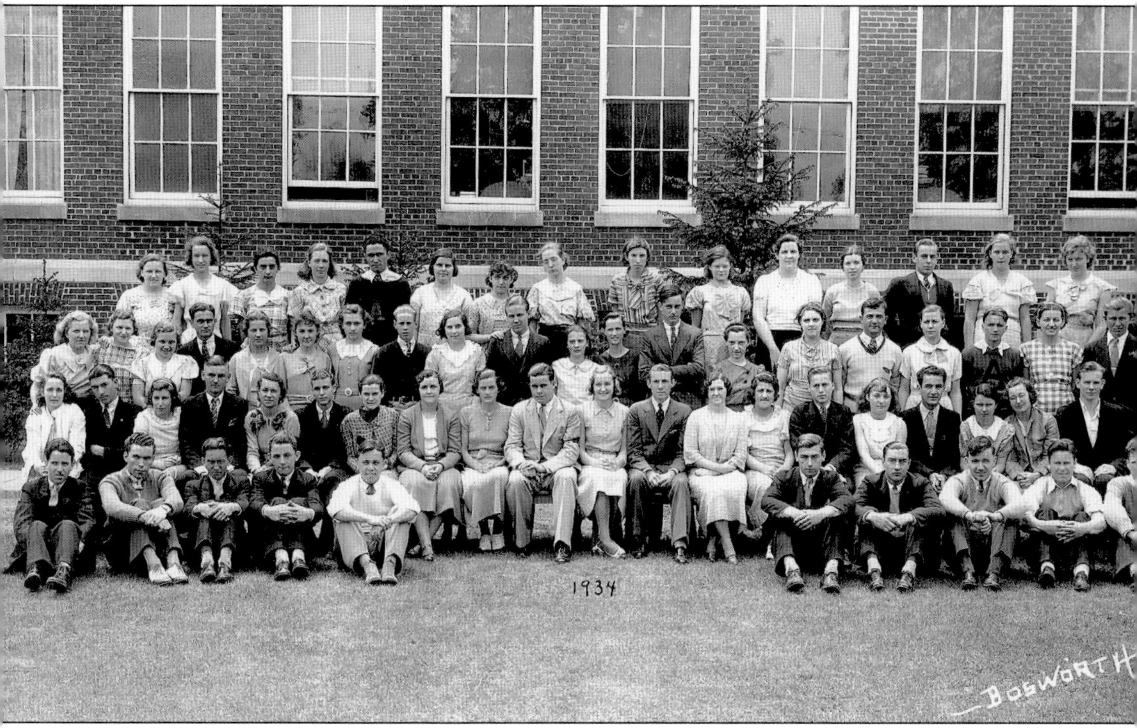

The Agawam High School class of 1934 poses for this photograph. The class motto was "The past is gone forever, the future's all our own." Class members are Elizabeth Abrams, Henry Alvergini, Lillian Ardizoni, Joseph Assad, Betsy Bailey, Harold Bailey, Mary Beauchane, Leonard Belcher, Frederick Bennett, Robert Bennett, Edward Bessette, Odette Bessette, Virginia Birchard, Eunice Bitgood, Elizabeth Bloom, Rose Brusseau, Winifred Carroll, Anna Cascella, Helen Cascella, William Cassens, Mary Chagnon, Michael Christopher, Evelyn Cowles, Paul Daubitz, Daniel DiDonato, Henry Fessler, Muriel Fraser, Donald Gensheimer, Henry Gensheimer, Bernice Halladay, Jane Hamblen, John Hastings, Shirley Hawkes, Robert Hennessey, Calvin Hewey, Aldah Holloway, Gertrude Jensen, Ronald Johnson, Irene Kalafut, John Kennedy, Elaine LaFleche, Jennie Lango, Evelyn Lewis, Lena Lodi, Frances Lucardi, Fern Miller, Raymond Montagna, Clayton Moore, Beverly Needham, Lydia Pisano, Samuel Provo, Helen Ramah, Marion Rising, Grant Sackett, Richard Shields, Robert Smith, Catherine Spaight, Walter Stepanik, Ernest Stone, Doris Svenson, Adele Swanson, Barbara Tulloch, Muriel Webster, Jennie White, and Edward Zielinski. (Agawam Historical Association collection.)

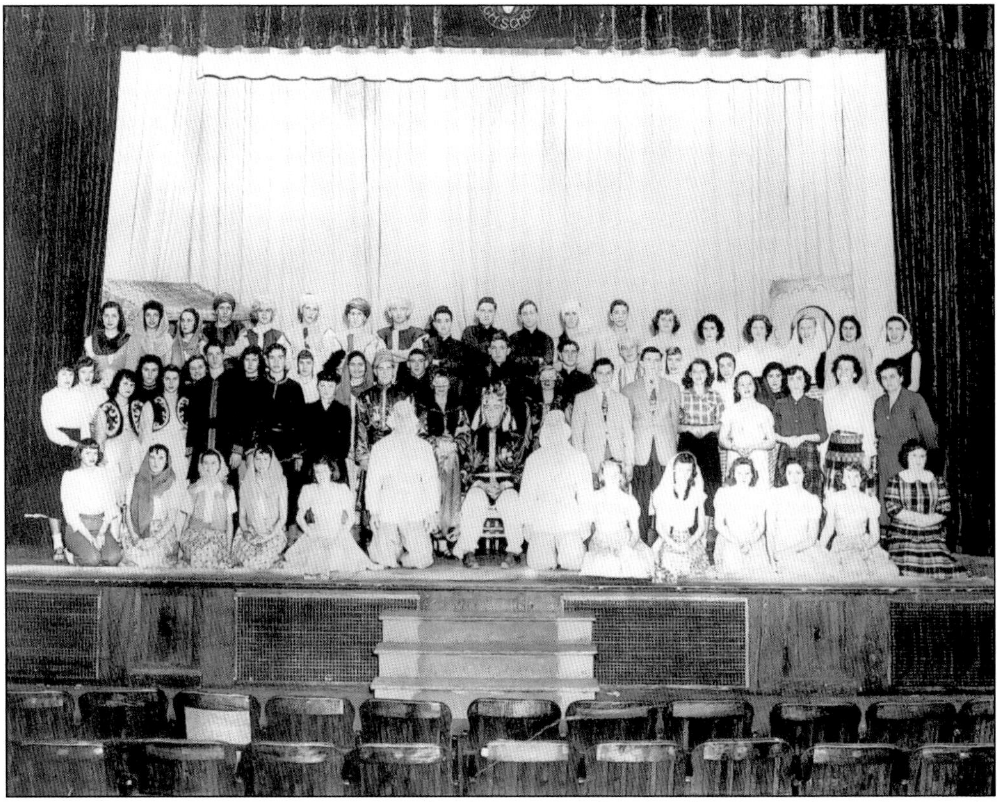

The cast of the 1949 Agawam High School musical *Belle of Baghdad* poses for a photograph. (Agawam Historical Association collection.)

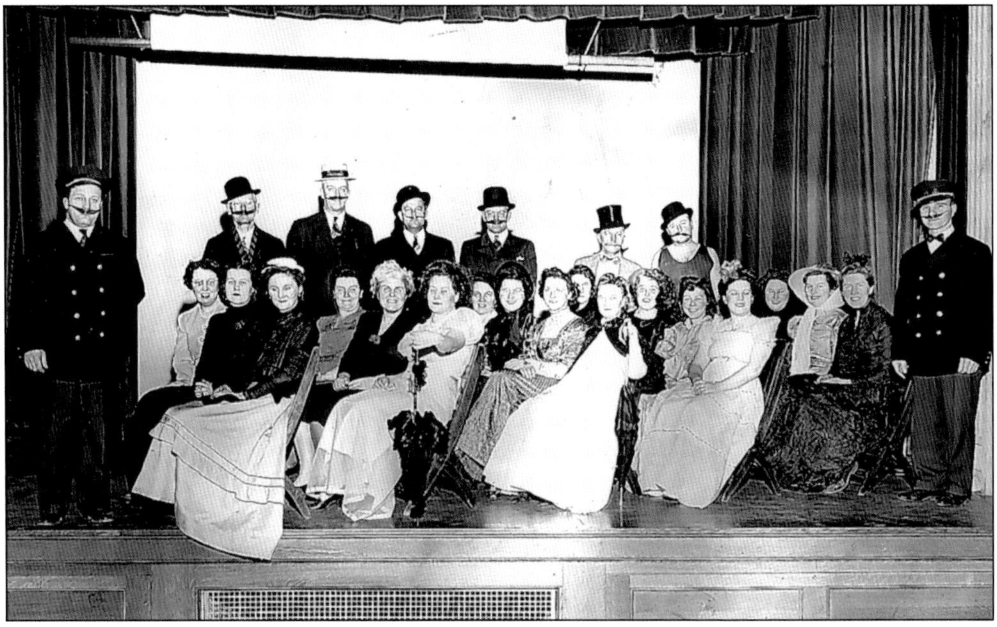

This PTA show took place in the late 1940s at Benjamin J. Phelps Elementary School (former Agawam Center School), at 689 Main Street. (Courtesy Joan Martel.)

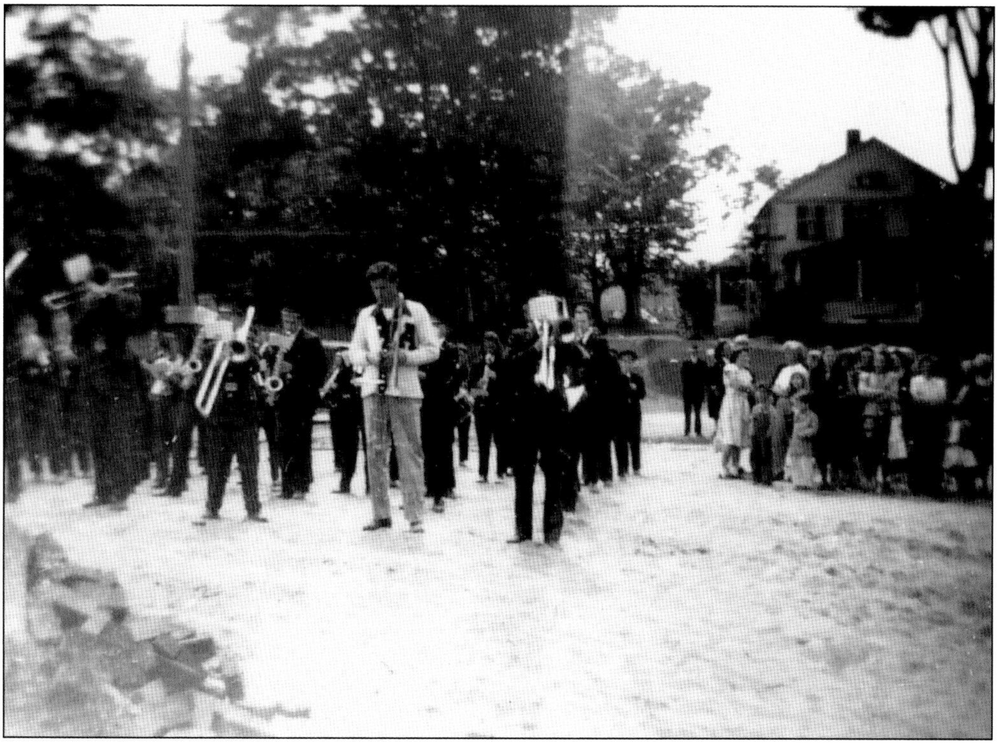

Above, a band plays at the laying of the cornerstone for Clifford M. Granger School. The school opened in 1950, replacing the old Feeding Hills Town Hall and Center School, which had stood in Feeding Hills Center since 1874. The new elementary school was named for the longtime school committee member (page 32). (Courtesy Anita Rising.)

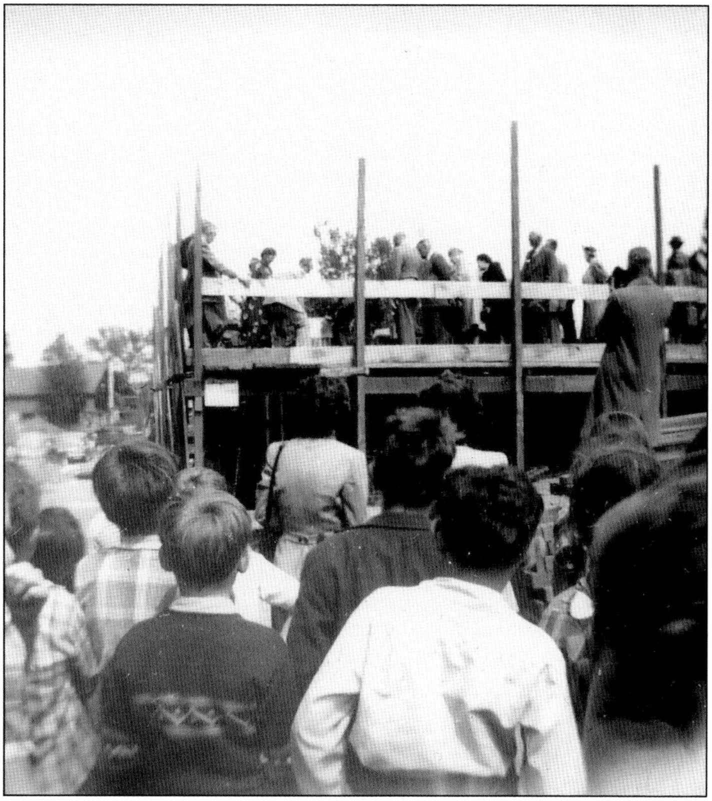

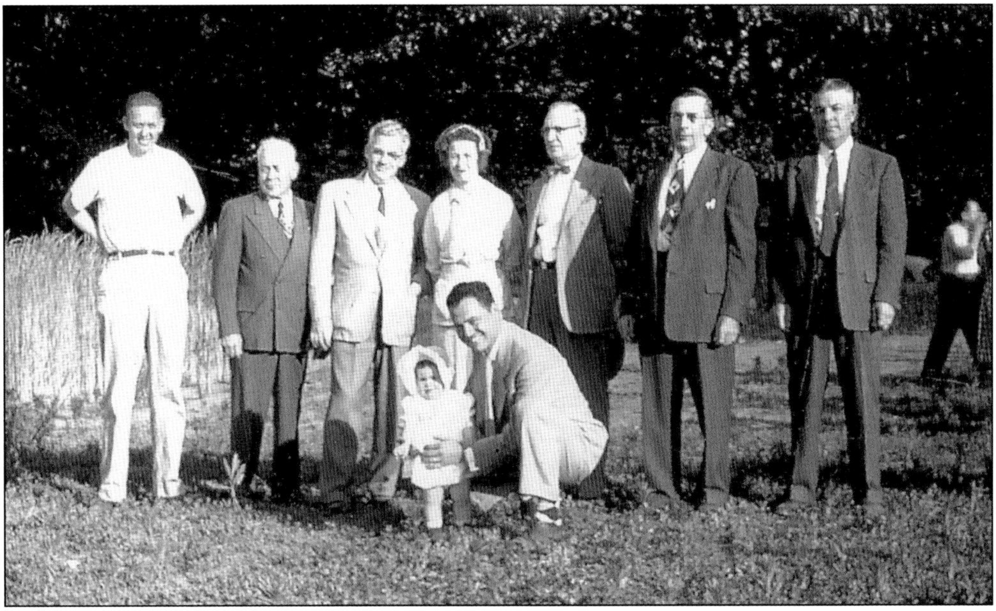

The high school building committee is pictured in 1954 at the groundbreaking for the new Agawam High School at 760 Cooper Street. Committee members are Benjamin S. Bassani (kneeling, with daughter Candy), William J. Coughlin, Roy K. Cowan, Raymond J. Deloghia, Wylie C. Hubbard, Irving R. LaFleur, Elizabeth B. Pond, and William Vigneaux. The new high school was dedicated on December 11, 1955. With many additions over the years, it has become the state's largest one-story high school. (Courtesy Candy [Bassani] Martin.)

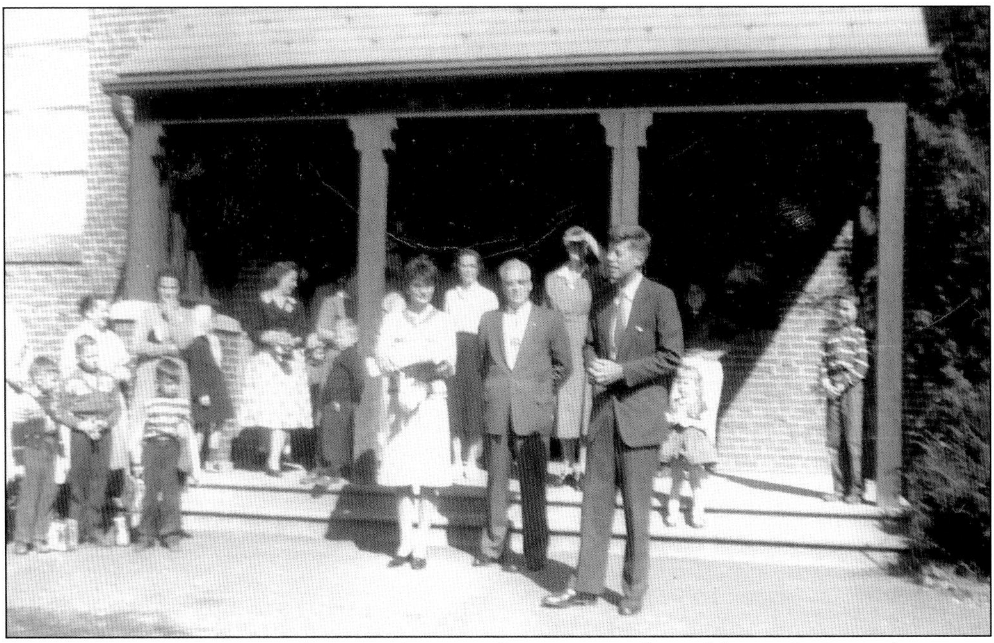

In this photograph by David Barnard, Sen. John F. Kennedy and his wife, Jacqueline, visit Clifford M. Granger School in 1958. Between them is Agawam police chief Kenneth Grady. (Courtesy Millicent Barnard.)

Four

Always a Party

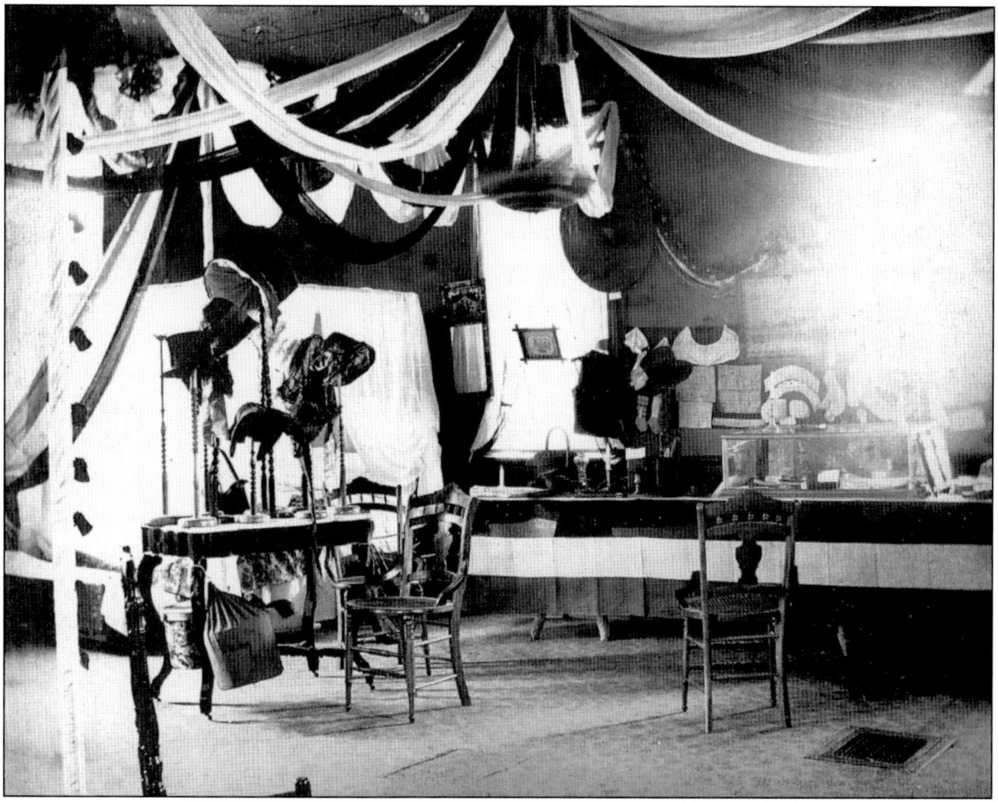

This Colonial exhibit at the old Agawam Town Hall on February 22, 1905, reminds us that at one time Washington's Birthday was more than just a day off. (Agawam Historical Association collection; gift of Donald Goss.)

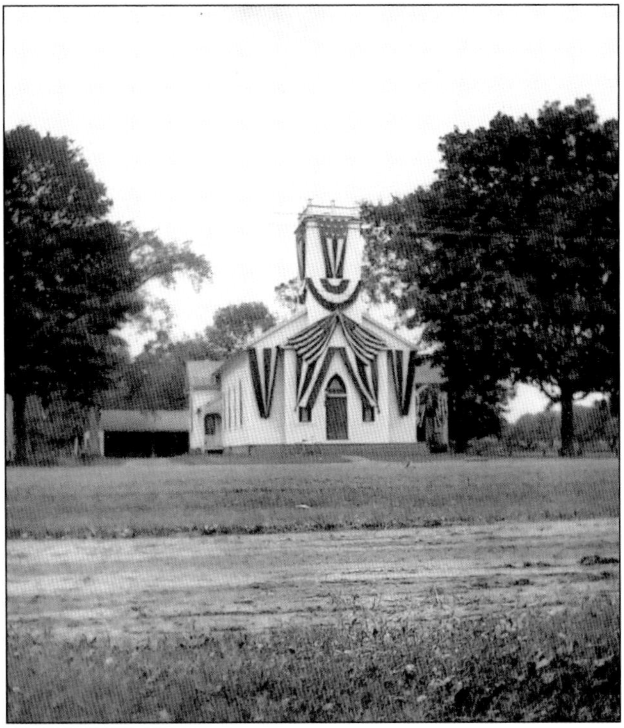

In 1904, it was voted at town meeting to appropriate $500 for the celebration of the 50th anniversary of the incorporation of the town of Agawam, to be held in August 1905. That sum is equivalent to more than $10,000 today. Here, the Agawam Baptist Church is dressed for the occasion. (Courtesy Paul Toelken.)

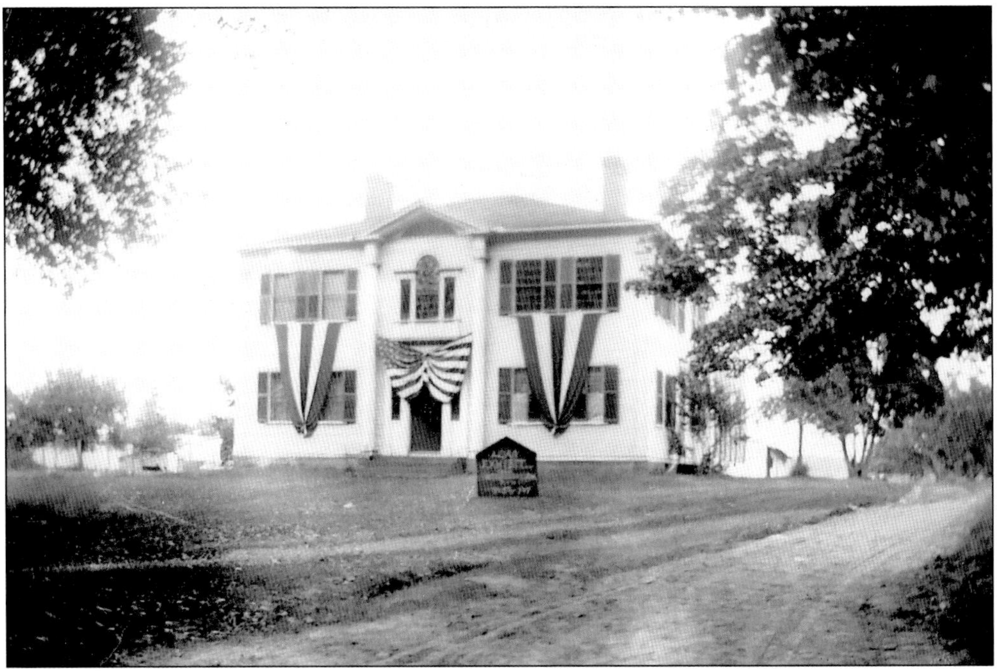

The Captain Charles Leonard House, then known as the Fowler House after the family who had long lived there, is shown as it looked at the time of the anniversary celebration on Wednesday, August 2, 1905. The house turned 100 years old that year, and several rooms of the house were open during the celebration as an example of Colonial life (pages 110–111). (Courtesy Paul Toelken.)

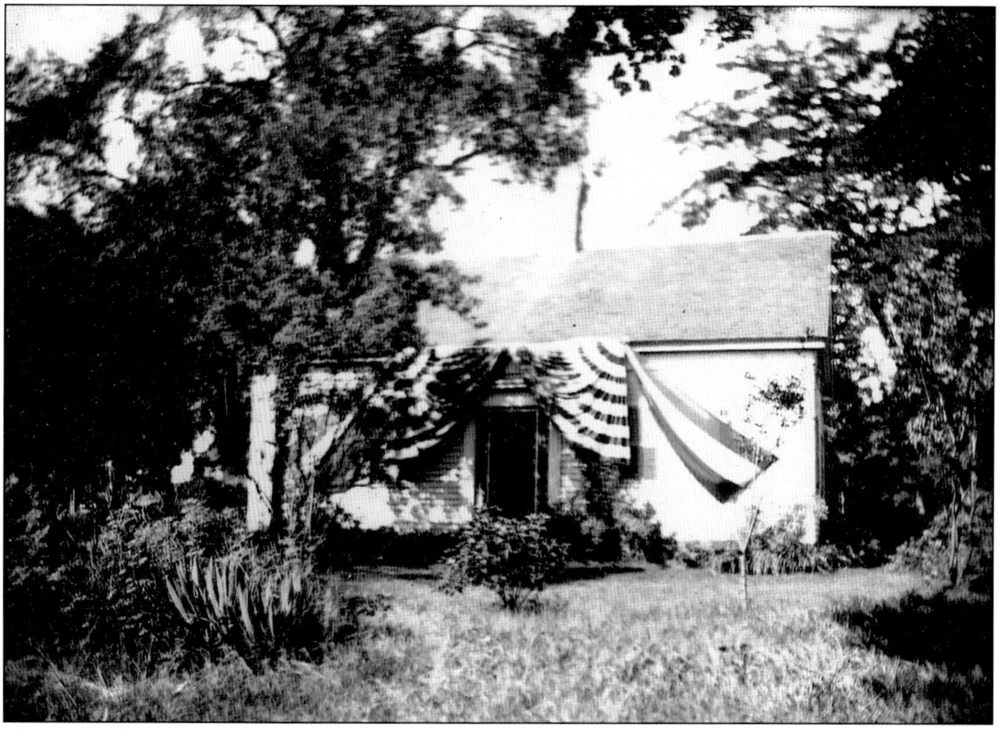

The Bodurtha home, at 41 Elm Street, is shown during the 50th anniversary celebration. Henry E. Bodurtha presided over the 10:30 a.m. opening ceremonies, which followed a 9:00 a.m. band concert by the 12th Regiment Band, directed by Fred Grady. (Courtesy Paul Toelken.)

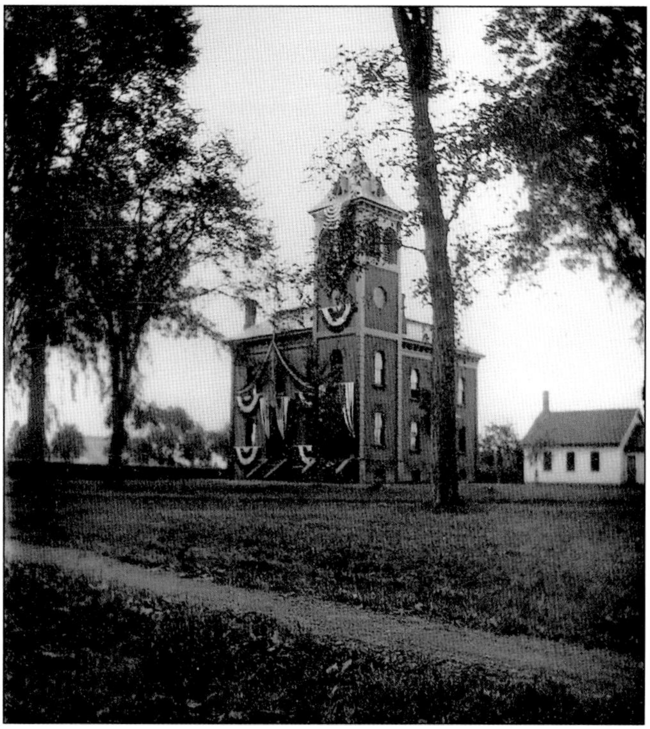

Shown here is Agawam Town Hall, with the primary school building to the right, in August 1905. Benjamin J. Phelps Elementary School and Veterans Green currently occupy this location at the corner of Main and School Streets. The 50th anniversary celebration concluded after a day of music, lunch, and "after dinner speaking" with "A Town Prospective" given by Charles Palmer Davis. (Courtesy Paul Toelken.)

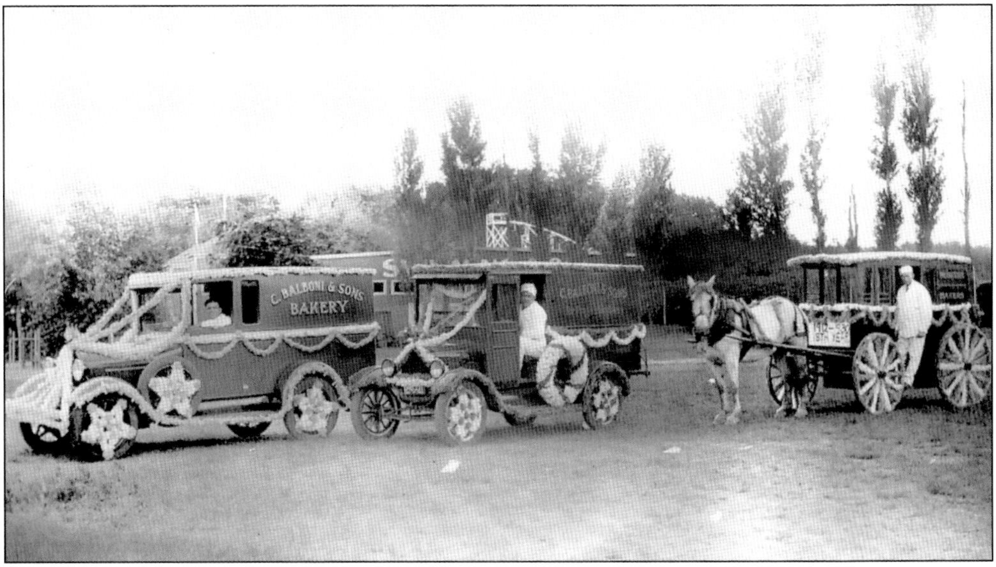

Just months after the stock market crash of 1929, Agawam residents voted to appropriate $1,000 for the celebration of the 75th anniversary of the incorporation of their town. Today's equivalent would be nearly $15,000. On August 12, 1930, a parade ran down Main Street to Riverside Park, where the Balboni Bakery fleet is seen decorated for the occasion. (Courtesy Mark Balboni.)

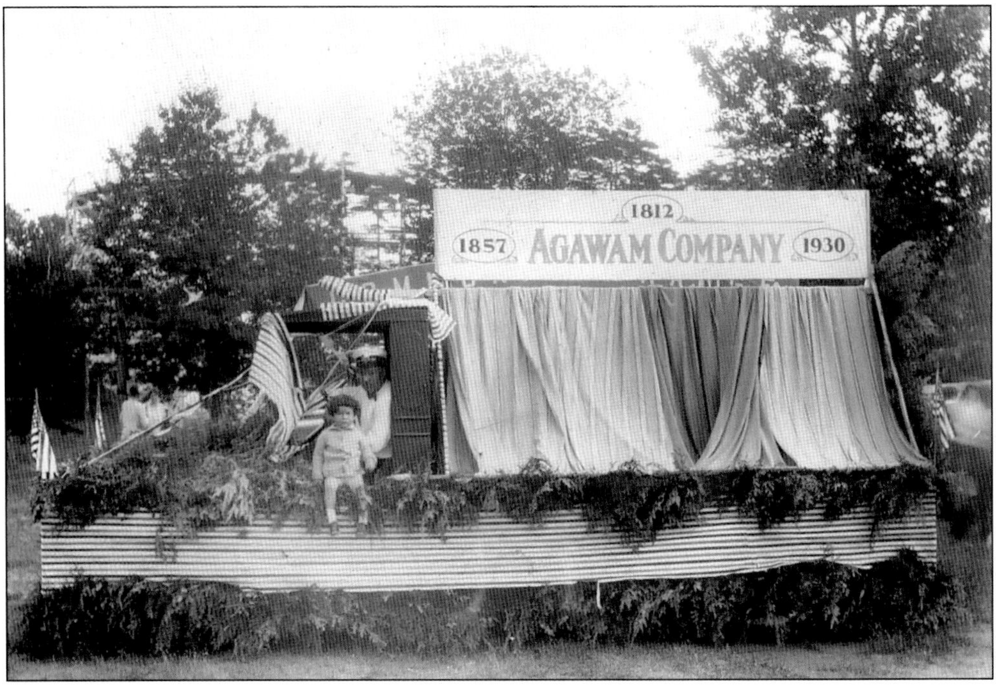

The author has an envelope that was mailed to the Agawam Company from a convent in Bavaria during the 1920s (with six million marks of postage affixed). The postcard attests to the worldwide popularity of the woolen mill's products, as well as the rampant inflation in Germany at that time. The company's entry in the 75th anniversary parade is seen here. The mill building on Elm Street still houses businesses. (Author's collection.)

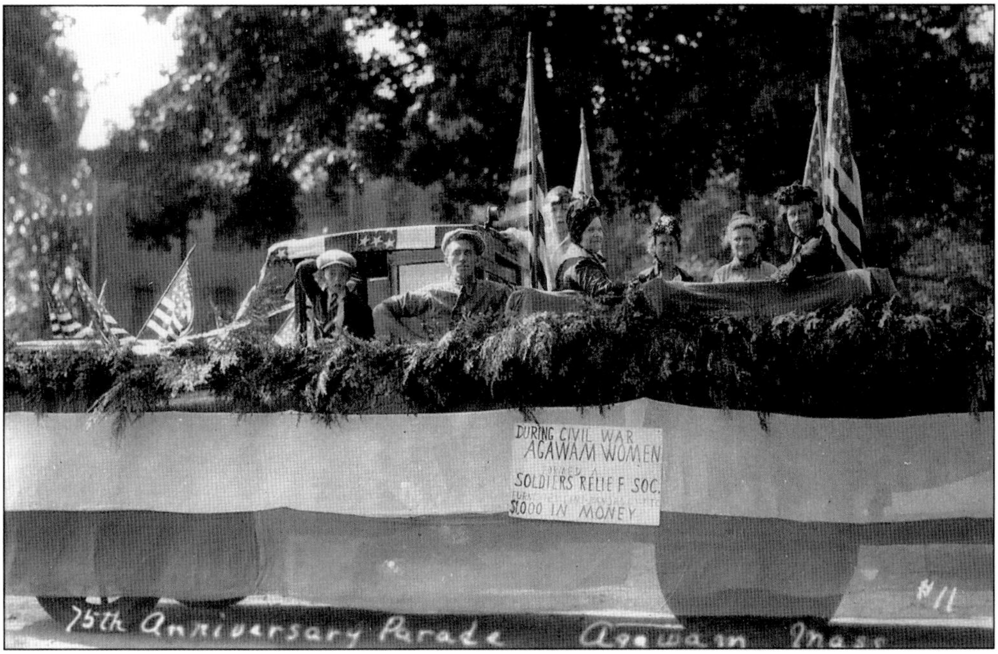

This 75th anniversary parade float represents the Soldier's Relief Society. Formed by Agawam women during the Civil War, the organization provided bandages and raised over $1,000 for Union troops. After the parade, *The Pageant of Agawam*, by George E. Pelletier, was performed at Riverside Park. (Agawam Historical Association collection.)

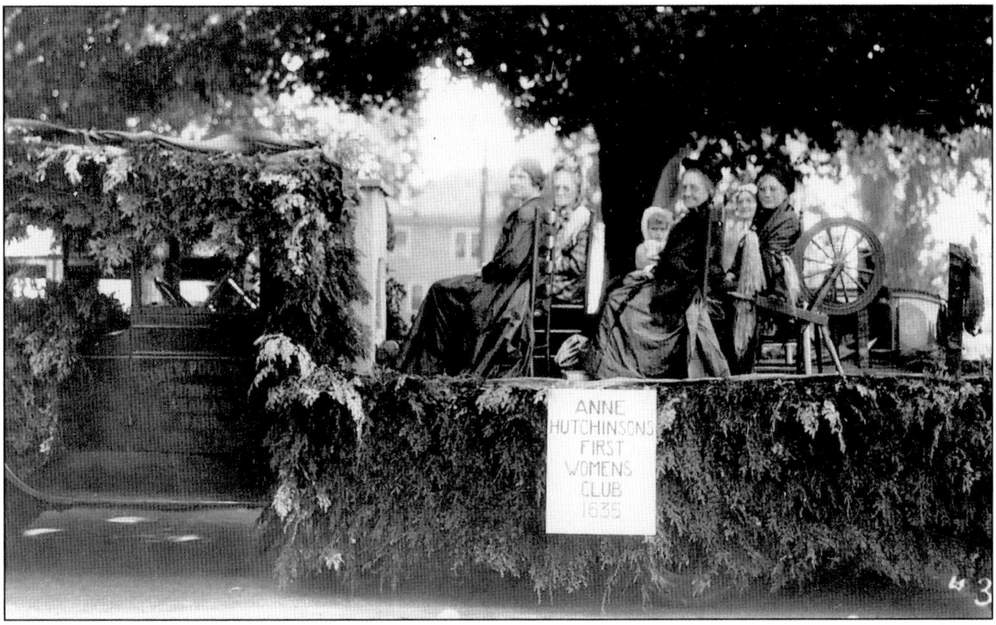

The Agawam Women's Club float commemorating Anne Hutchinson's first women's club is seen here in the 1930 parade. As an example of how important agriculture was in Agawam's past, both the 1905 and 1930 celebrations were held not on the actual May 17 anniversary date, but in August, during the lull between haying and filling the silo. (Agawam Historical Association collection.)

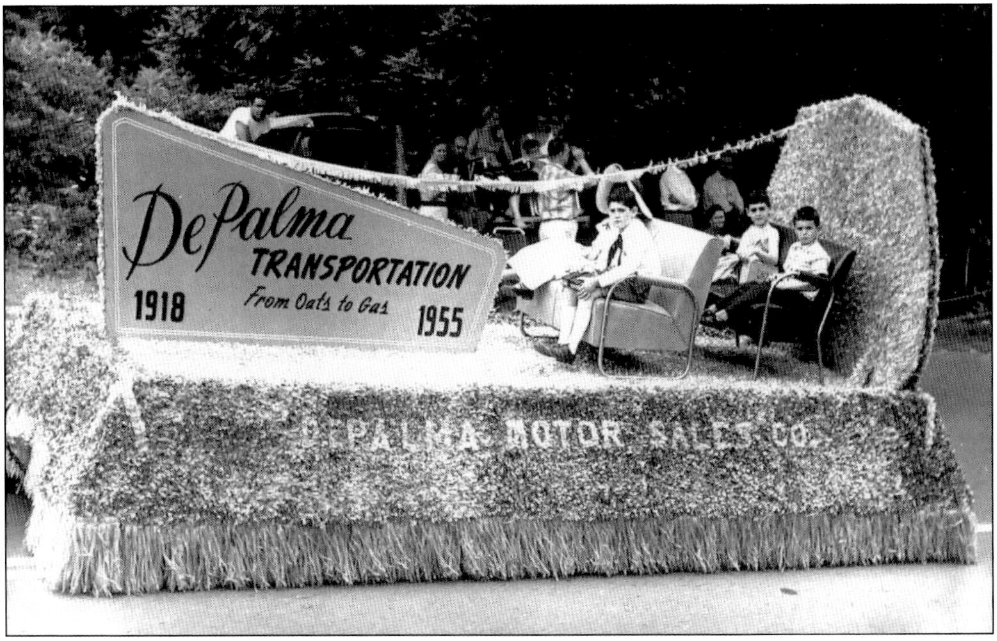

The town of Agawam celebrated the 100th anniversary of its incorporation in high style, spending close to $22,000, an equivalent today of nearly $154,000, for a four-day extravaganza in June 1955. Seen here is the DePalma float from the centennial parade. The people seated on the float include Donald Roy, Sue Ellen Roy, and Steve Ferrari. (Courtesy Mary [DePalma] Ferrari and Phyllis Ferrari.)

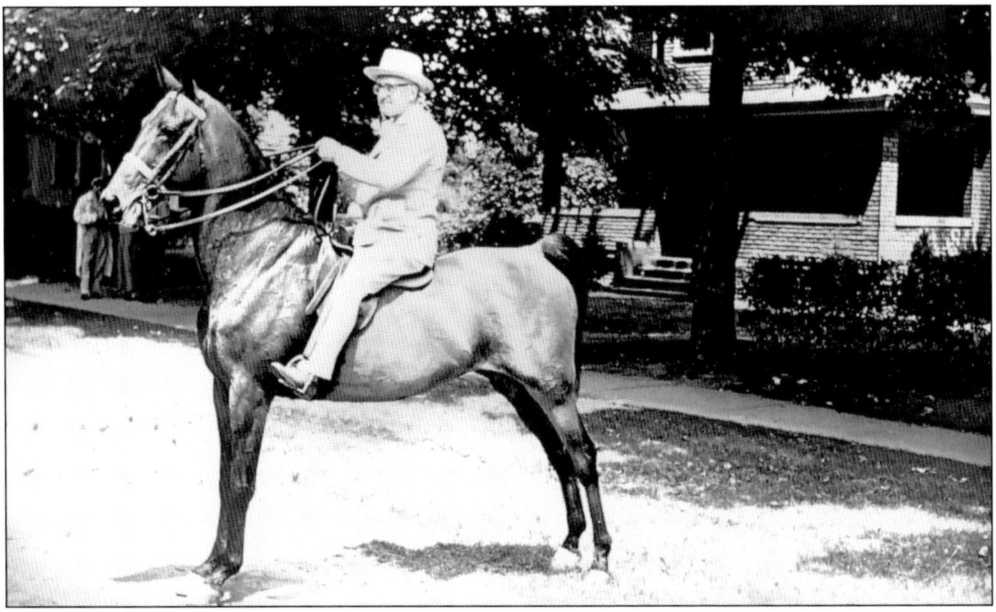

The centennial parade stepped off at 1:00 p.m. on Sunday, June 19, 1955. Units assembled at Phelps School and proceeded north on Main Street. Agawam truant officer Sherman Huntley rode in the parade atop George Reynold's horse Mindy. He was remembered by his friend Reynolds in the inscription on the back of this photograph as a "great guy." (Courtesy Jeffrey Reynolds.)

The parade passed a reviewing stand at town hall that included local officials, Lt. Gov. Sumner Whittier, and the mayors of Northampton, Springfield, and Holyoke, and it ended at the then new Agawam (Food Mart) Shopping Center at Walnut and Springfield Streets. The town was so proud of the shopping center that it appeared on the commemorative centennial plate issued that year. Seen in the photograph to the right, the Agawam Chamber of Commerce float hosted centennial queen Marilyn Wilson and her court. (Courtesy Marian Bradford.)

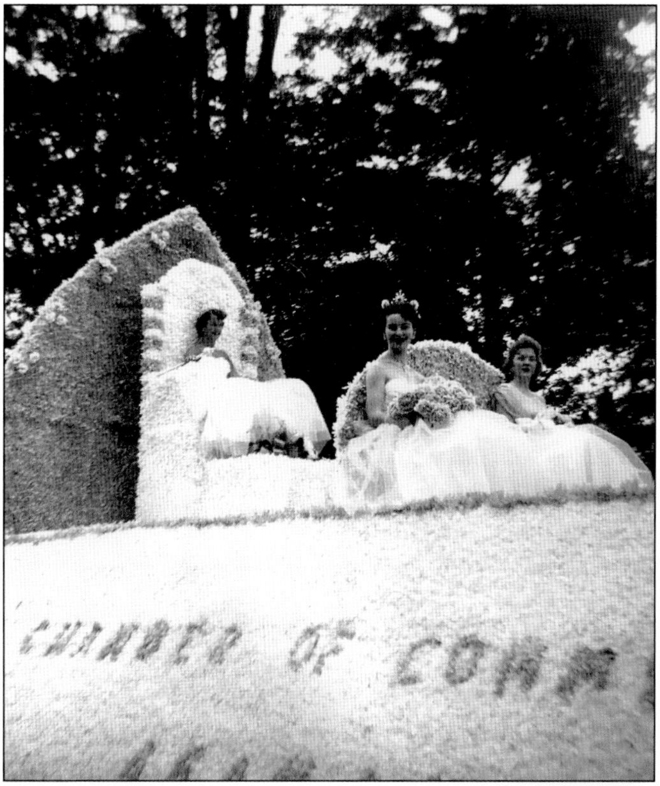

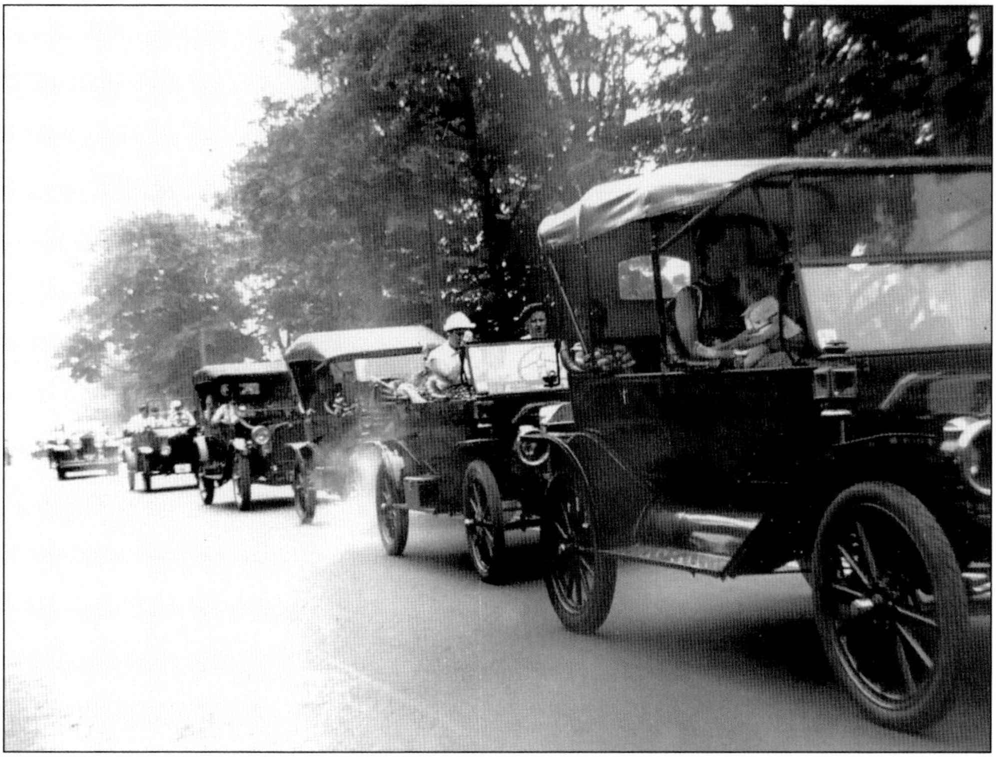

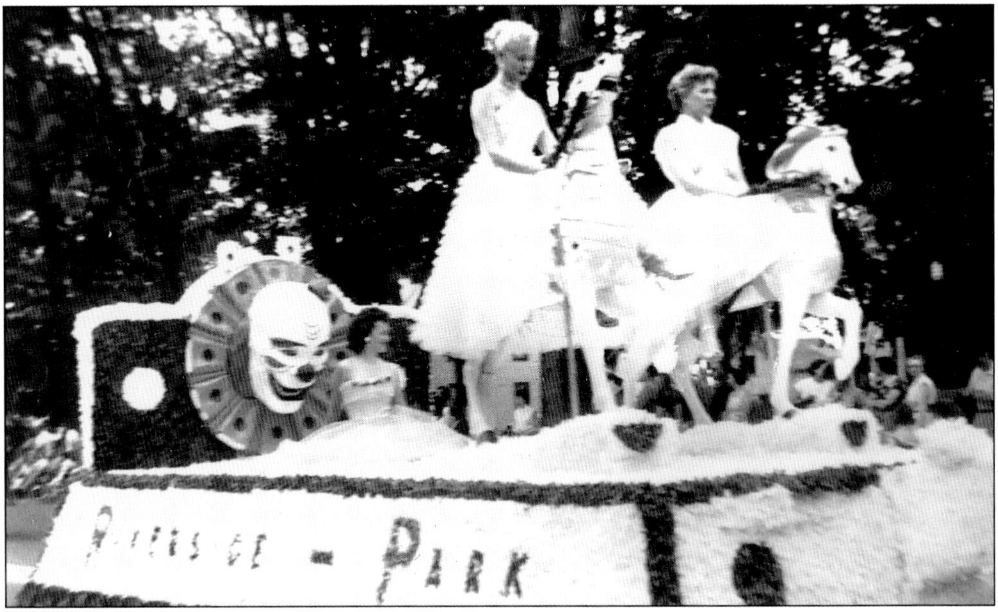

The centennial parade hosted floats by the Springfield South End Merchants Association, Twin Brook Dairy Farms, Hampden Brewers, civic groups, and local churches and businesses, among many others. There was also a huge rolling birthday cake sponsored by the neighboring town of Southwick. Above, Barbara Cheney, Jessie Rivers, and Frances Radwilowicz grace the Riverside Park float. According to the July 10, 1955, edition of the *Springfield Sunday Republican* "Rotogravure" section, an estimated 40,000 spectators witnessed the procession, many from bleachers built along the route. (Courtesy Marian Bradford.)

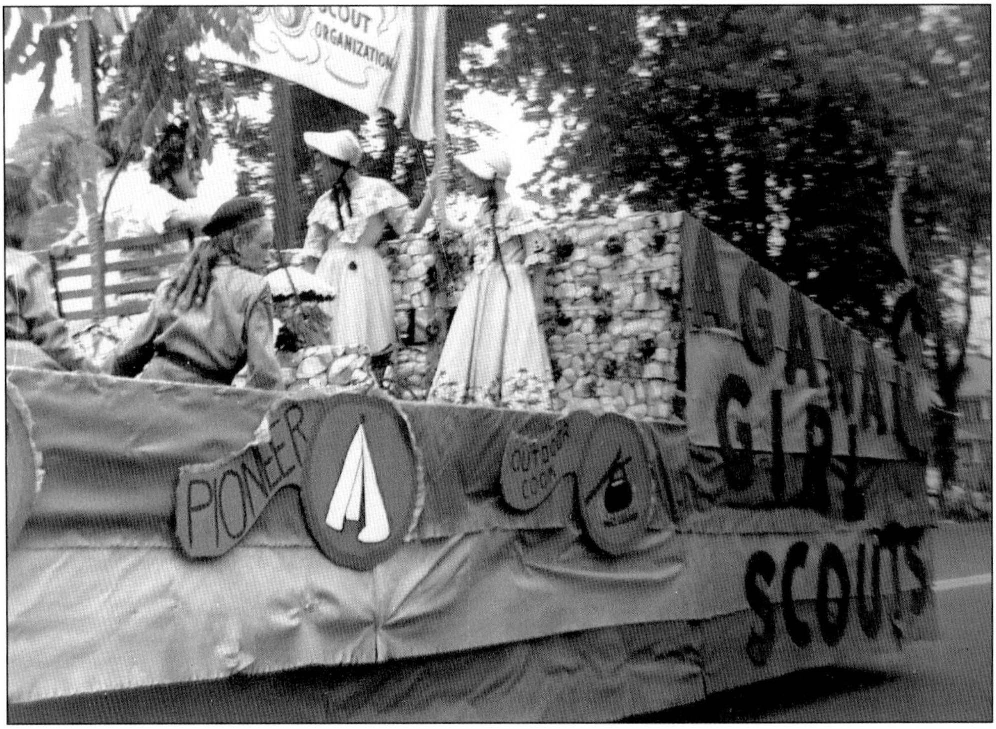

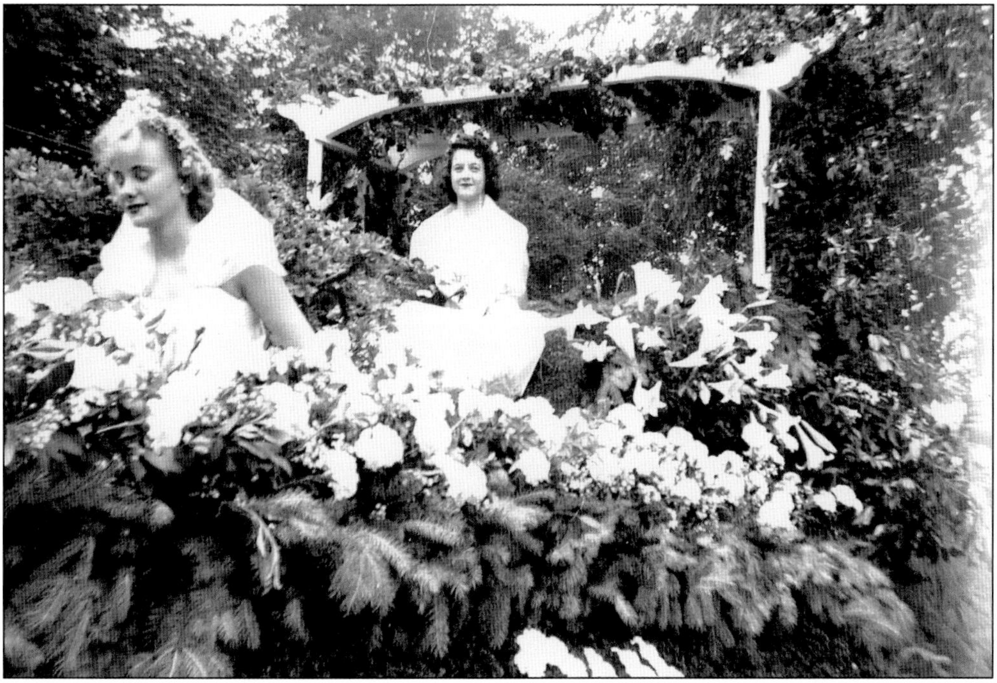

Above, Marjorie Haseltine is seen atop the elaborate Aitken Florist float. Below, Donald Catchepaugh sports the beard he grew for the centennial bearded man contest. Others who grew whiskers for the occasion included Duane Stebbins, Bud Soper, Raymond Vandergrift, Clifford Safford, Basil Pederzzani, and Edward Kryzoski. (Above, courtesy Marian Bradford; below, courtesy Virginia Catchepaugh.)

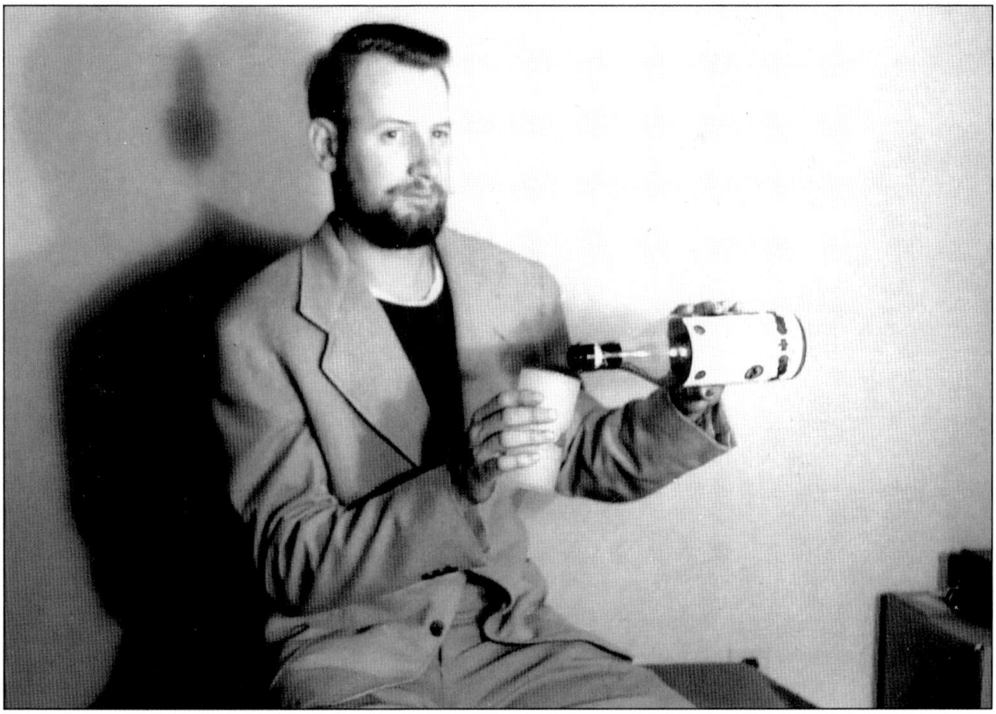

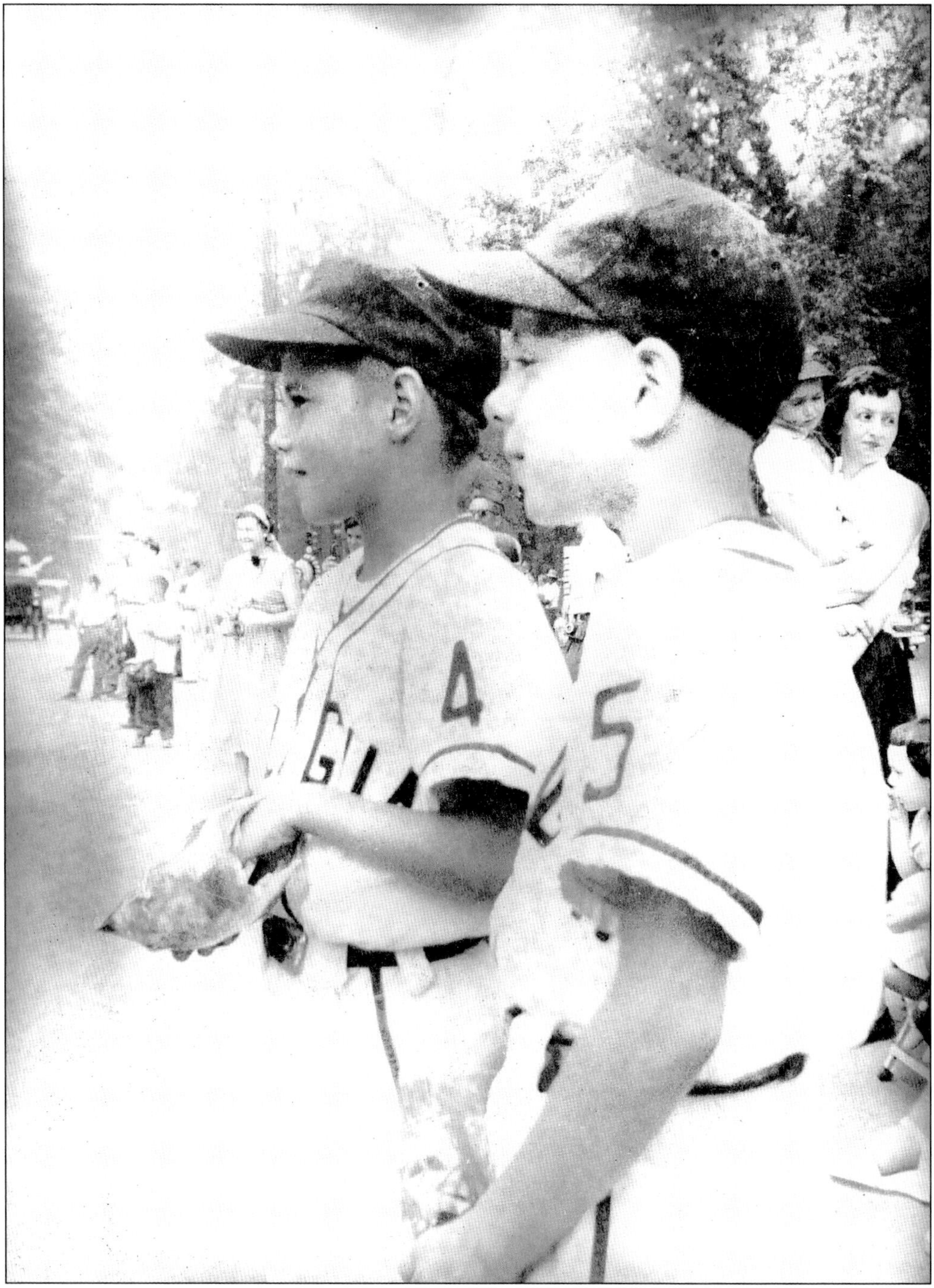

Billy Ferranti (No. 4) and Jeffrey Reynolds enjoy the centennial parade from their vantage point on the south side of the corner of School and Main Streets. Both boys were members of the Deloghia Jets, who had played the Barker Cubs the previous day as part of a centennial celebration doubleheader at Granger School. Other teams participating were the Food Mart Aces and Chriscola Bears. (Courtesy Jeffrey Reynolds.)

Five

The Fruit of Their Labor

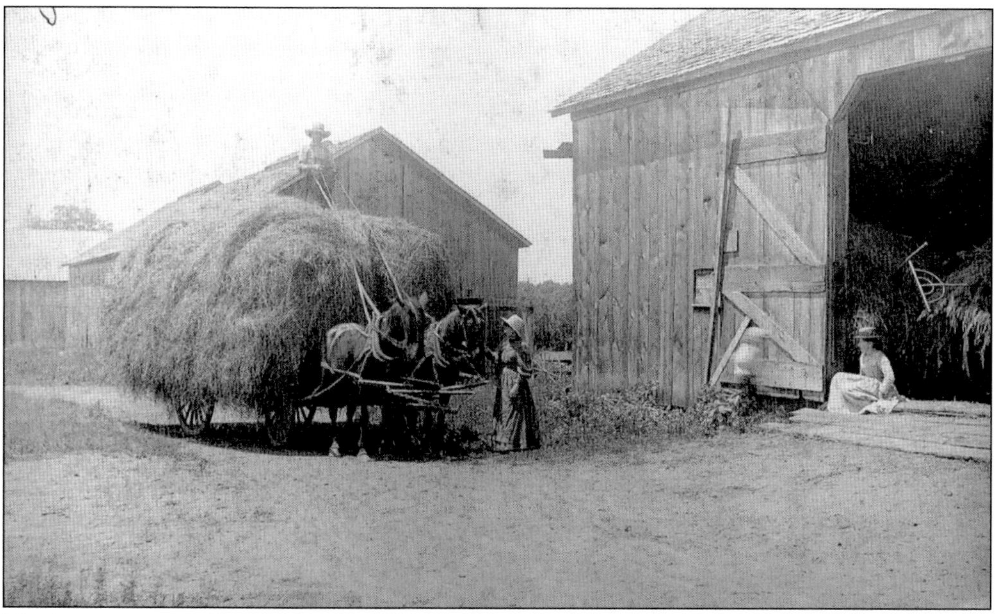

The hay wagon at the W. H. Porter Farm on Silver Street is shown *c.* 1891. The Porter family moved here in 1887. When the Porter farm was sold in the 1950s, the homes on Porter Drive were constructed there. The Porter house, at the corner of Silver Street and Porter Drive, burned in 1964. (Courtesy Mr. and Mrs. John Porter.)

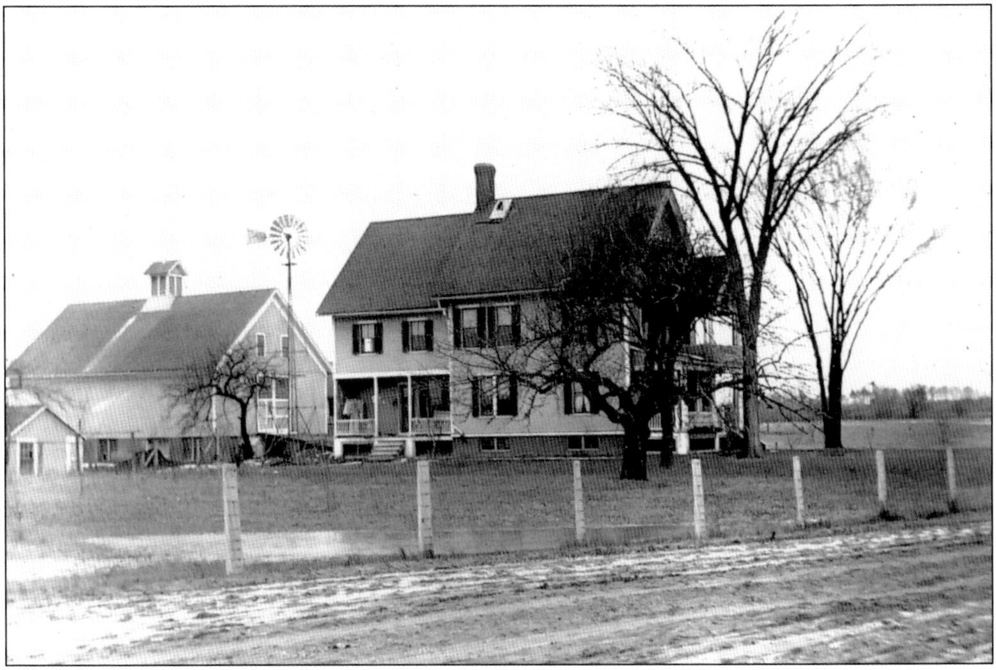

The Merrell farm was a large concern on River Road whose fields were replaced by the homes on Merrell Drive by the mid-20th century. The old Merrell farm house, barn, and windmill are seen here in the early 1900s. The house remains and is located at 717 River Road. (Agawam Historical Association collection.)

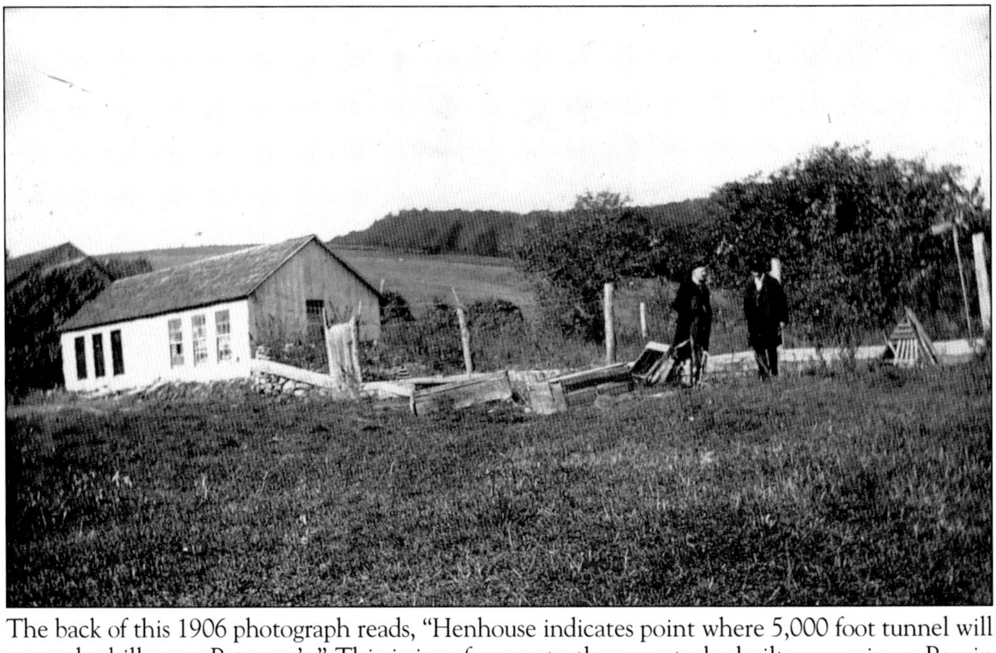

The back of this 1906 photograph reads, "Henhouse indicates point where 5,000 foot tunnel will enter the hill, near Peterson's." This is in reference to the soon-to-be-built reservoir on Provin Mountain and the city of Springfield water main that would cross several Feeding Hills properties near the Westfield end of North West and North Westfield Streets. (Author's collection.)

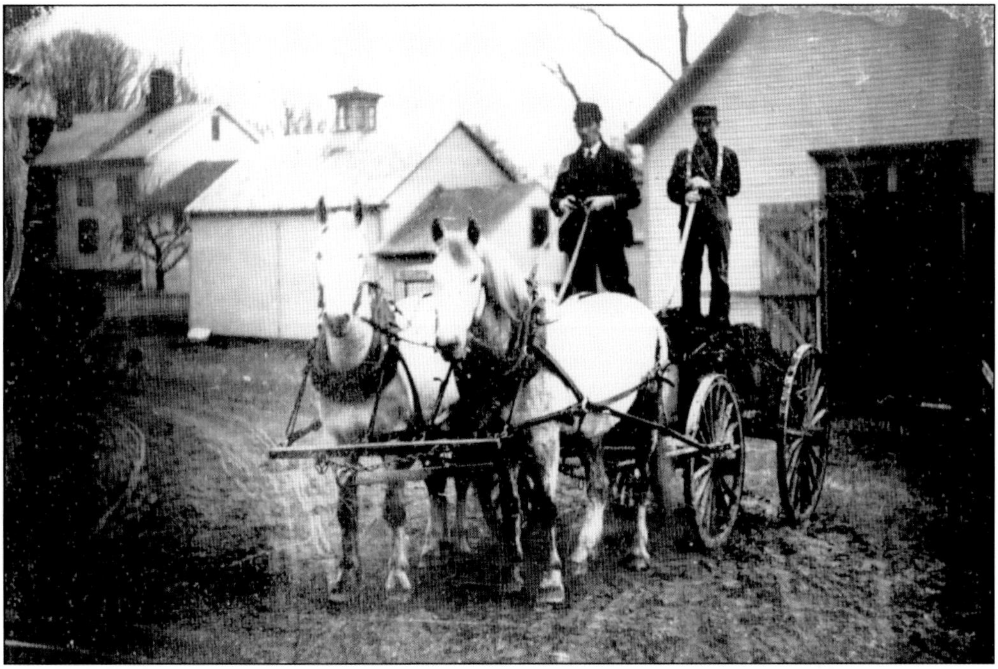

Preston Worden and his hired man are seen c. 1918 at the large dairy farm he operated at 2 Main Street, where Rocky's currently stands. In 1955, the Worden house was moved to the corner of Walnut and Springfield Streets by the Bottaro family, who operated Betty's Olde Towne House there for many years. Worden was very active in town affairs. (Agawam Historical Association collection.)

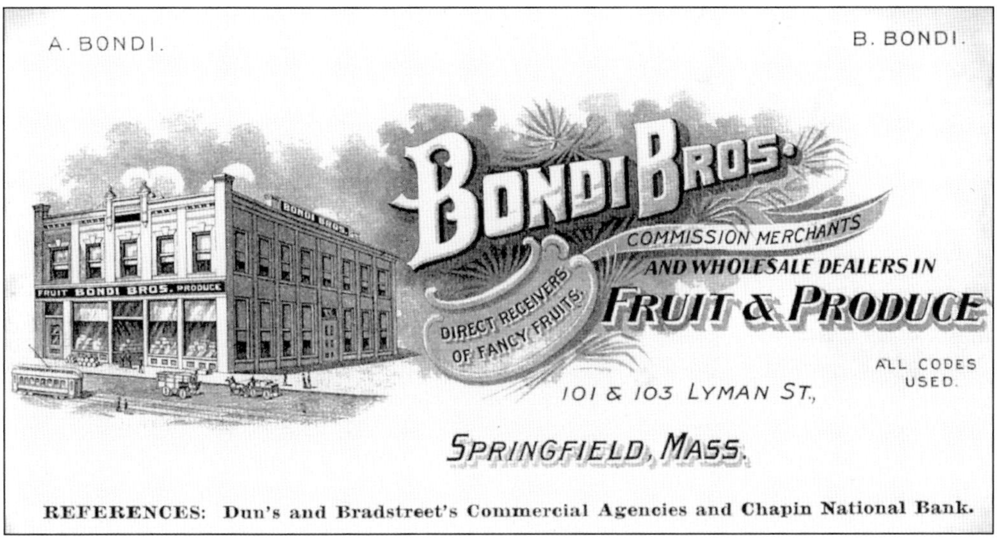

In 1896, Humbert and Amedeo Bondi took over their father Luigi's wholesale fruit and produce business on Lyman Street in Springfield and renamed it Bondi Brothers. Luigi is best known for his $550 purchase of "certain real estate," which later became home to the Bondi's Island regional wastewater-treatment plant. (Author's collection.)

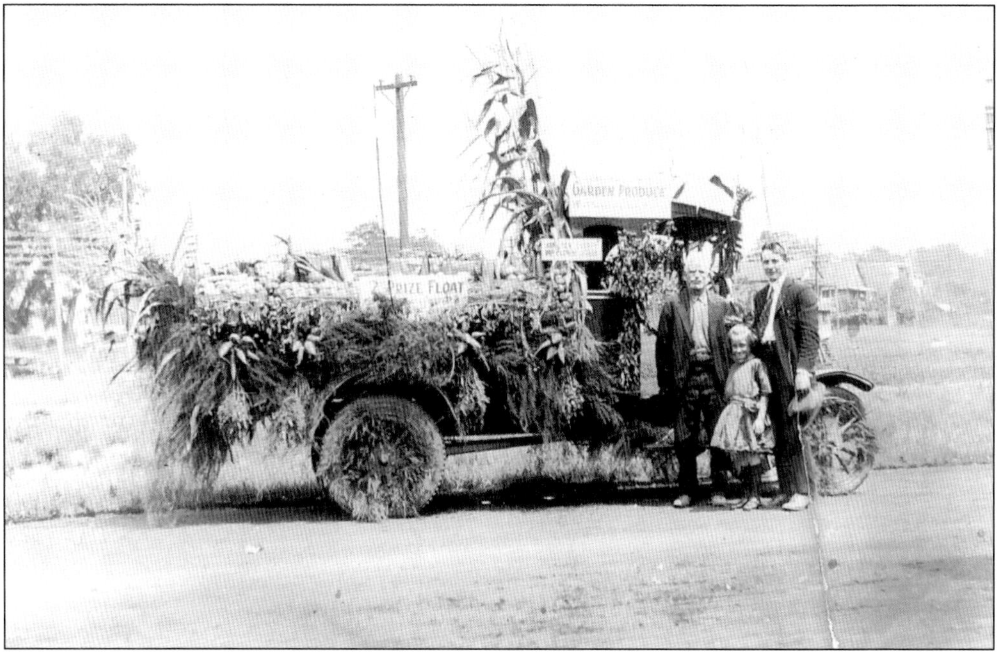

This Hampden County Improvement League float featuring produce grown by the Cesan and DePalma families won second prize at the Hampden County Memorial Bridge dedication parade on Thursday, August 3, 1922. Seen here are Felix DePalma, Anita Cesan, and her father Daniel. (Courtesy Anita [Cesan] Rising.)

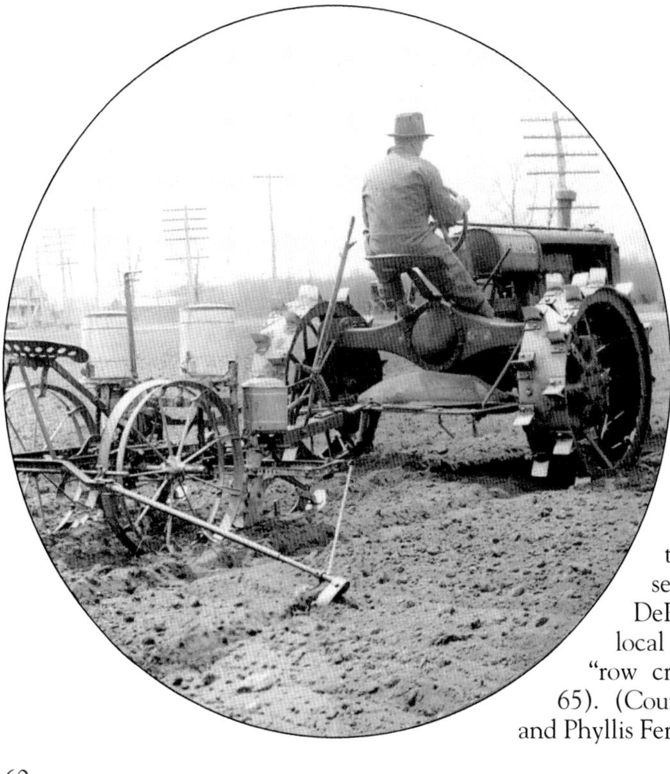

Frank Chriscola, who with his brothers ran Chriscola's Farm Equipment on Suffield Street for many years, remembers that until Louis DePalma bought this tricycle-type Farmall in 1932 (page 61), seen here with corn planter on DePalma's Garden Street farm, local growers preferred wide-set or "row crop" style front wheels (page 65). (Courtesy Mary [DePalma] Ferrari and Phyllis Ferrari.)

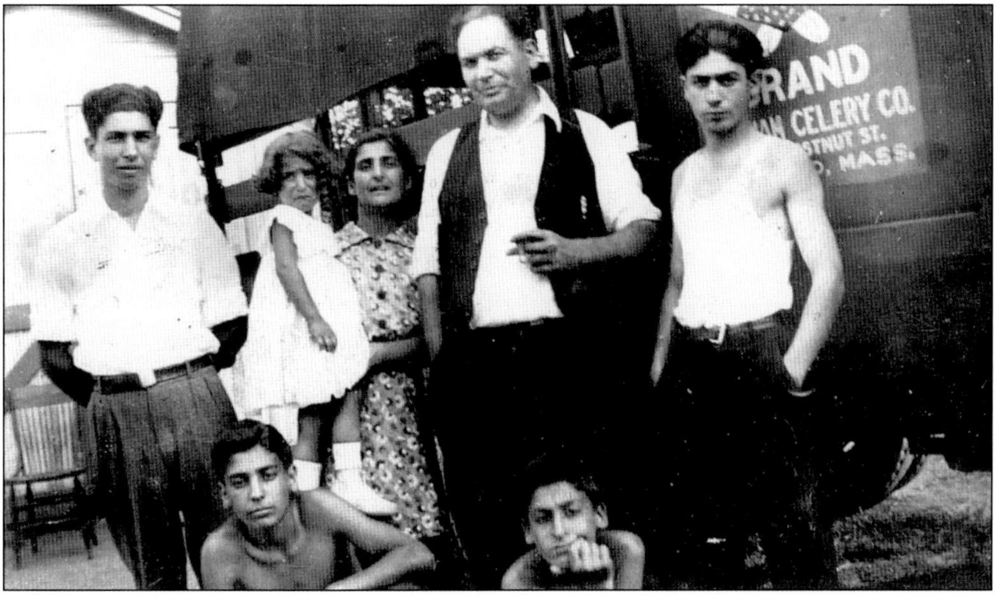

Cincotta Farms was started in 1936 by Louis Cincotta, shown here surrounded by family. Family members are, from left to right, Manuel, Teresa, Angela, Louis, Felix, and (in front) Joseph and Louis. For many years, the Cincotta family operated the Agawam Celery Company from their Springfield Street location, and they continue to operate a year-round farm stand there. (Courtesy Felix Cincotta.)

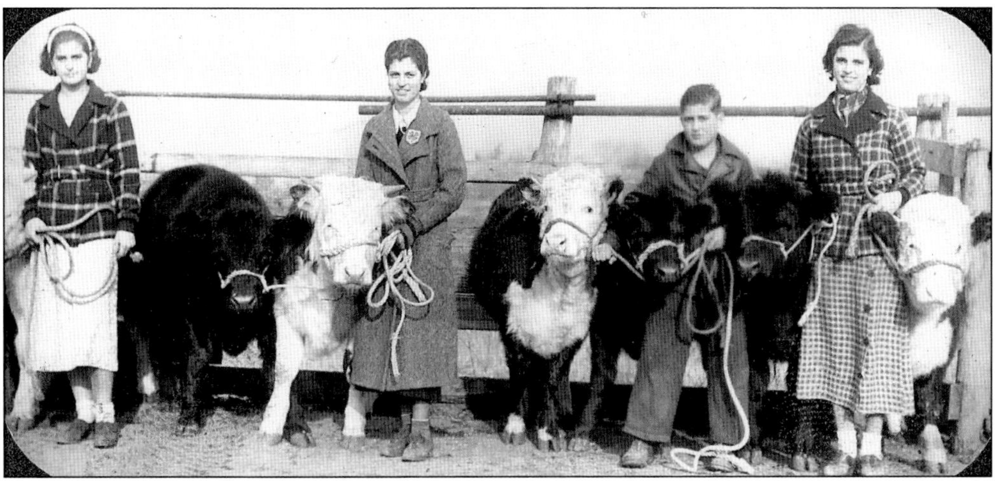

Mary, Sabatina "Sabby," Phil, and Esther DePalma are shown at the 1937 Eastern States Exposition 4-H Baby Beef competition. The DePalma children won several champion and runner-up ribbons in the years they participated in this contest. (Courtesy Mary [DePalma] Ferrari and Phyllis Ferrari.)

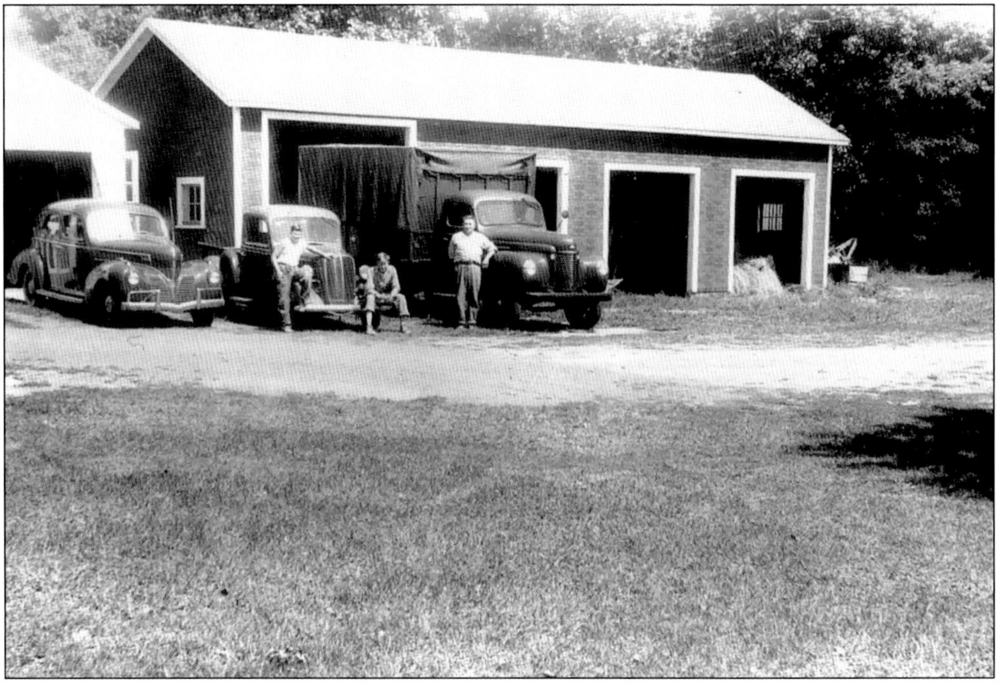

Edward and Richard Stepanik pose with their father, John, at their Twin Oaks Road farm in the 1940s. The John Stepanik farm was later divided between Richard (Twin Oaks Road and Shoemaker Lane) and Edward (North West Street and Southwick Street). John Stepanik's grandsons continue to farm the family land. (Courtesy Eleanor Stepanik.)

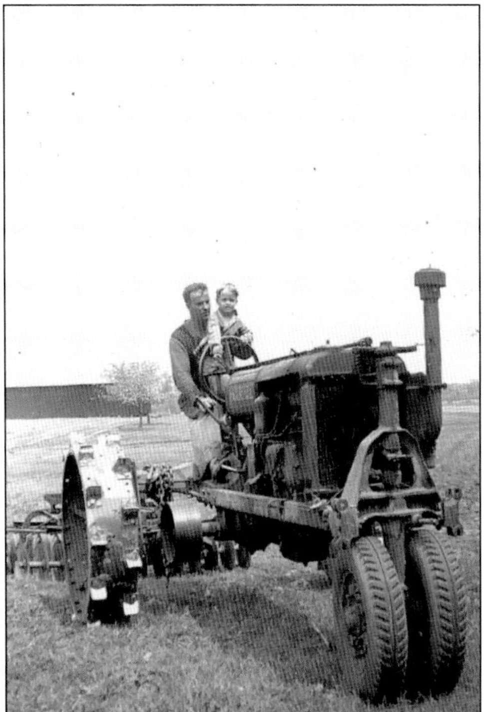

Leonard Rising Sr. and Jr. are shown on the Rising farm, at 942 Shoemaker Lane, in the mid-1940s. This photograph clearly illustrates the tricycle-type wheel arrangement mentioned on page 60. Steel wheels were common during the 1940s, when rubber was needed for the war effort. (Courtesy Anita [Cesan] Rising.)

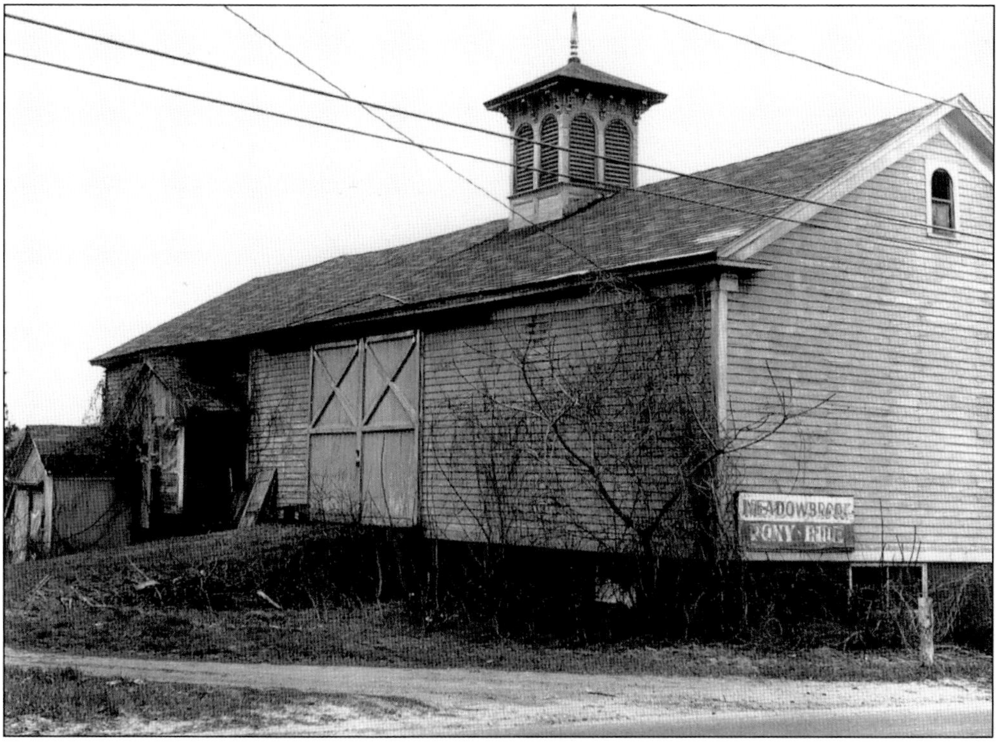

The large barn seen in this Jean Welt Taylor photograph was part of the Samuel Johnson farm near the corner of Southwick and South West Streets until it was torn down. The cupola survived even longer, becoming a familiar sight along the side of South West Street. (Agawam Historical Association collection.)

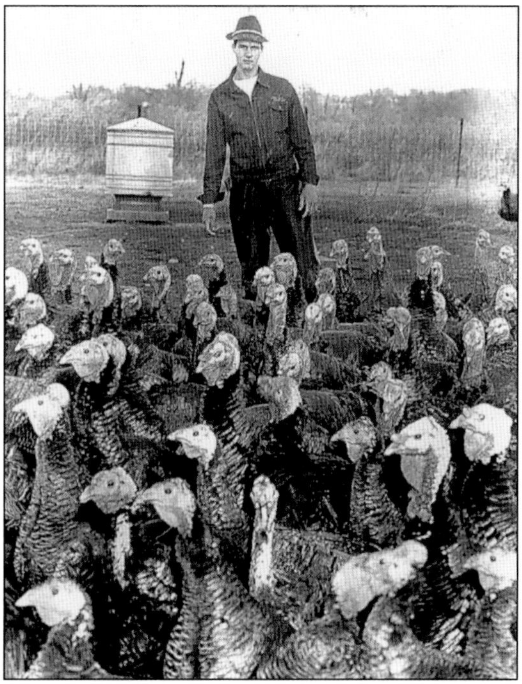

Michael Juzba tends the turkey flock at Wanieski Farms on South Westfield Street c. 1950. Founded by Henry, Michael's uncle, and Matthew Wanieski, Wanieski's is well known for their outstanding meat products and pot pies. (Courtesy Diane and Christopher Juzba.)

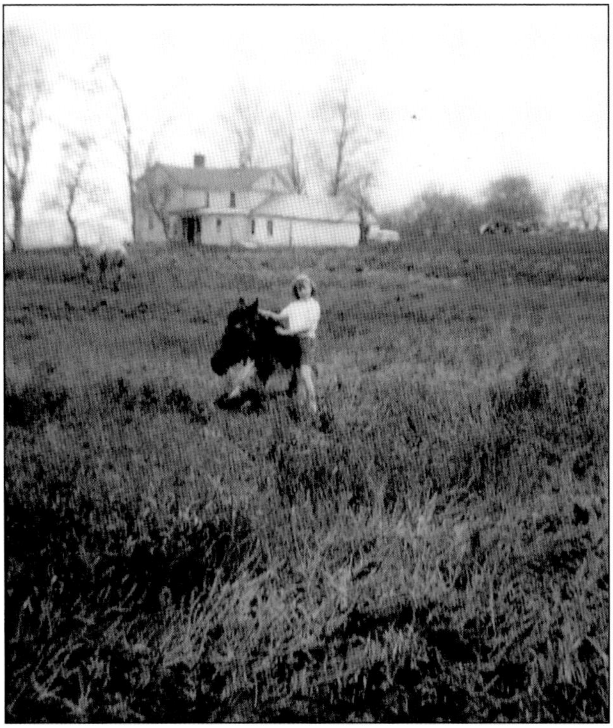

A 1919 town directory lists Giuseppe Cecchi (the author's great-grandfather) as living in "the Patch." By 1924, he had purchased the Hubbard Farm at the corner of Shoemaker Lane and Suffield Street, where he lived with his family, including sons Peter and Erminio. His former home at 32 Shoemaker Lane is seen here from Suffield Street. (Courtesy Barbara and Peter Cecchi.)

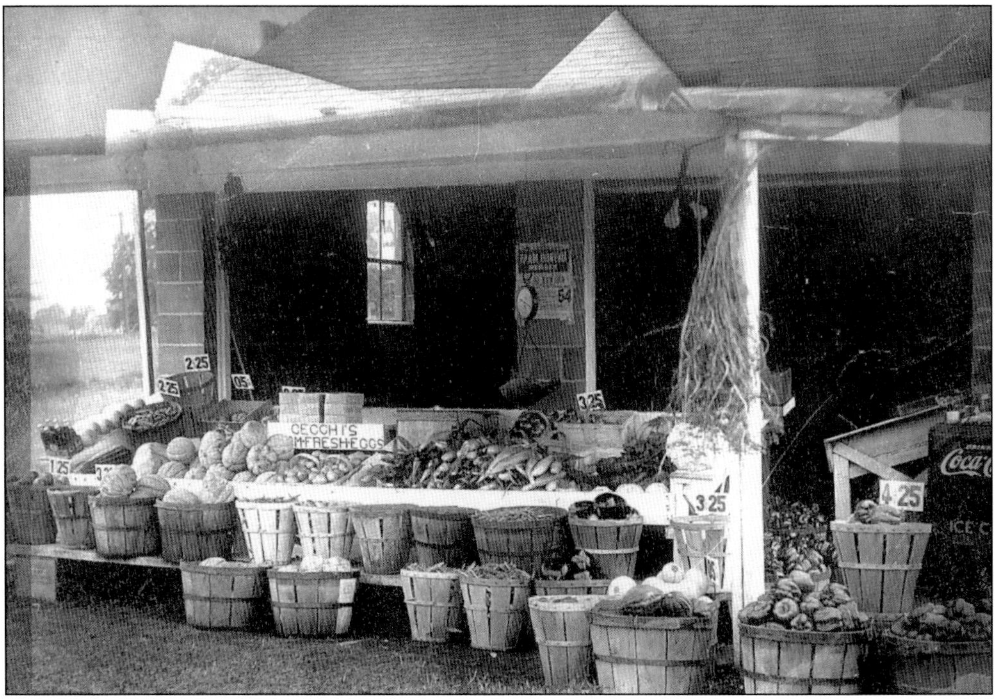

In 1948, a cement-block farm stand was built at the corner of Shoemaker Lane and Suffield Street, where Peter Cecchi Jr., wife Barbara, and son Edward continue to sell plants. Later, some 55 acres of the original farm and the old Cecchi home were sold, and they are now part of the Crowley horse farm. (Courtesy Barbara and Peter Cecchi.)

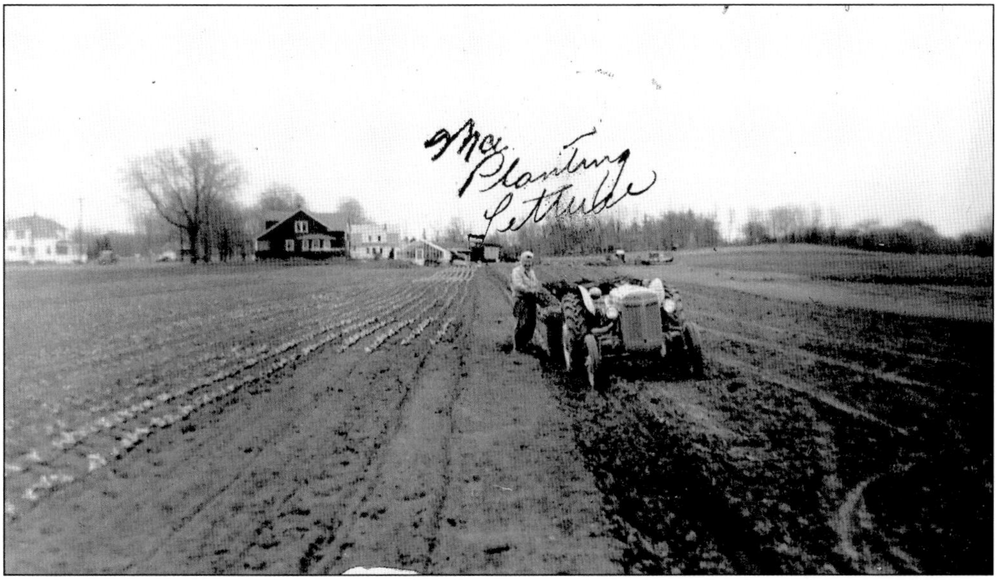

In 1946, Erminio (the author's grandfather) and Anna Cecchi moved to Springfield Street. Anna Cecchi is seen here planting lettuce *c.* 1949. The tractor in the photograph sports the row-crop wheel setup mentioned on page 60. The dark house and glass greenhouse seen here have both been demolished and replaced with modern greenhouses. The white house at left center is the Sacred Heart Church rectory. (Courtesy Anna Cecchi.)

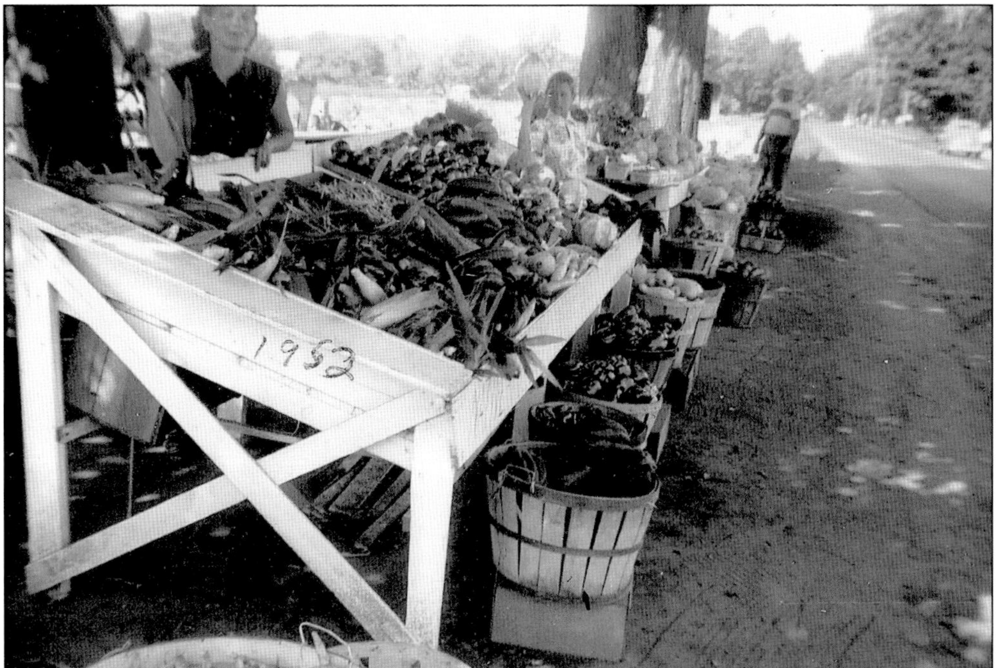

Before the current farm stand was built in 1953, produce was sold from tables under the trees in front of the Cecchi home at 1131 Springfield Street. Seen here are Carol (Cecchi) Kaleialoha and Robert Cecchi (the author's father), who currently operates the farm with his sons Robert Jr. and Michael. (Courtesy Anna Cecchi.)

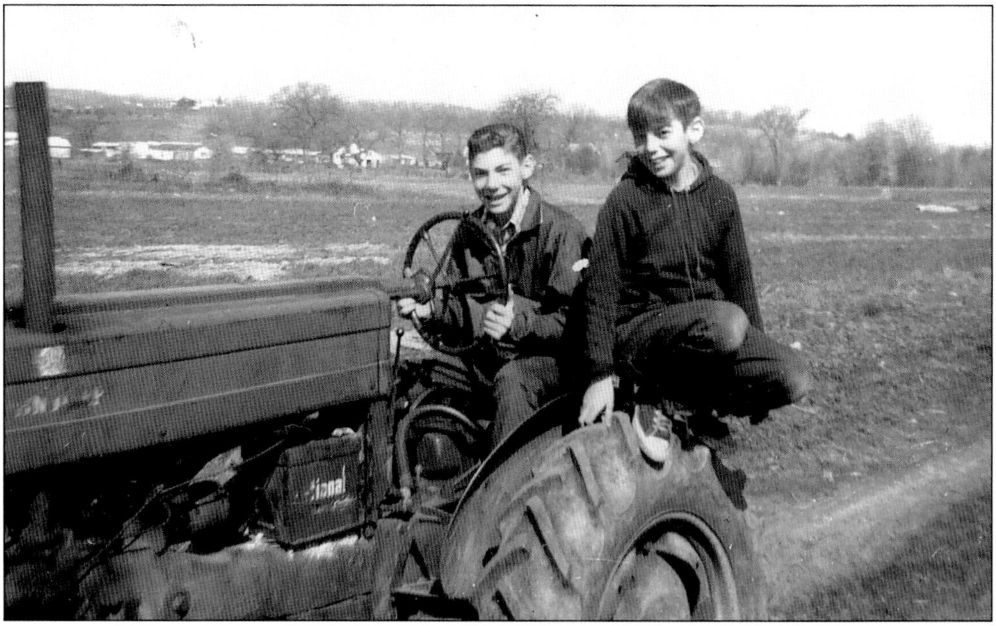

Albert and Felix Cincotta are pictured on their John Deere tractor in the 1950s. The Feeding Hills Stop & Shop currently occupies the former Elmer Cleary farm, seen in this view looking west from the Cincotta property on Springfield Street. (Courtesy Felix Cincotta.)

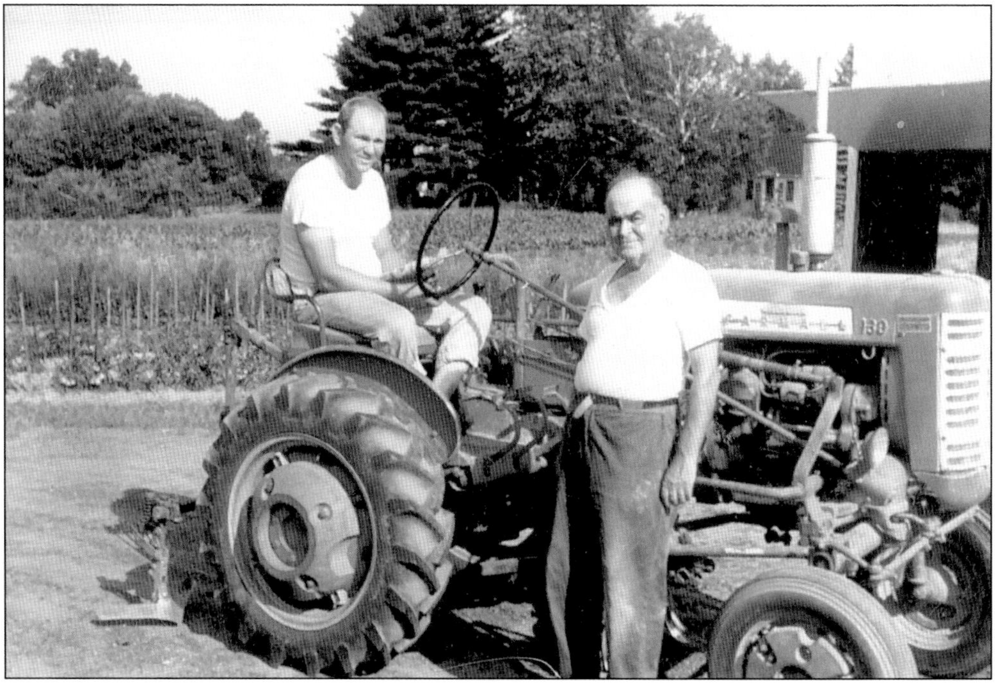

Edward Stepanik is seen here with neighbor and fellow grower George Morgenstern. Stepanik's sons continue the family business. Donald raises greenhouse tomatoes, and Alan grows bedding plants and hanging baskets on the Stepanik family's Southwick Street and North West Street property. (Courtesy Eleanor Stepanik.)

Six

Business As Usual

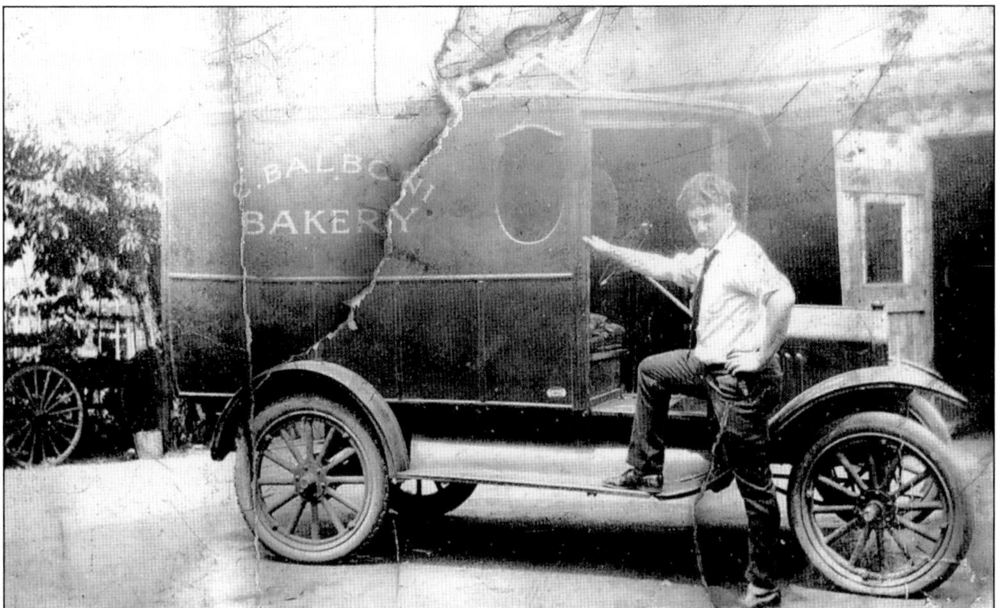

The Balboni Bakery has been located in North Agawam since 1912. Famous for their delicious star bread (the recipe for which has not changed in over 90 years), the King Street bakery is now run by fourth-generation bread makers. Seen *c.* 1920 with his delivery truck is Carlo Balboni. (Courtesy Mark Balboni.)

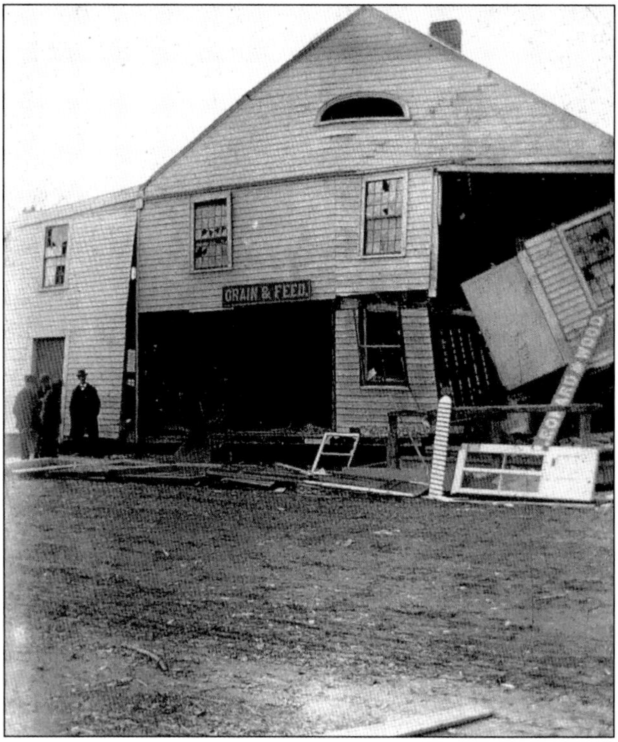

William H. Granger (fourth from the left) is seen at the Leonard and Wood feed store in Feeding Hills after it was partially destroyed by a grain dust explosion in the 1890s. (Courtesy Paul Toelken.)

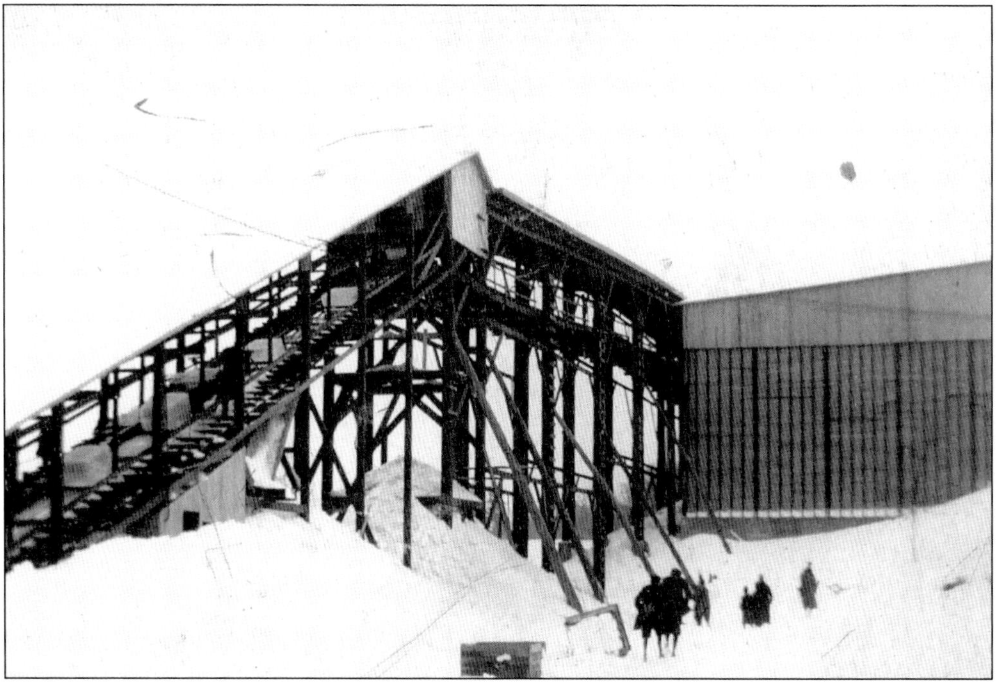

Before the advent of electric refrigerators, iceboxes required a year-round supply of ice to keep things cool. In 1909, the Frye family constructed this large icehouse on Silver Lake, the capacity of which was doubled with a 1920 addition. The company's offices and distribution center were located in Springfield. (Courtesy Norman Roberts.)

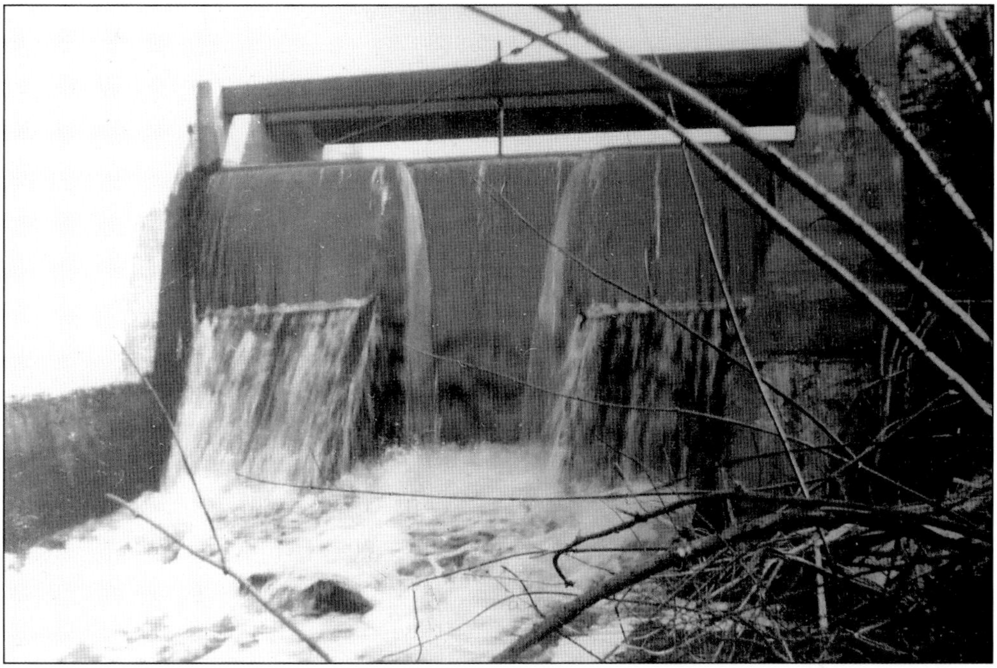

The Agawam Company woolen mill on Elm Street was powered by a dam on Mill (or Factory) Pond. A 1955 flood washed out the dam, which was never rebuilt. There is no more Mill Pond. (Courtesy Paul Toelken.)

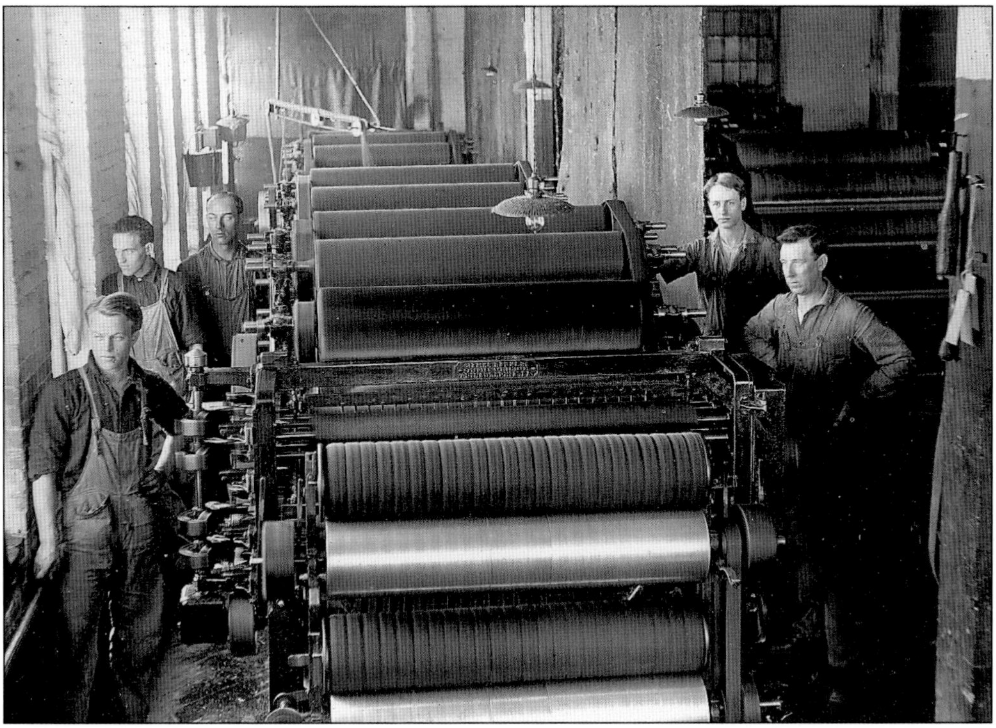

Richard E. Toelken is in the back right of this 1910 view of the Agawam Company woolen mill. (Courtesy Paul Toelken.)

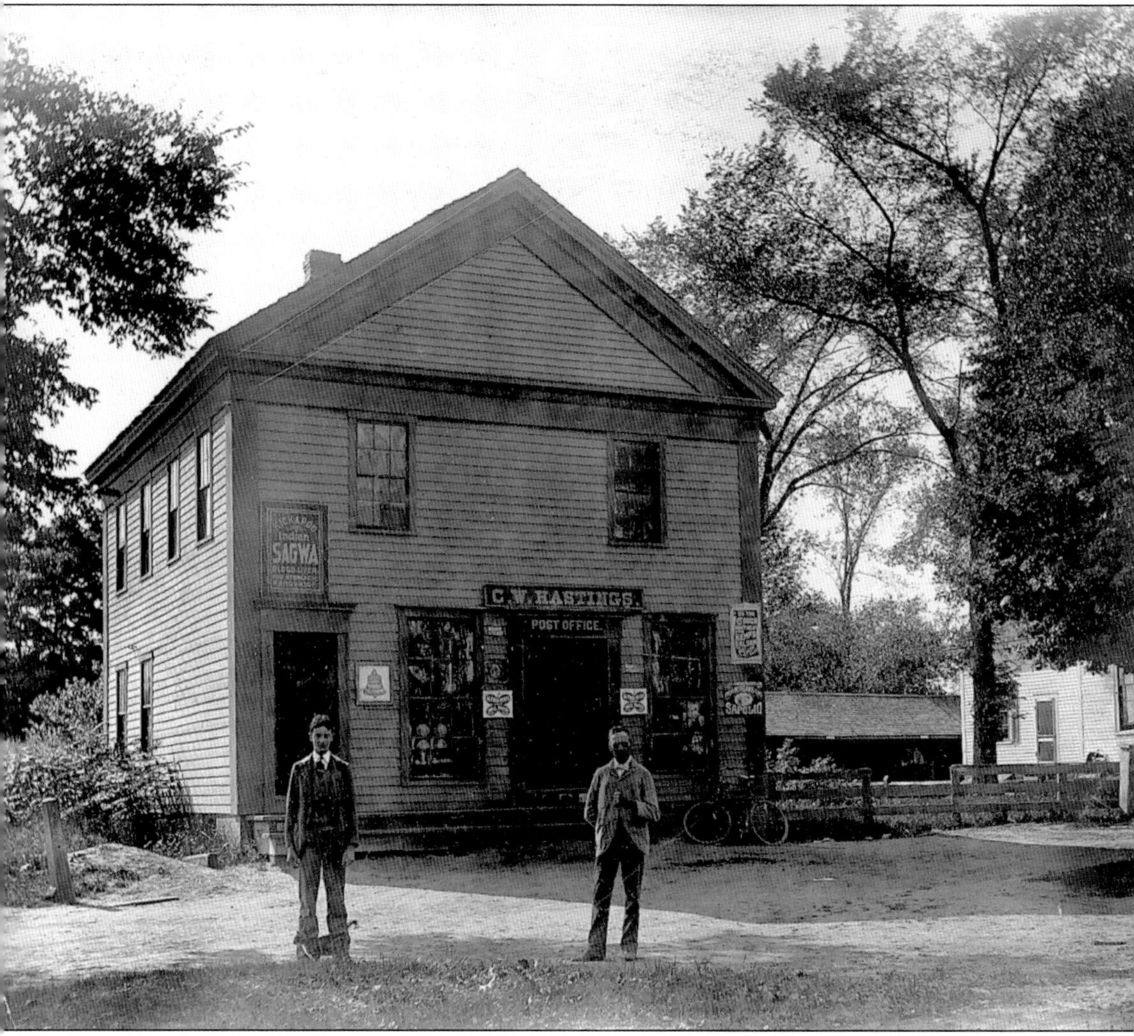

The day Charles W. Hastings and Ellen Thompson were married, May 5, 1879, the newlyweds moved to Agawam, where Hastings had purchased a general store on Main Street next door to the Agawam Baptist Church, near the corner of Elm Street (current location of the Agawam Public Market). The original store (seen here) was built in 1859 by Edward and Stephen Bodurtha and later moved to Central Street, where the building still serves as a residence. A new building was constructed in the first decade of the 20th century. Among the inventory in 1897 was "2/3 dozen Dandelion Extract, 1 pair Frog Mouth Gloves, 5 bottles Laudanum, 1 Panama Hat, 1 dozen collars, 1 plow, 1 tobacco needle, and 1 harmonica." The Hastings store boasted the first telephone in Agawam, which was connected to the Hastings home, at 684 Main Street, with only a bell because Hastings felt he could not afford two telephones. Hastings also served as Agawam postmaster, a position he held for nearly 50 years. He died on April 10, 1936, at age 80. (Courtesy Henry C. Hastings.)

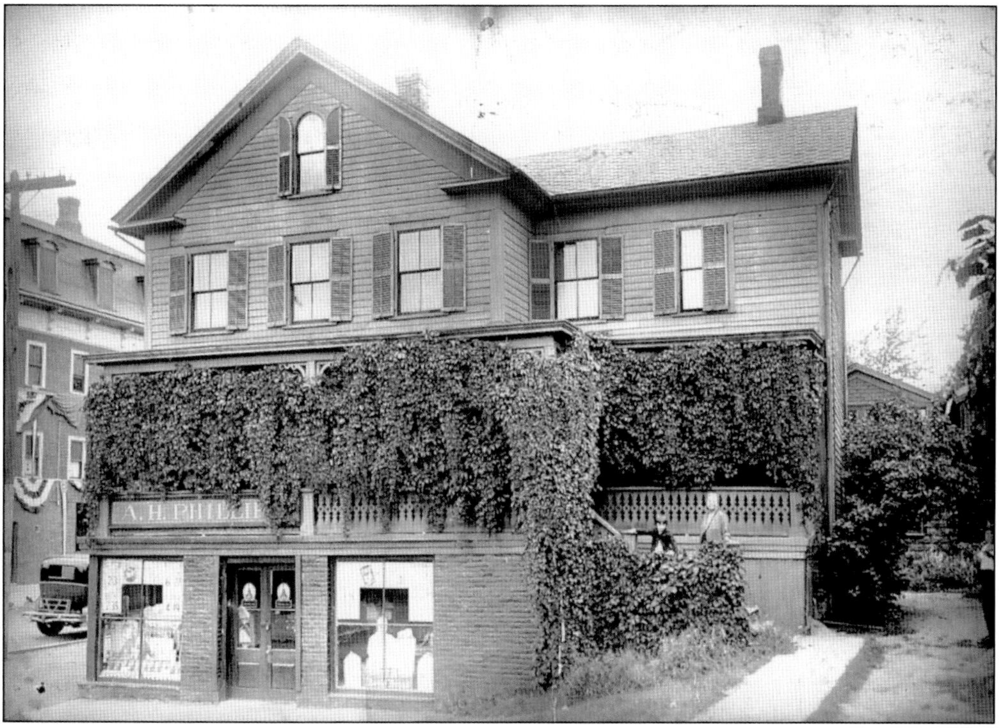

Shown here is the A. H. Phillips store, located at the corner of Bridge and River Streets, where the former Tinti's Restaurant (and current Masonic Hall) stands. Neither this building nor the imposing structure seen to the left remains at this North Agawam location. (Agawam Historical Association collection; gift of Phyllis Mason.)

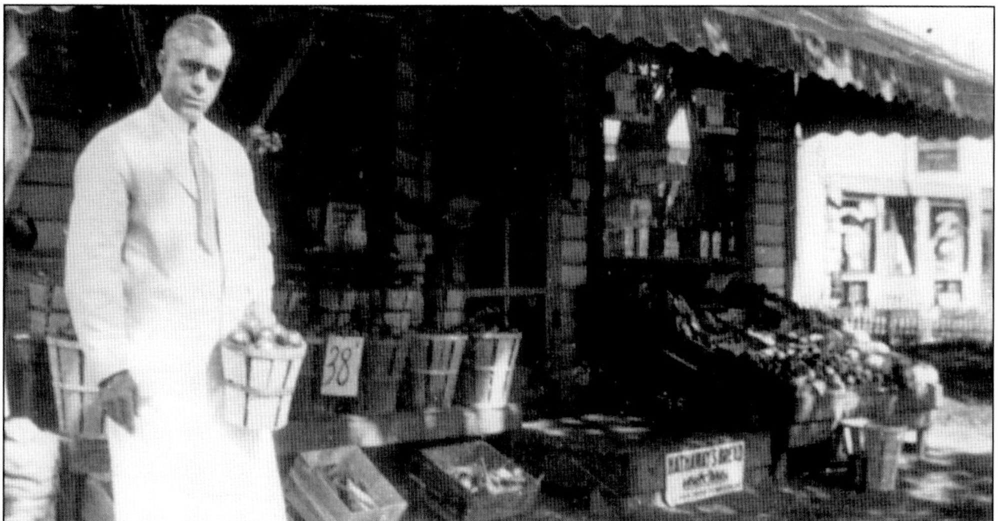

During the 1930s, Frank E. Draghetti used his World War I bonus to open this fruit and produce business on the corner of North and Springfield Streets at O'Brien's Corner. Barely visible to the right is the McGrath-Brewin Block, which was home to Doc's Barber Shop, the Old Agawam Cafe, and Sarat Ford. It was ordered demolished by Agawam mayor Richard A. Cohen in 2004. (Courtesy Alice [Draghetti] Smith.)

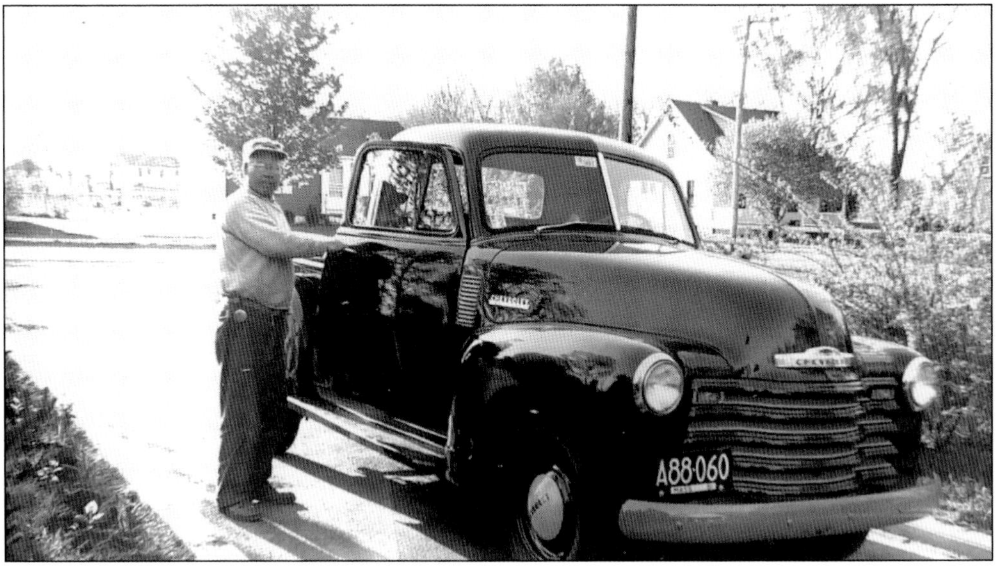

Seen here in 1951 is Lucas Subotin of 1141 Main Street. He was the builder of many Agawam homes. (Courtesy Jennie and Joseph Della-Giustina.)

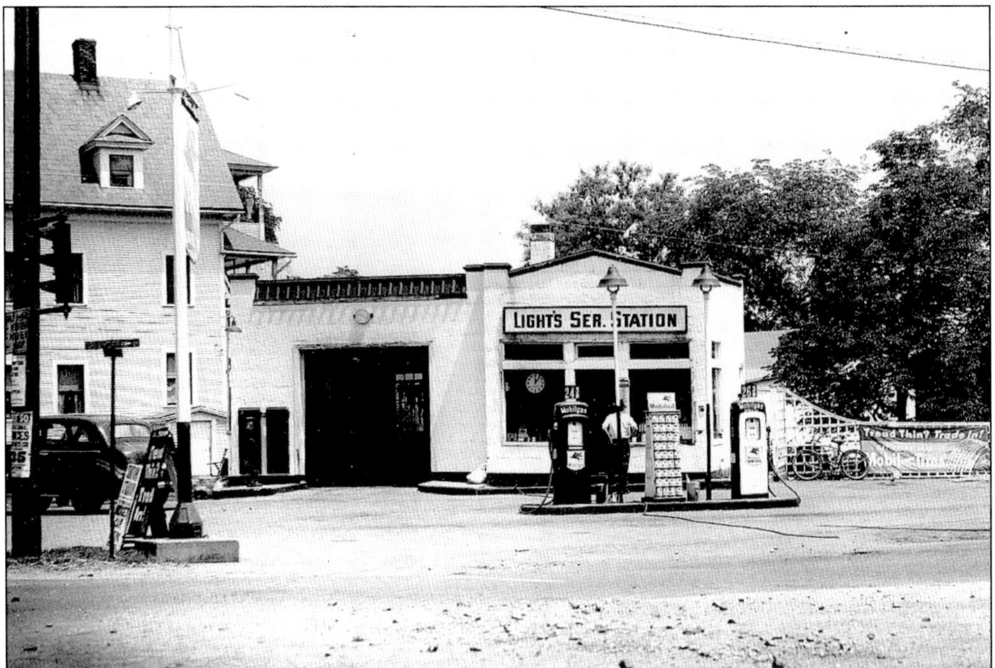

Light's Service Station was located at the corner of Springfield and North Westfield Streets for many years. Even though this business replaced the charming Jimmie Moore house that had earlier stood on this corner, it seems quaint itself when compared to the scene one finds at that intersection today. (Courtesy Helen Light.)

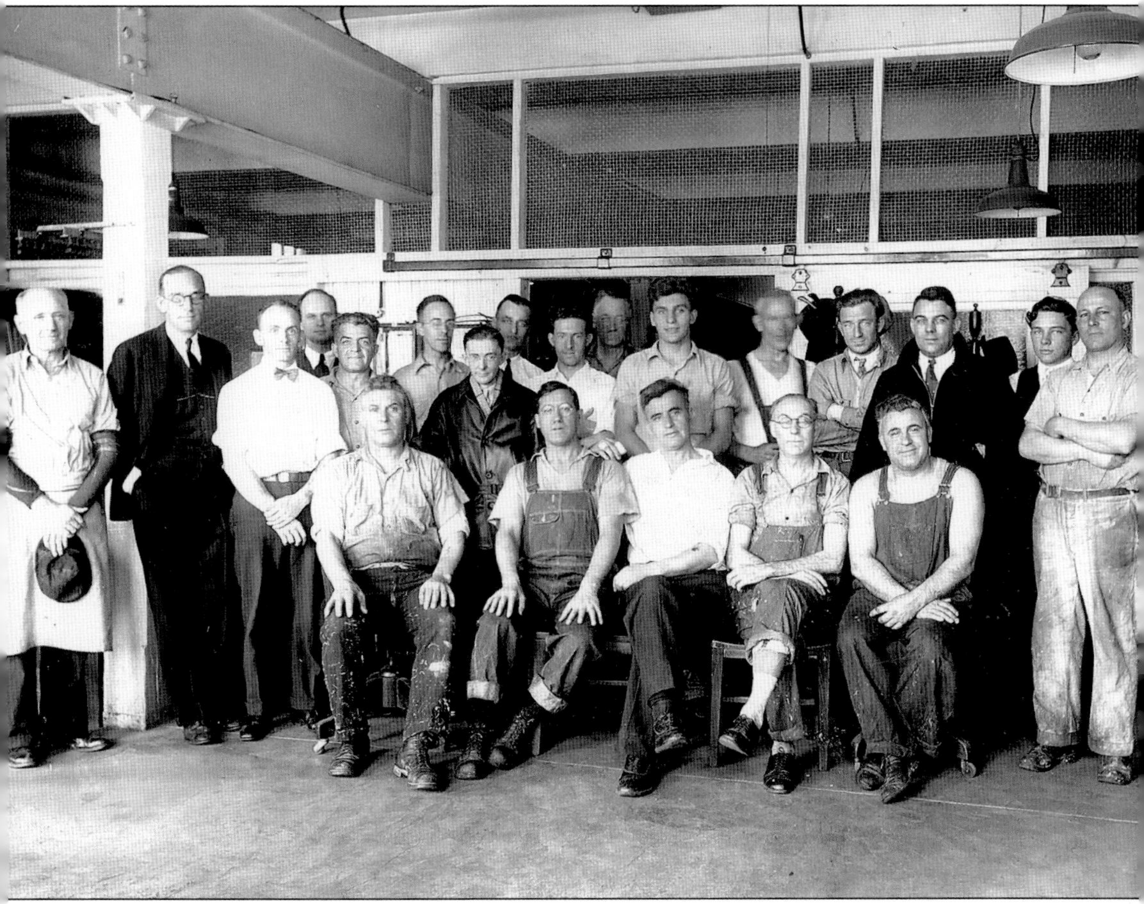

George Beauchane (seated, third from the left) poses with coworkers c. 1945 at Strathmore Paper in West Springfield. For decades, the paper mills on the Agawam River in North Agawam (Worthy Paper on the Agawam side, Southworth and Strathmore on the West Springfield side) employed many Agawam residents, especially the French Canadian and later Italian immigrants who settled in that area. All three mills were known for their fine printing papers. The Worthy Paper Mill closed in the 1930s, and the building burned in 1975. The Strathmore mill, the first of five Strathmore mills in the state, closed in the 1970s and was demolished in 1996. Only the Southworth Company mill remains. It has been in continuous operation since 1839. The late Ben Bassani, who grew up in North Agawam, told the author you would know what color paper they were making on any given day, because if you went swimming in the river downstream from the mills, you would emerge dyed that color. (Courtesy Ellen Janik.)

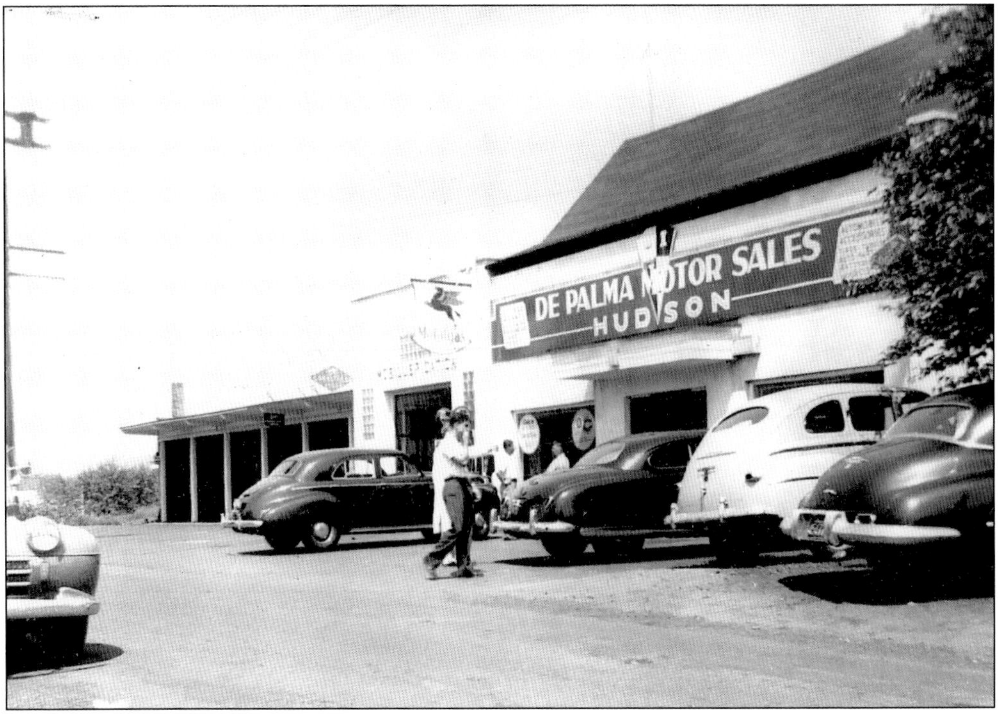

DePalma Motor Sales, located at 71 Garden Street, is shown here in 1949. The dealership sold Hudson motorcars, Norge and Crosley electrical appliances, and farm freezers. This building later housed the DePalma Transportation school bus fleet after the auto dealership moved to Springfield Street in the early 1950s. (Courtesy Mary [DePalma] Ferrari and Phyllis Ferrari.)

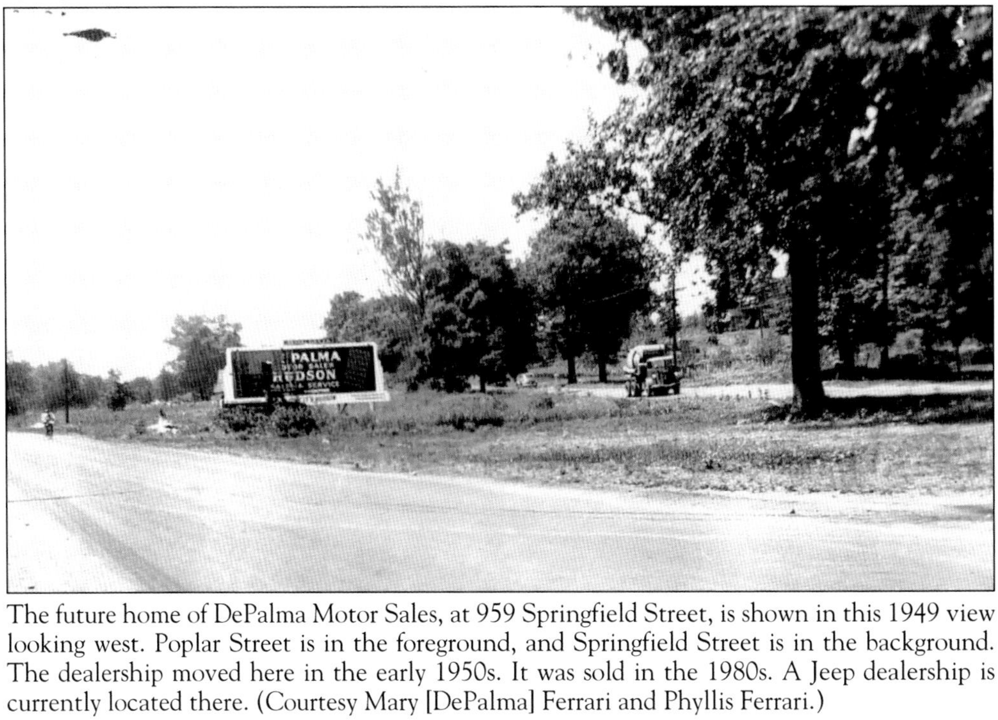

The future home of DePalma Motor Sales, at 959 Springfield Street, is shown in this 1949 view looking west. Poplar Street is in the foreground, and Springfield Street is in the background. The dealership moved here in the early 1950s. It was sold in the 1980s. A Jeep dealership is currently located there. (Courtesy Mary [DePalma] Ferrari and Phyllis Ferrari.)

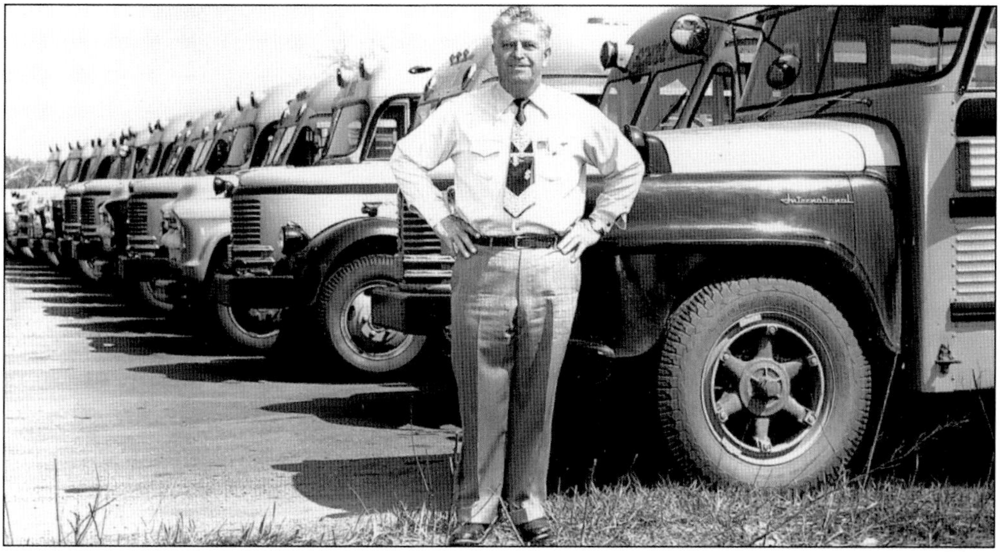

Louis DePalma poses with his fleet in the mid-1950s. In the early years of his business, DePalma transported students in used bakery delivery trucks (similar to that on page 67) in which he had cut out windows and installed removable seats, enabling him to also use the vehicles to haul produce from the family farm (page 60). (Courtesy Mary [DePalma] Ferrari and Phyllis Ferrari.)

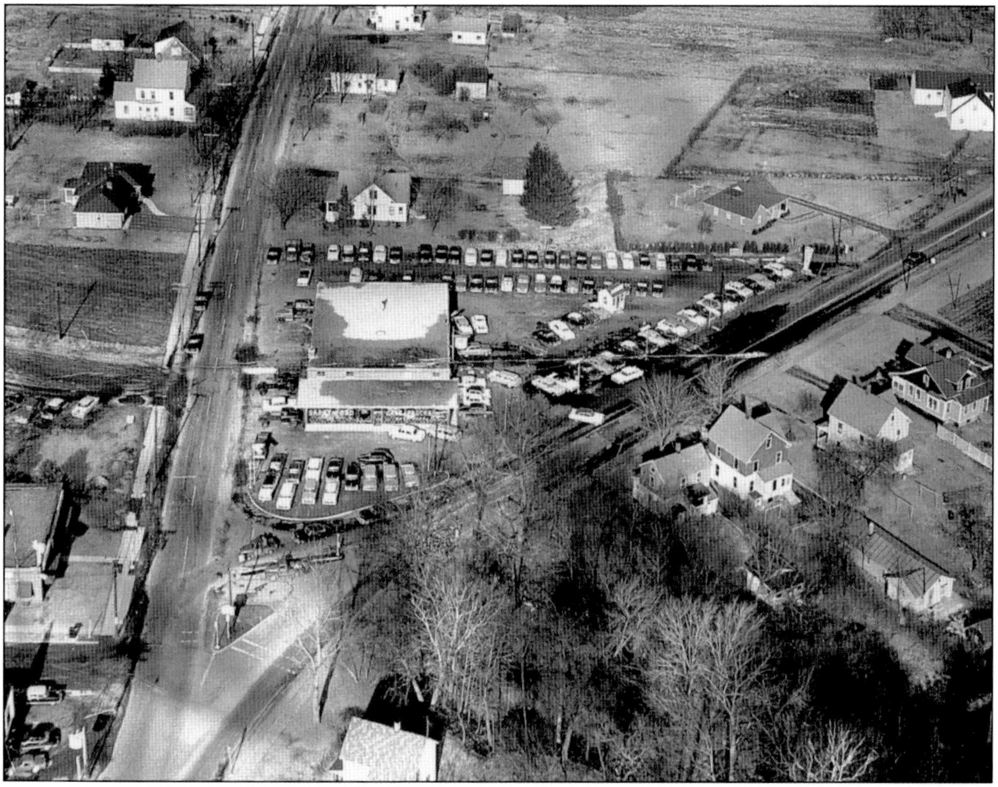

Sarat Ford was founded in 1929 by John Sarat in the O'Brien's Corner building that is barely visible at the lower left. It moved to the corner of Maple and Springfield Streets in 1955. It has since expanded to replace the houses seen to the right. (Agawam Historical Association collection.)

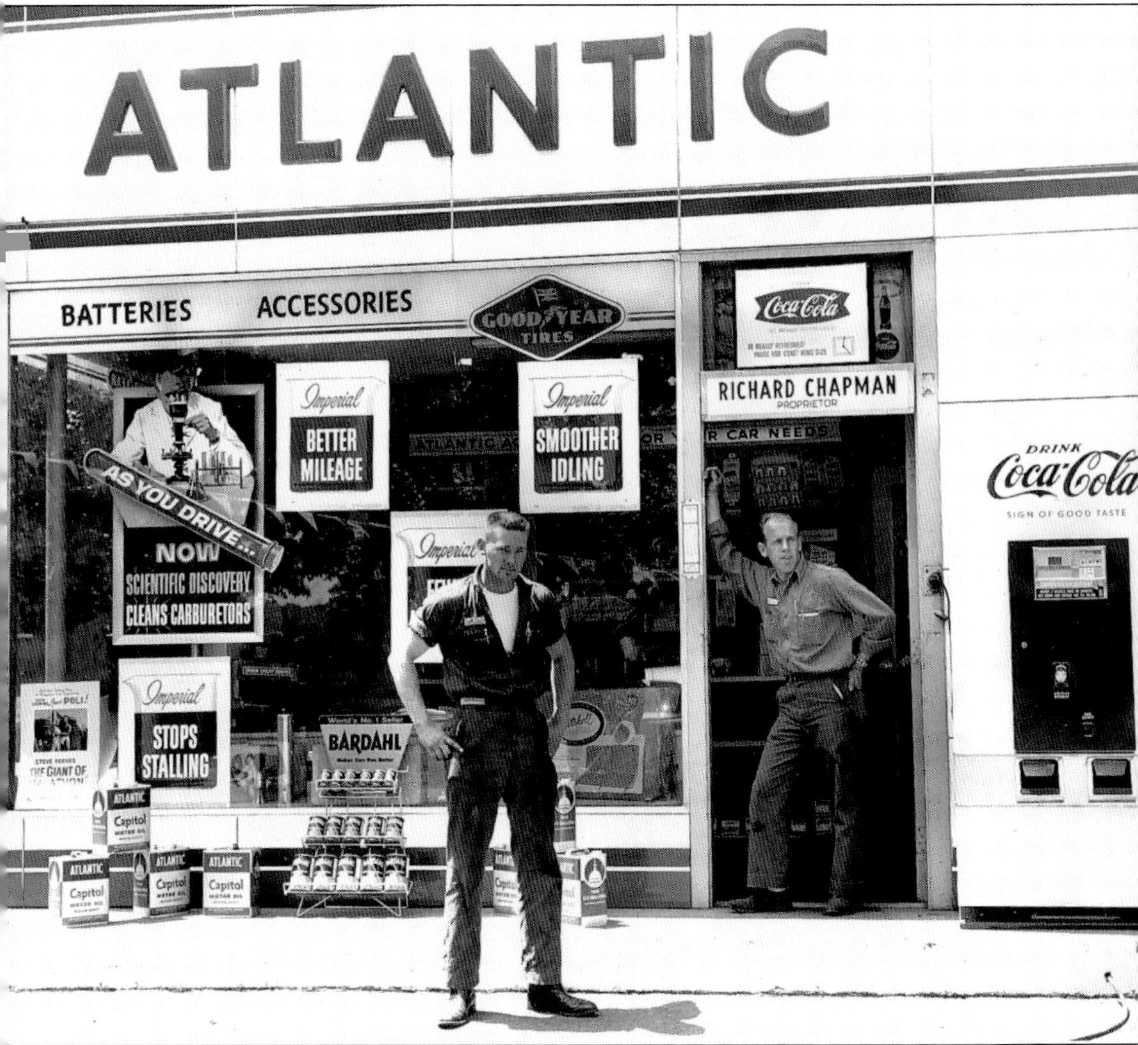

Bill Flood (left) and Dick Chapman are seen at Chapman's Atlantic Service Center, at 981 River Road at the corner of School Street, in the mid-1950s. Recalling those simpler times, Chapman said, "Things were different then. You didn't worry about anything. If you had money for bread you were happy." The site is now occupied by an ice-cream stand and a welding shop. (Courtesy Dick Chapman.)

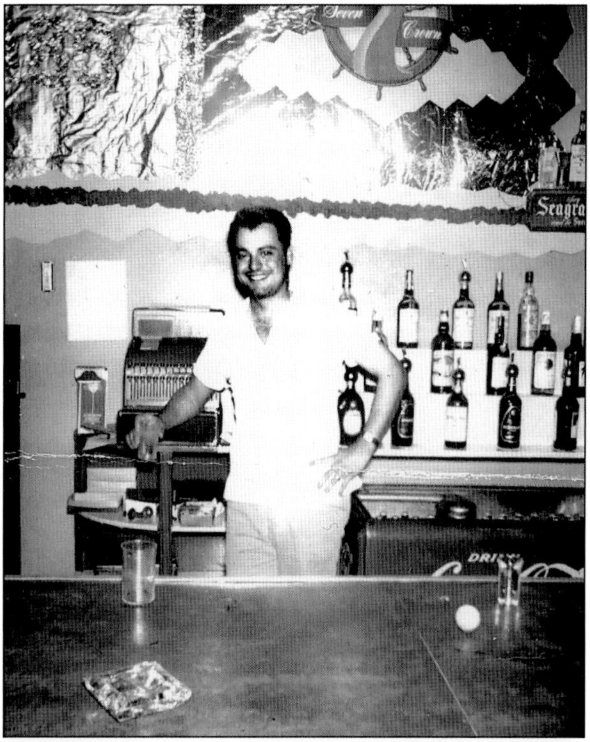

Ben Bassani briefly owned Lou's Lounge, at 295 Springfield Street, during the 1950s. He also tended bar there. Bassani later served on the Agawam School Committee, high school building committee, and finance committee. Always headed somewhere, he often used his signature phrase, "Gotta go." (Courtesy Candy [Bassani] Martin.)

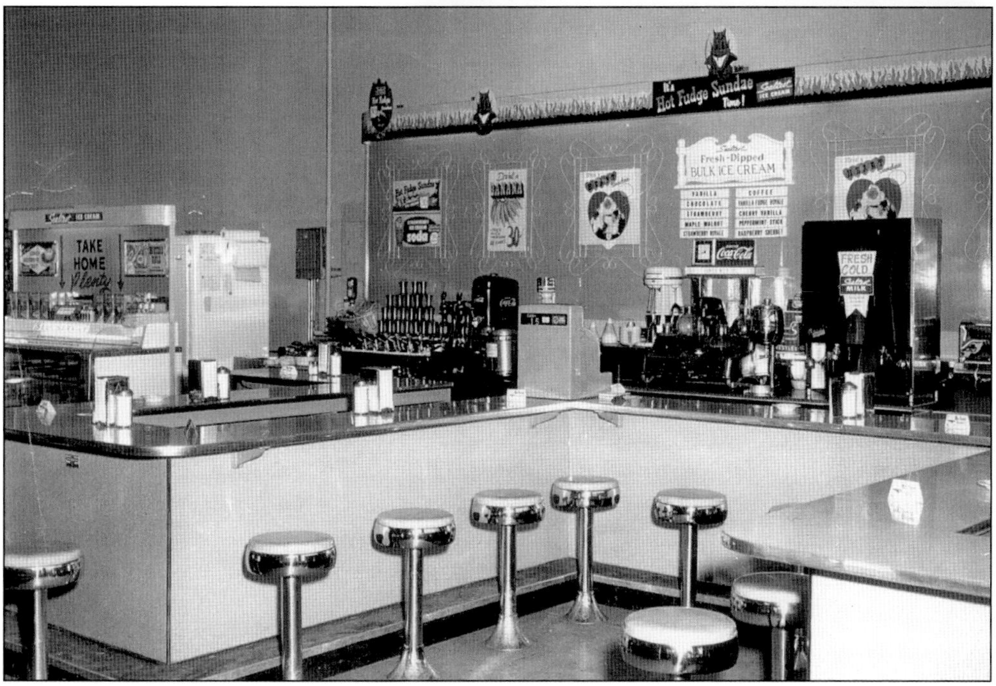

A popular meeting spot in the late 1950s was the lunch counter at the Agawam Pharmacy on Main Street, which featured hot fudge sundaes for 30¢ and ice-cream sodas for 25¢. Agawam Center lost its pharmacy in the 1990s, but it regained a gathering place when the Russo family opened Giovanni's Bakery there at that time. (Courtesy Edward Shore and Theresa and Tony Russo.)

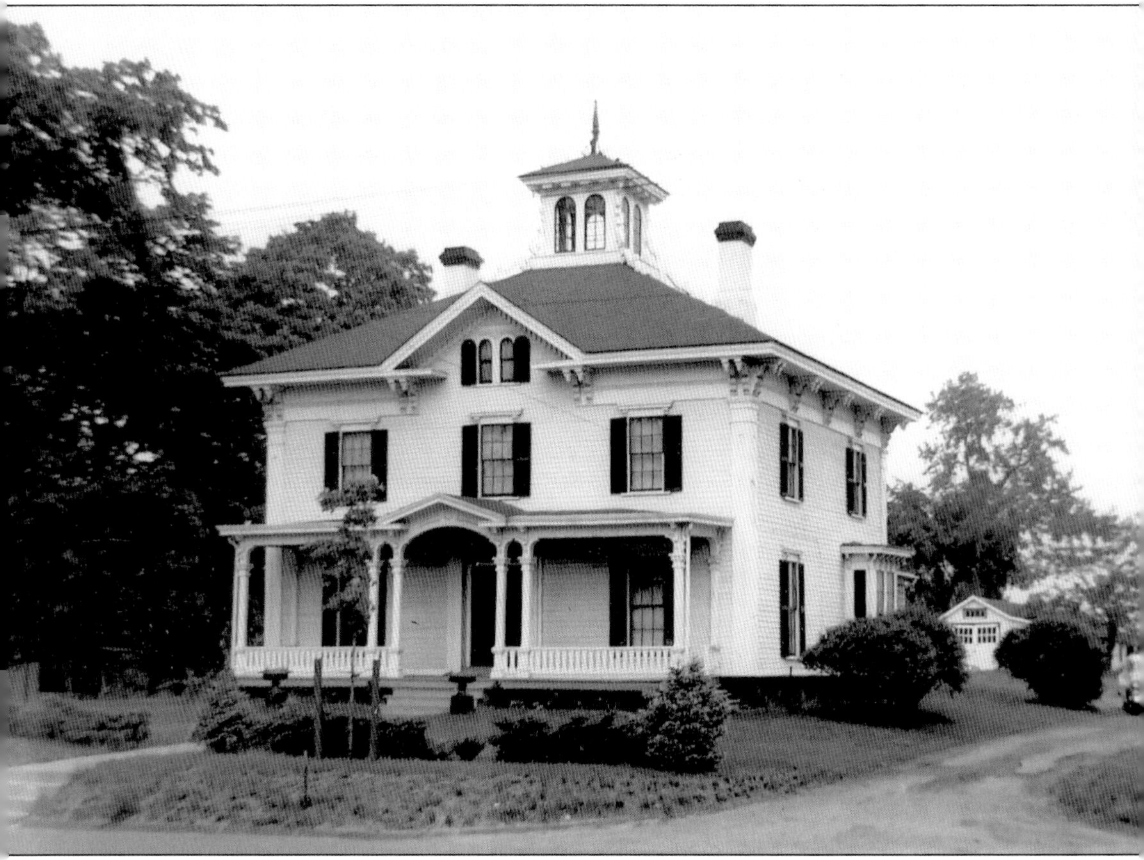

Although Robert E. Cooper began construction of this imposing residence at 159 Main Street in 1861, it was not finished until after his return from service in the Civil War. John Caldon Sr. purchased the 18-acre property in 1917 and operated a celery and asparagus farm there for many years. In the years after his 1945 death, the land was sold to Tinti's (now Carando) and Buxton (now Southworth). In 1957, Arthur J. Leary Jr. renovated the building and opened the Country Squire Furniture Shop. As the business grew, additions were constructed in 1961 and 1968. Cooper's, a curtain and gift shop, was later added to the rear of the property. Operated by Leary's daughters since before his death in 2004, both businesses continue to thrive and are considered Main Street landmarks. (Courtesy Martha [Leary] Trevallion.)

Seven

ROBINSON STATE PARK

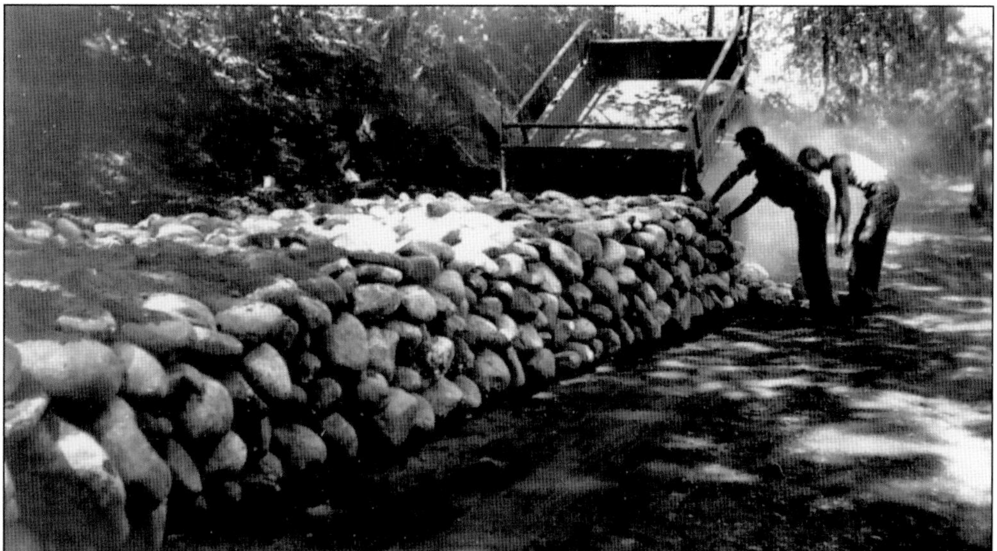

Area resident John C. Robinson spent 15 years acquiring more than 700 acres that he deeded to the state in 1934 to form the core of what was at first known as the Agawam River Parkway, seen here under construction in 1936, due to its location along the Agawam River. Today, John C. Robinson State Park consists of 811 acres. (National Archives; author's collection.)

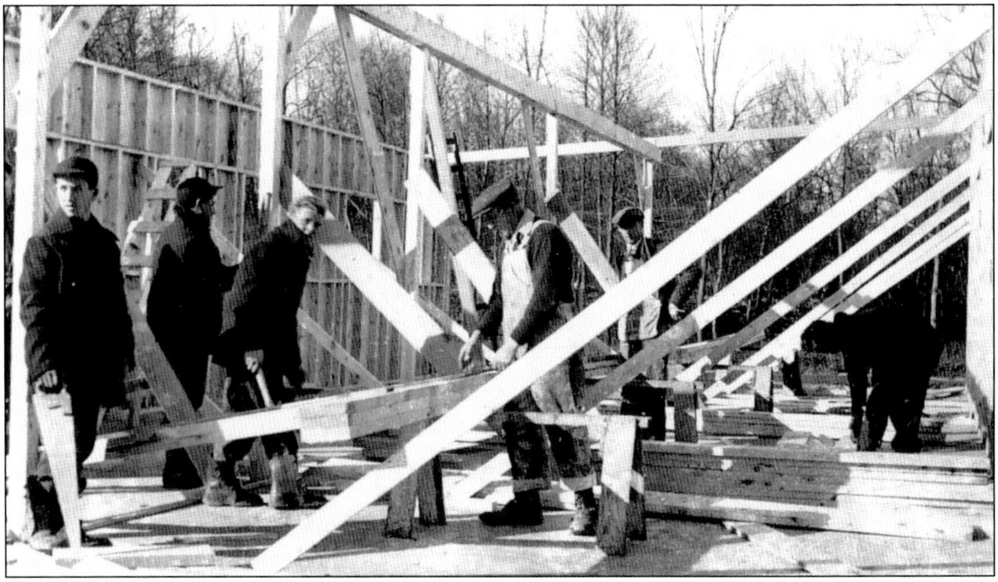

In May 1935, work began under the auspices of the Emergency Relief Administration (ERA) when land was cleared for an athletic field. A Civilian Conservation Corps camp (No. SP-24) soon followed (seen here under construction), and the CCC took over the building of the park. (National Archives; author's collection.)

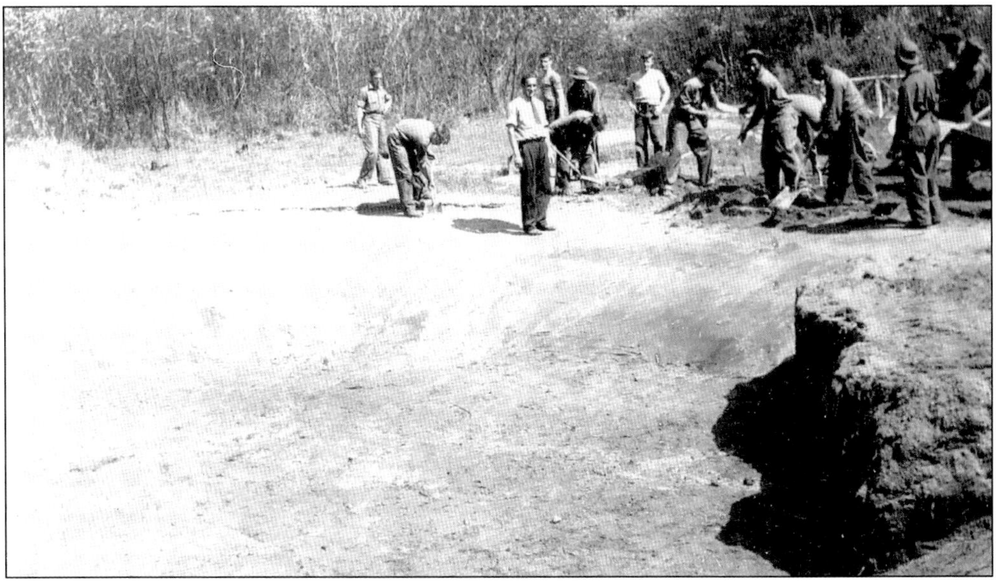

A December 1935 narrative report by park superintendent John M. Malone describes John Robinson as a "frequent visitor" and "ready to donate more land to enlarge the park area." It continues, "This park area becomes more interesting with each study and we will be able to provide swimming pools that are sadly lacking in this area." This photograph, from a June 1936 progress report, shows the watering holes under construction. (National Archives; author's collection.)

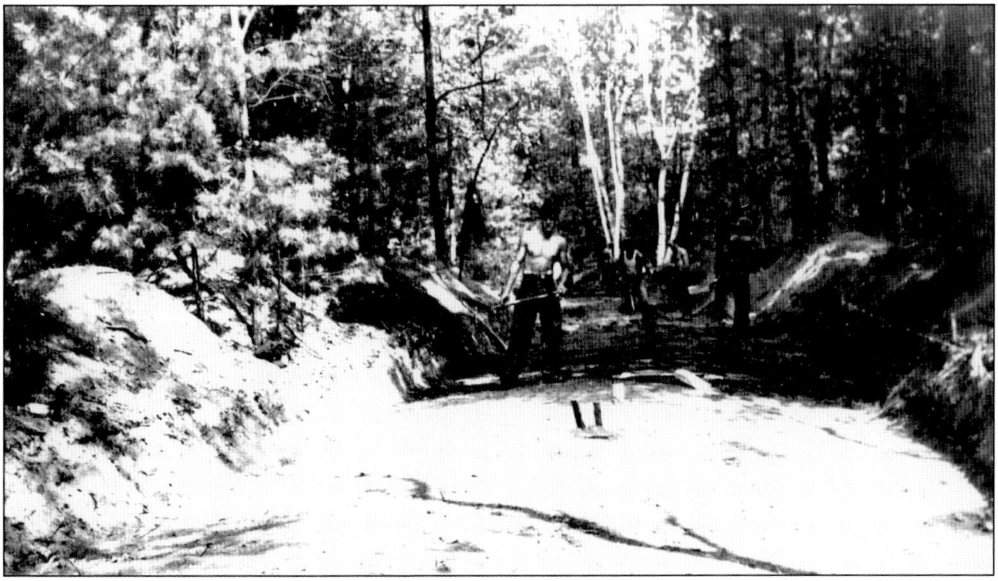

A March 1936 narrative report filed after that year's devastating flood stated, "Too much cannot be said of the work of the C.C.C. boys" who provided assistance to Westfield, West Springfield, and Springfield and earned a letter of appreciation from the mayor of Westfield, who also filed with the report. Here, the park's Provin Mountain Road is seen under construction in 1936. (National Archives; author's collection.)

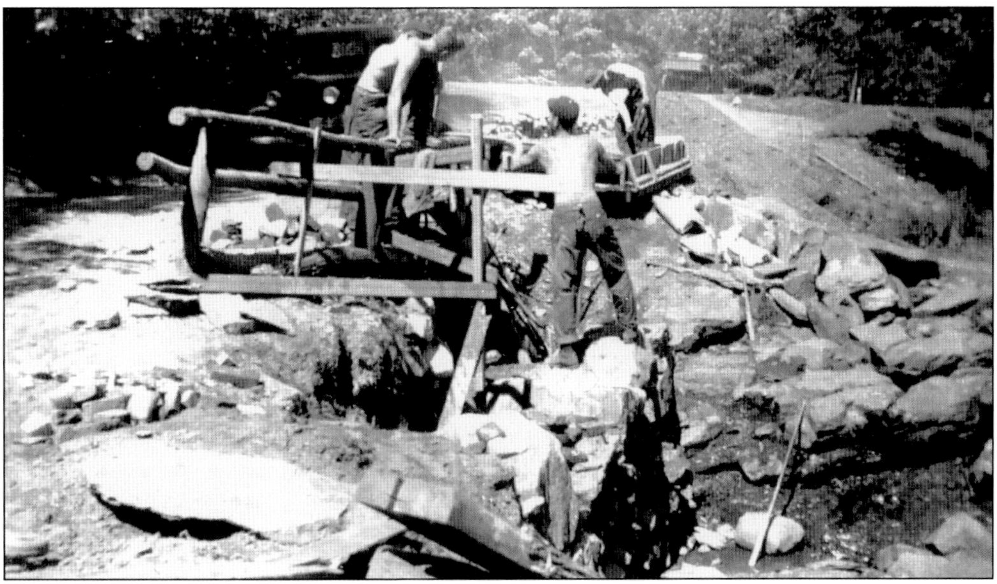

Three meals a day were provided for the CCC boys, who most likely worked up quite an appetite building the park. On July 20, 1938, a dinner consisting of cucumbers, celery-tomato soup, roast veal, mashed potatoes, summer squash, gravy, coffee, bread and butter, lima beans, and blueberry pie was served to 183 men. The *total* cost was $20.75. (National Archives; author's collection.)

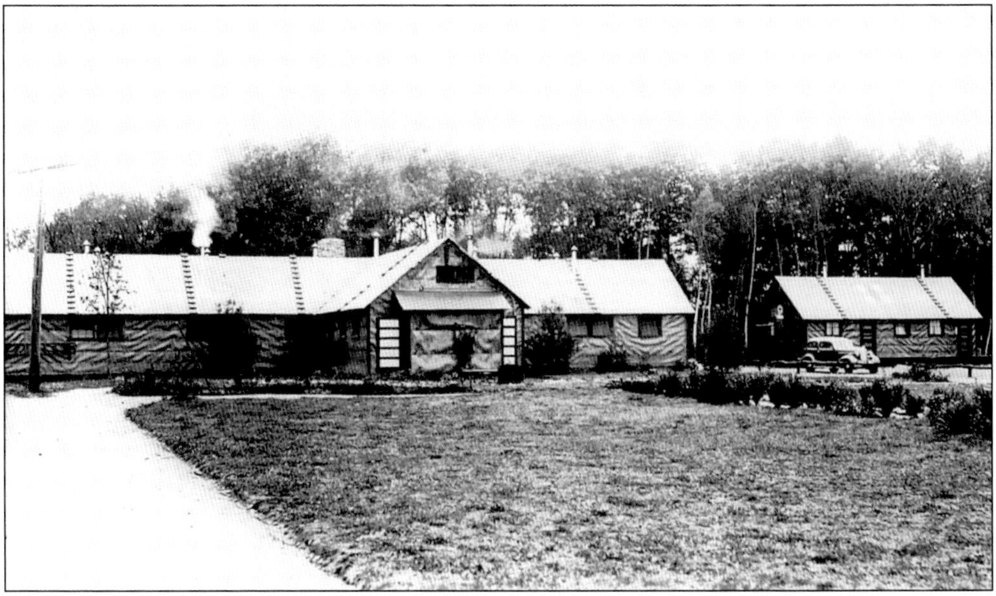

The headquarters and infirmary of the 2103 Company of the CCC in Agawam are seen here. The CCC camp inspection report dated November 29, 1939, notes, "Community relations have been excellent for this camp in the past years. This camp has rated high in past years, for work service, general morale and general condition of the camp buildings and area." (National Archives; author's collection.)

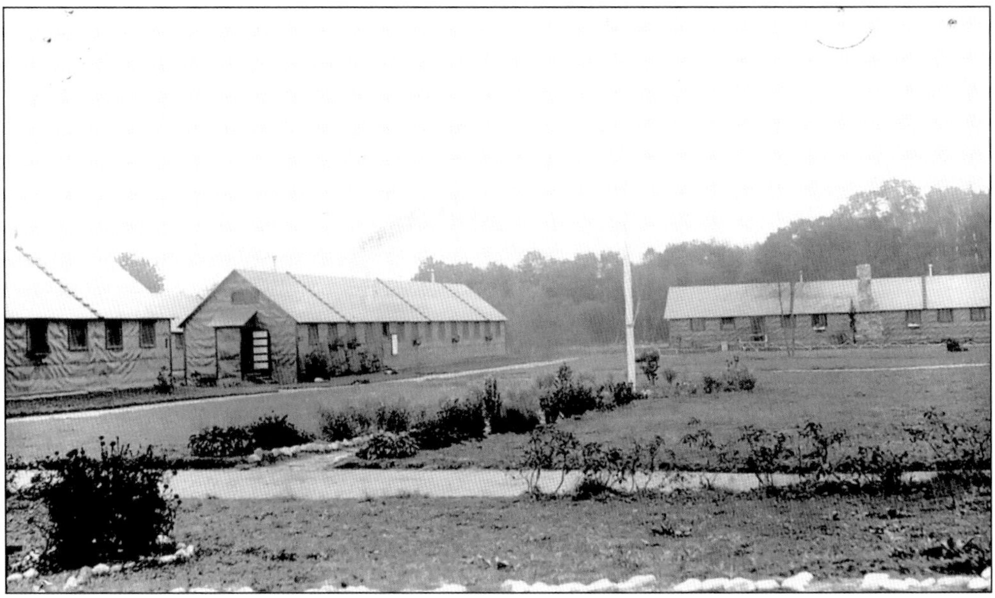

Pictured here are the schoolhouse and recreation hall of the 2103 Company of the CCC in Agawam. Here, "Educational and Welfare Activities" such as grammar, spelling, truck maintenance, leathercraft, piano, boxing, and Ping-Pong were provided for camp residents. A 1935 report states, "Church services are held at the camp each Sunday and Holy Day for the Catholic boys." (National Archives; author's collection.)

Eight

On the Move

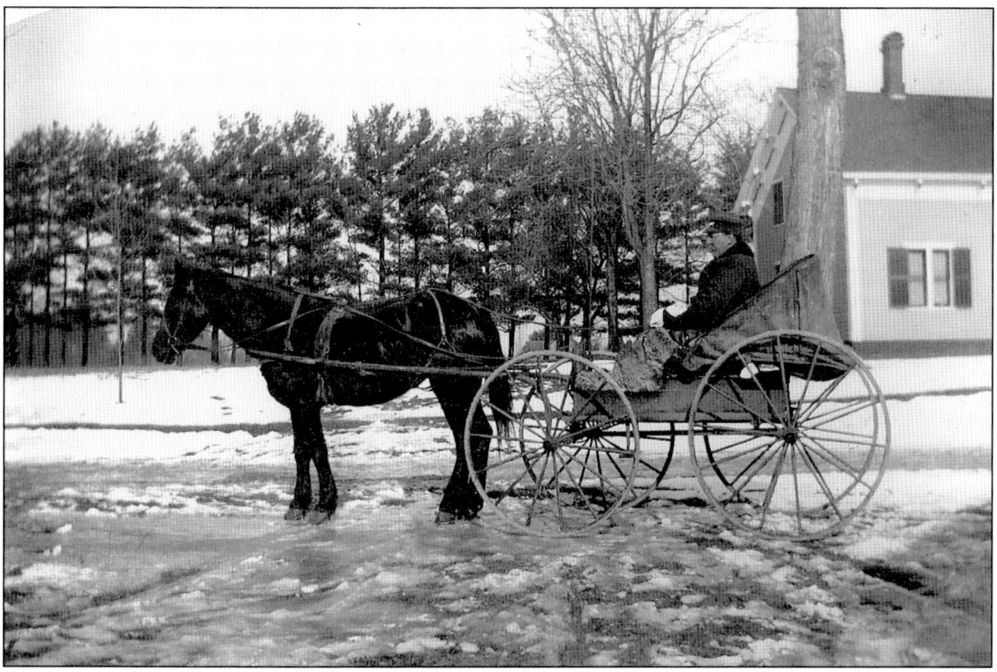

Monroe Hayward was an early letter carrier after rural delivery service was established here in 1900. He is seen here with a horse and buggy in front of the Samuel Bodurtha House, located at 142 Silver Street, which still stands. Described in *Chowder without Tomato* as "the village strongman," he later became the namesake of Monroe Street. (Agawam Historical Association collection; gift of Donald Goss.)

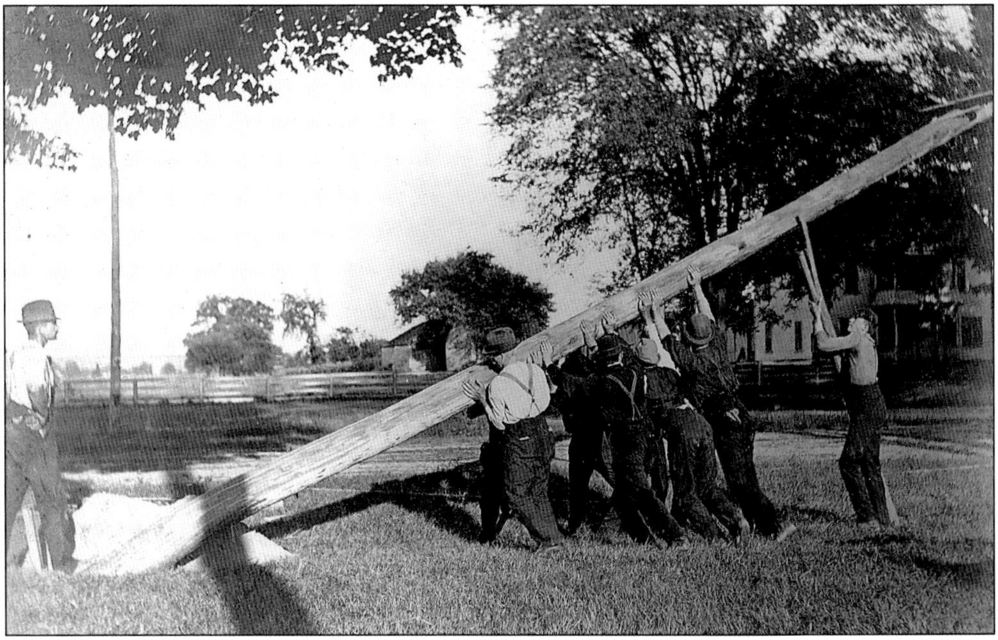

In 1900, the Springfield Street Railway built a trolley line from the newly built Agawam Bridge (the old covered bridge it replaced had burned the previous year) at the foot of Main Street to the Connecticut state line. Service to Feeding Hills from the bridge followed in 1902. Seen here on Main Street are construction crews erecting poles to carry the wires that powered the trolley cars. The *c.* 1795 Lt. William Allen House, at 722–726 Main Street, can be seen on the right in both photographs. The Victorian-era porch was removed in the early 1930s. (Courtesy Henry C. Hastings.)

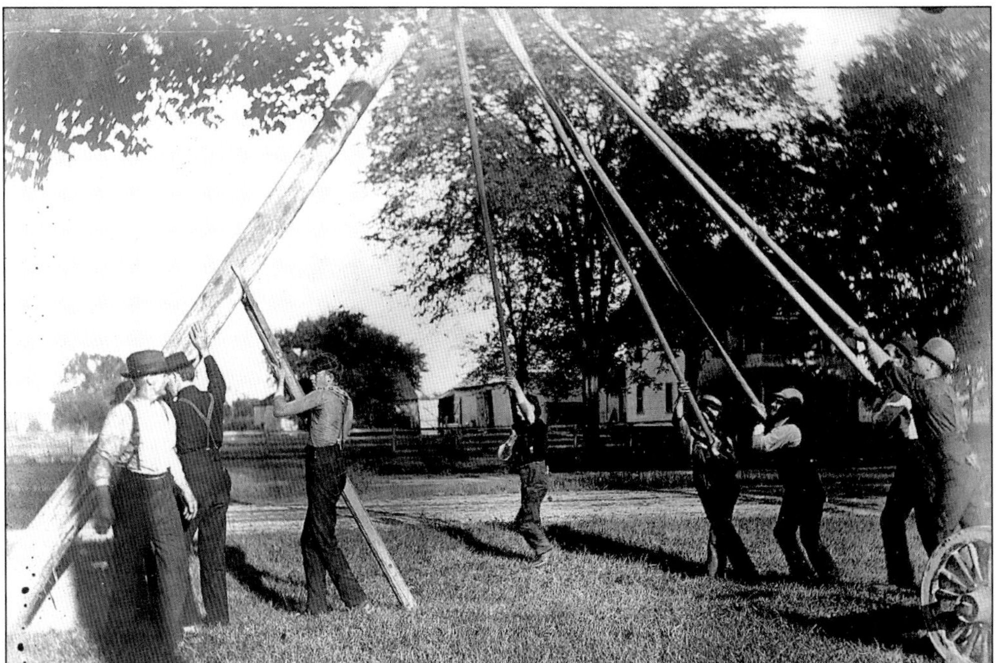

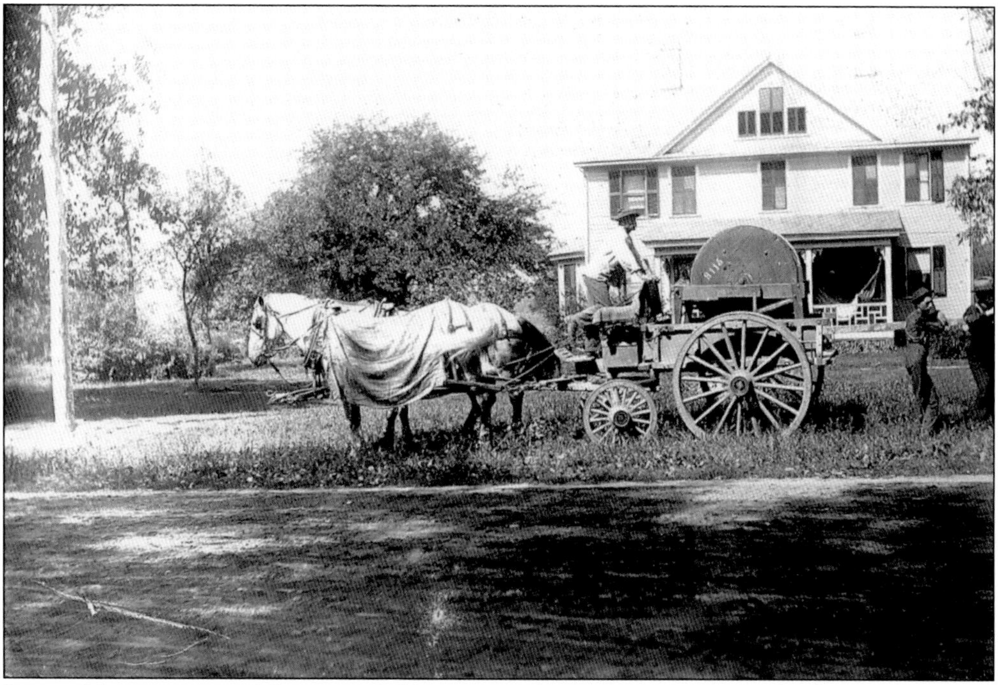

Pictured here are two of the Springfield Street Railway Company's specialized wagons used for the installation of the overhead wires that powered the line's trolley cars. The *c.* 1795 Allen-Hastings House, which still stands at 692 Main Street minus the triangular dormer and large front porch, is seen in the background. Once trolley service was established, up to a dozen cars at a time could be seen on Main Street heading to and from Riverside Park during the summer months. (Courtesy Henry C. Hastings.)

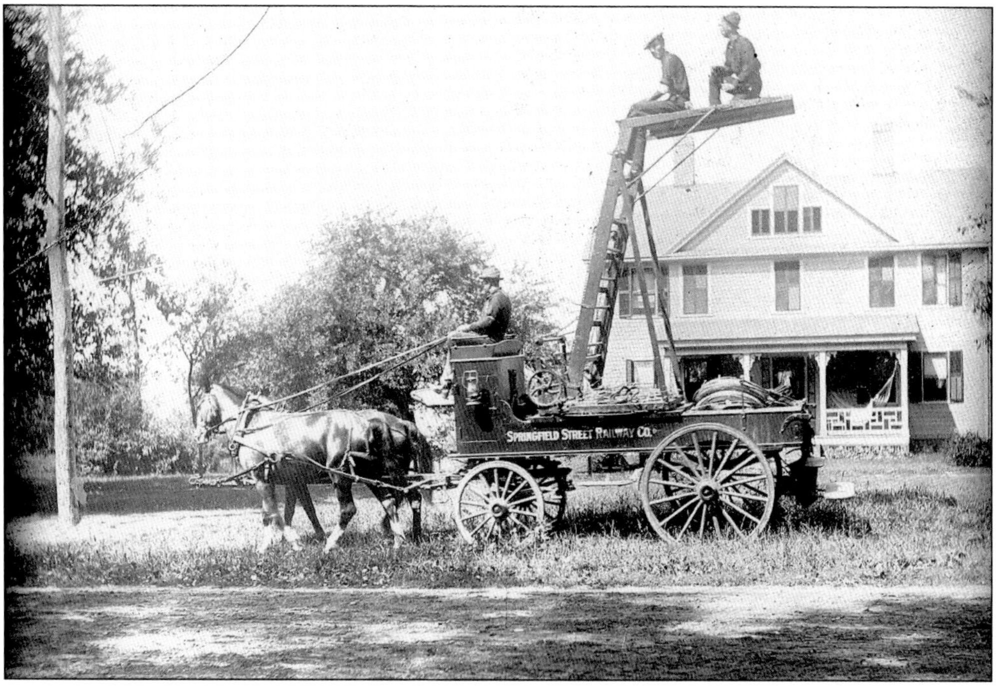

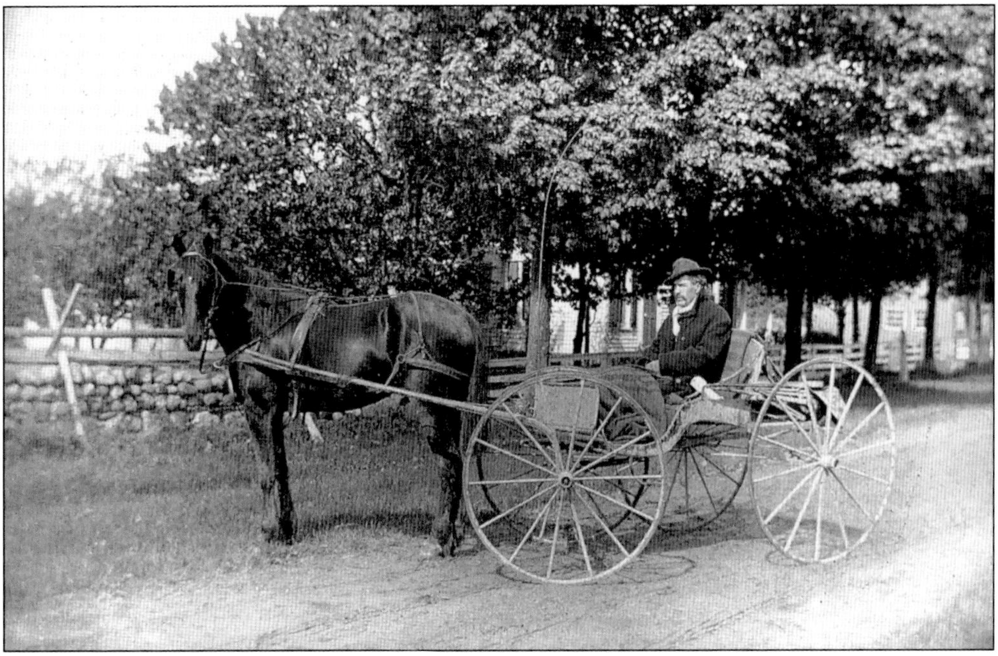

Storekeeper and Agawam postmaster Charles W. Hastings delivers groceries in his horse and buggy (pages 11 and 70). (Courtesy Henry C. Hastings.)

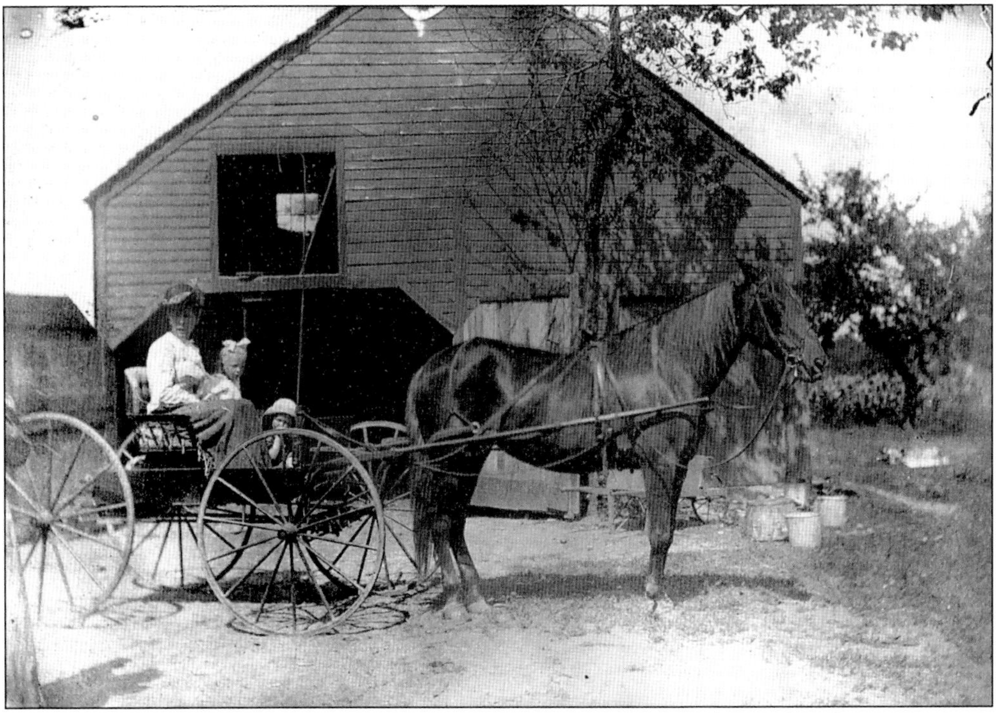

Hendrick Fickweiler took this photograph of Helena Toelken, Helen Fickweiler, and Louise Shields in a horse-drawn buggy near the Toelken-Fickweiler-Moore house, at 43 Perry Lane, where the Toelken family and their descendants lived from 1897 to 2001. (Courtesy Paul Toelken.)

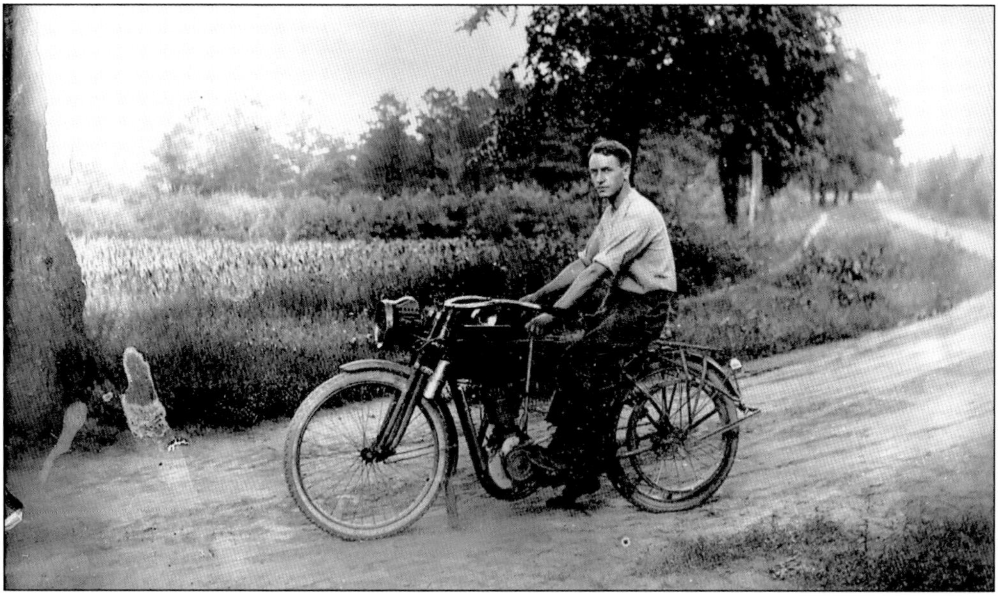

This 1911 photograph of Richard E. Toelken on his belt-driven Harley-Davidson motorcycle was taken looking east from the front of the Toelken house, at 43 Perry Lane on the corner of Elm Street, which is seen here on the right. The Harley's maximum speed was 40 miles per hour. (Courtesy Paul Toelken.)

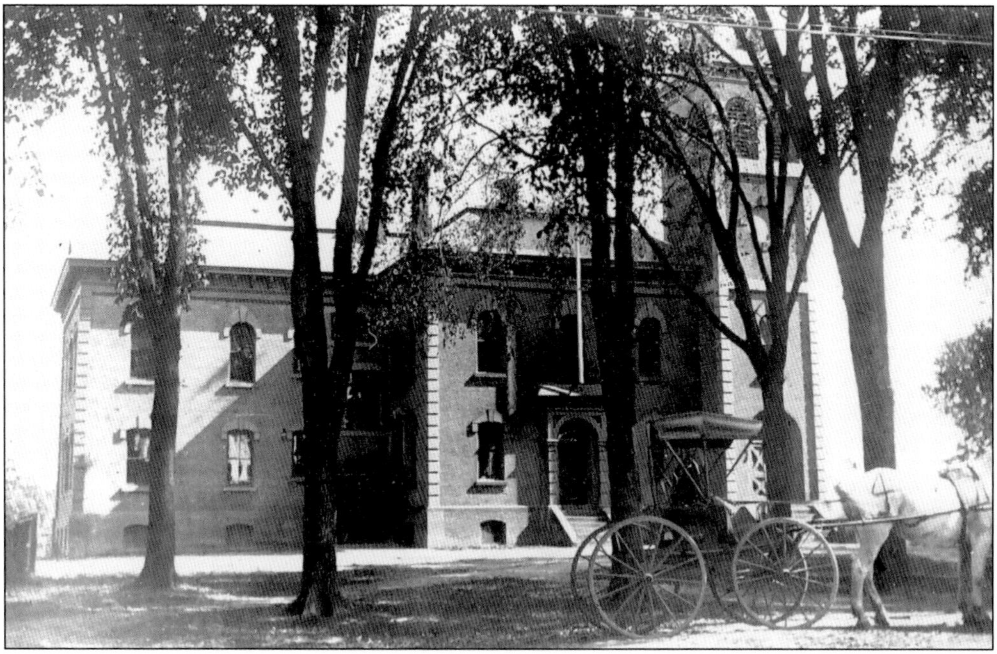

A horse-drawn buggy is pictured outside the old Agawam Town Hall on Main Street *c.* 1912. Town meeting day was described in the following manner in *Chowder without Tomato*: "On the appointed day, rigs began appearing at the Town Hall grounds. Horses were tied to every available hitching post in the neighborhood, and when the hitching posts were all taken, hitching weights were thrown out of the vehicles to hold the horses." (Courtesy Paul Toelken.)

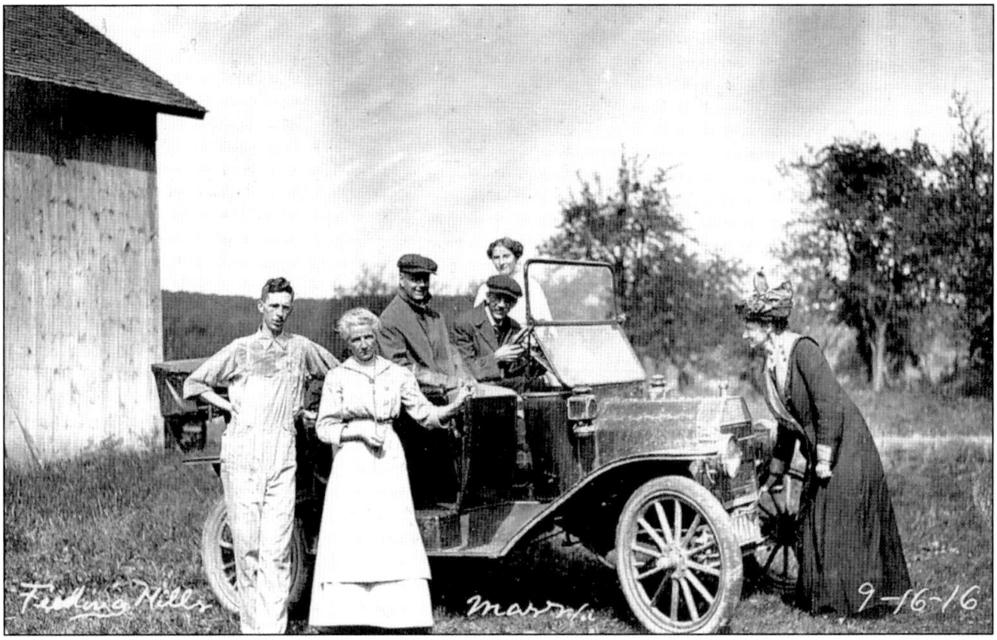

Women have apparently been treated as equals in this town for quite some time, as is evidenced by this photograph taken on September 16, 1916. Attempts to identify these motorists by tracing the registration number on the license plate have been unsuccessful. (Author's collection.)

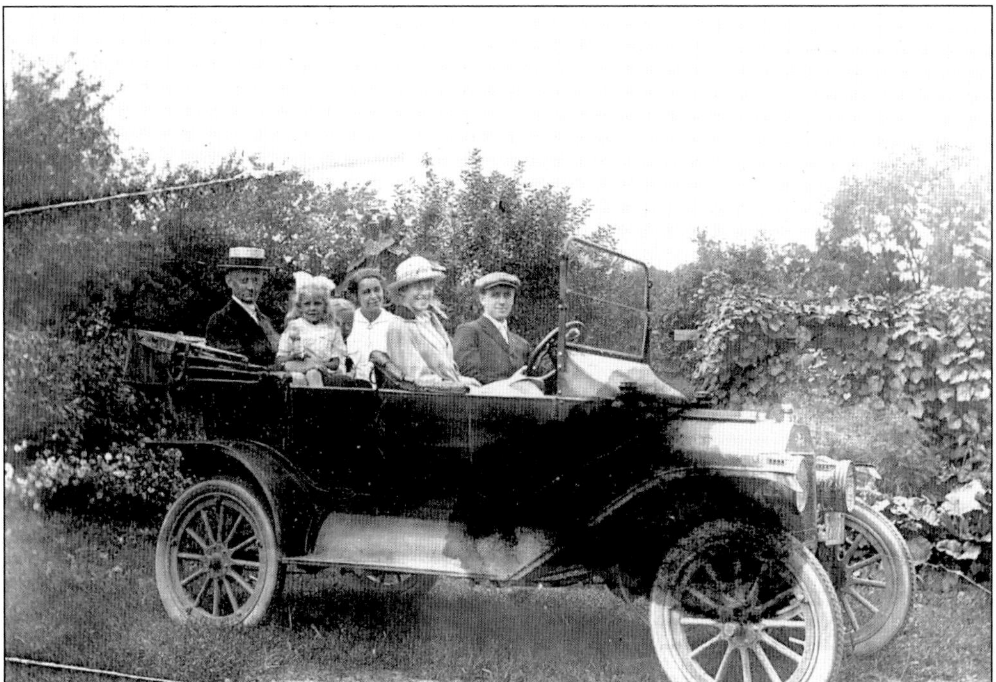

Richard E. Toelken is at the wheel of this Ford. Irene Crouss is in the passenger seat, and the Fickweiler family is in the rear seat. A 1956 ditty entitled "Motoring in Agawam" bemoans the quality of Agawam roads. (Courtesy Paul Toelken.)

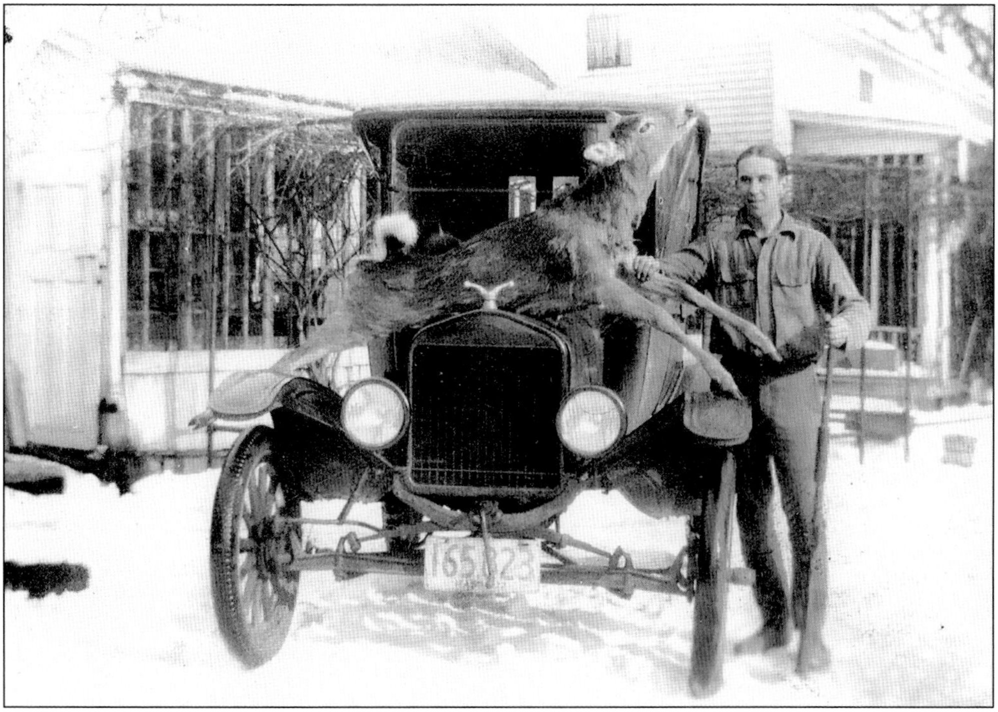

John Schwartz shows off the spoils of a hunting trip at the Schwartz Farm, at 639 River Road, in this 1922 photograph. (Courtesy Jeffrey Reynolds.)

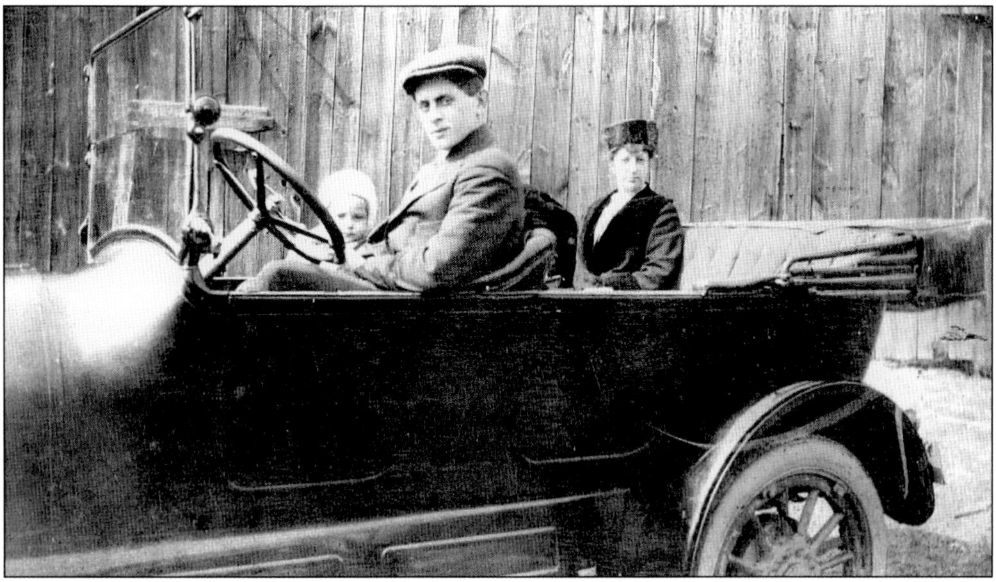

Young Anita Cesan (later Rising) is shown with her father, Daniel Oscar, and mother, Grace Blackburn Cesan, in their open touring car. (Courtesy Anita [Cesan] Rising.)

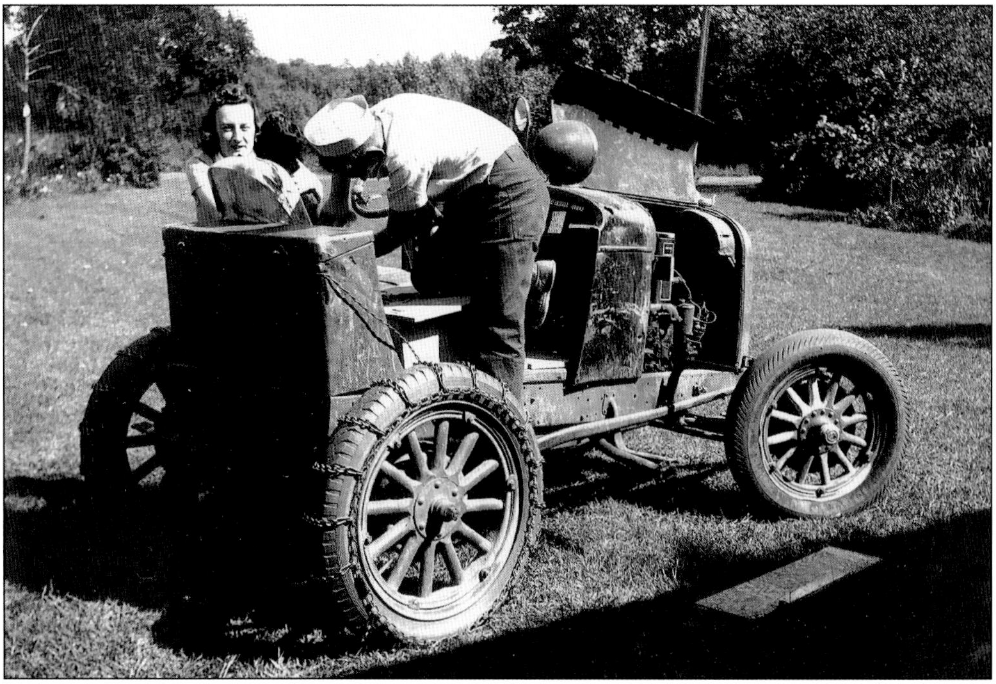

During the Great Depression, the Johnson family, who lived at 491 North West Street, could not afford a team of horses. However, they were able to arrange a trade of a week's worth of carpentry services (about $20) for a tractor with a Mr. Peterson (page 58) farther up the road. Peterson's son stripped down a 1927 Chrysler touring car, replaced the rear end with an old Ford Model T truck worm drive, and added a Dodge transmission. The Johnsons used this tractor on their farm to plow, harrow, cut, and rake hay. Above, Jarl Johnson fixes the seat while his sister Alva watches. Below, Johnson is seen dragging a large elm stump with the tractor. This tractor is still in the barn on the Johnson property. (Courtesy Jarl Johnson.)

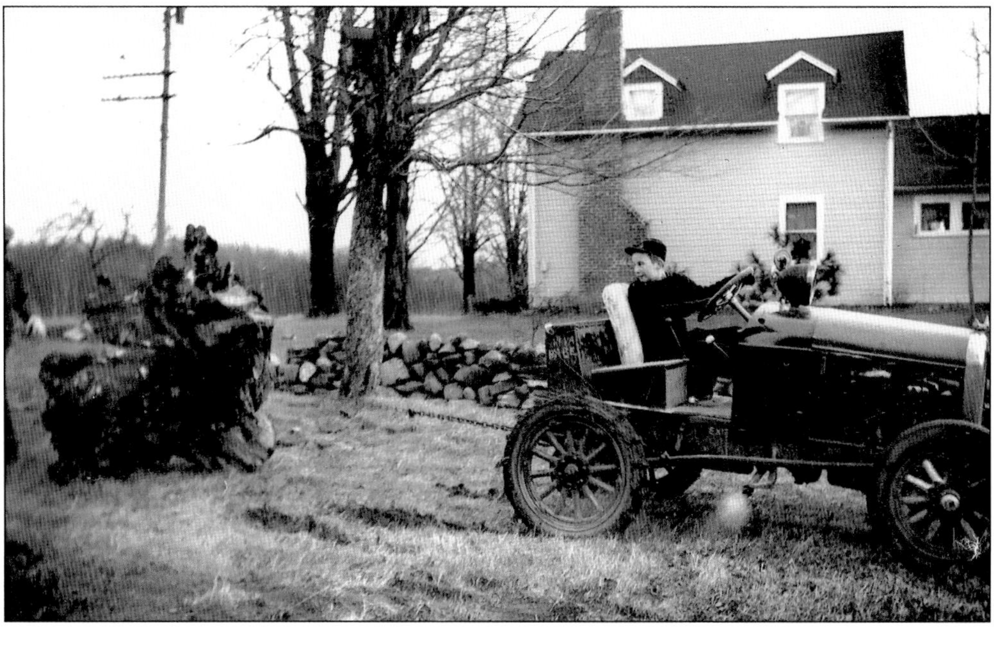

Alfred Beauchane is shown in front of his Model A coupe on Homer Street. (Courtesy Ellen Janik.)

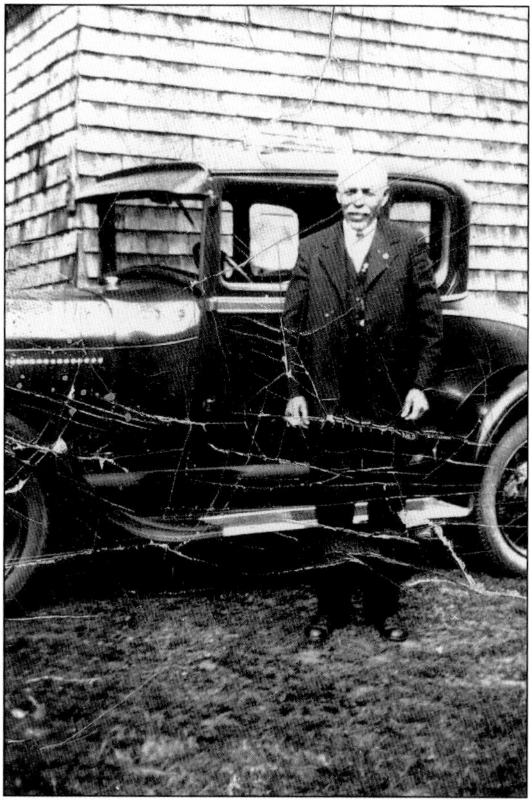

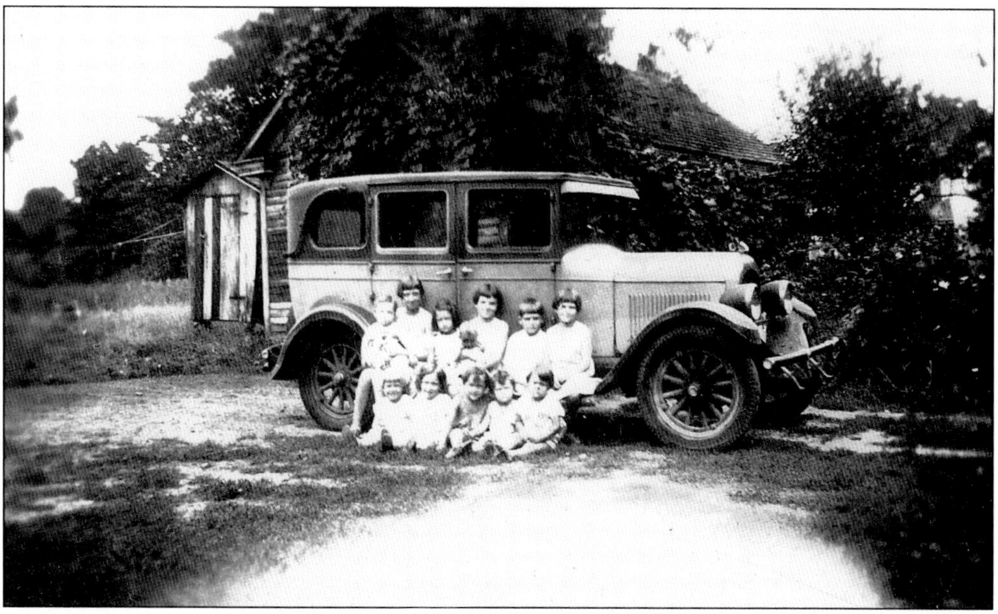

The Haseltine family and cousins pose on the running board of the family sedan at their School Street home in 1930. (Courtesy Marian Bradford.)

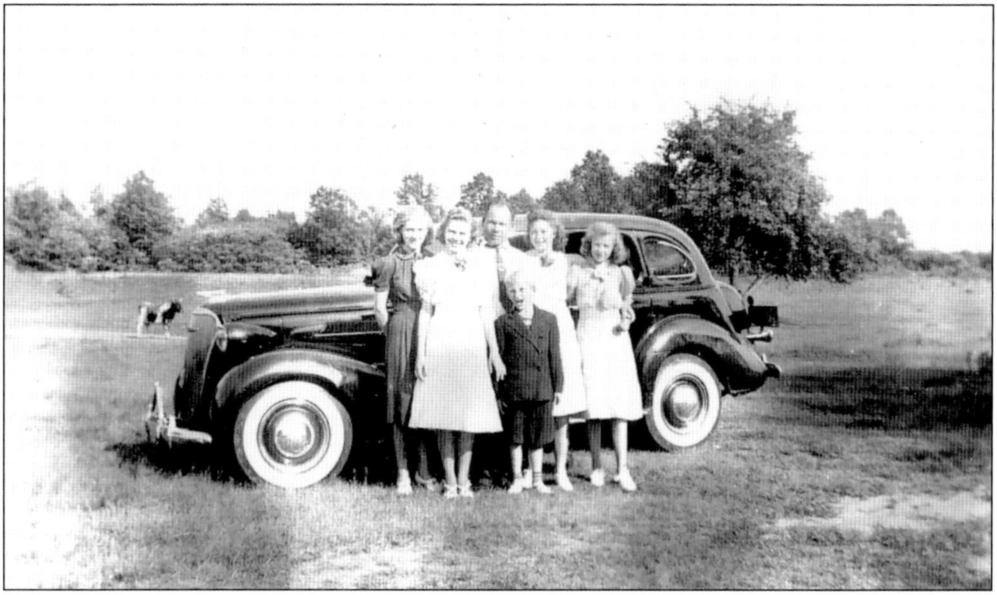

Lucas Subotin poses with his family and their Terraplane in the late 1930s. Family members are, from left to right, Zoafia (later Dempko), Helen (later Lawrenchuck), Lucas, Jennie (later Della-Giustina), Mary, and (in front) Stanley. (Courtesy Jennie and Joseph Della-Giustina.)

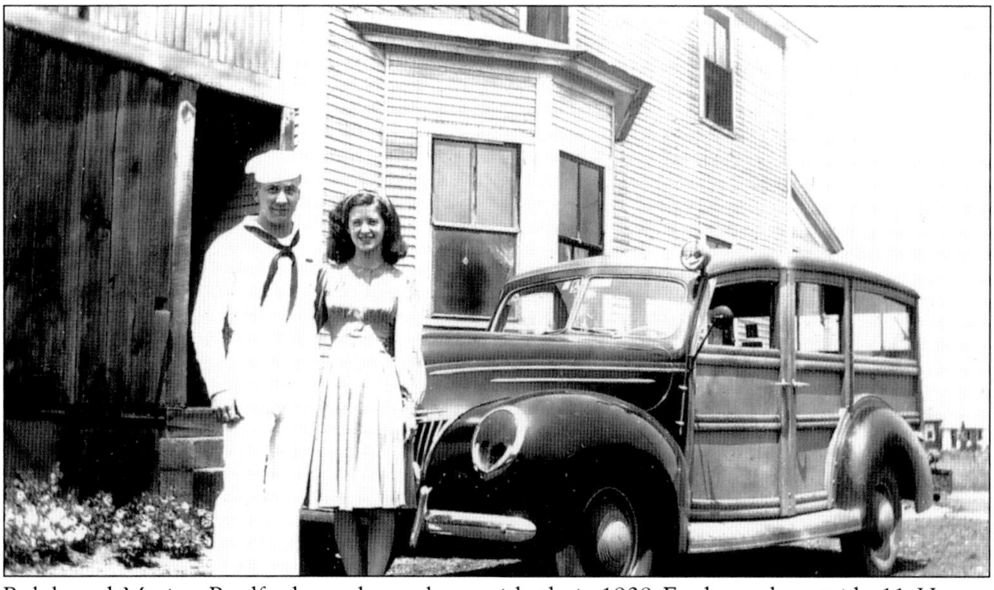

Ralph and Marian Bradford are shown here with their 1939 Ford woody outside 11 Homer Street on July 8, 1943. (Courtesy Marian Bradford.)

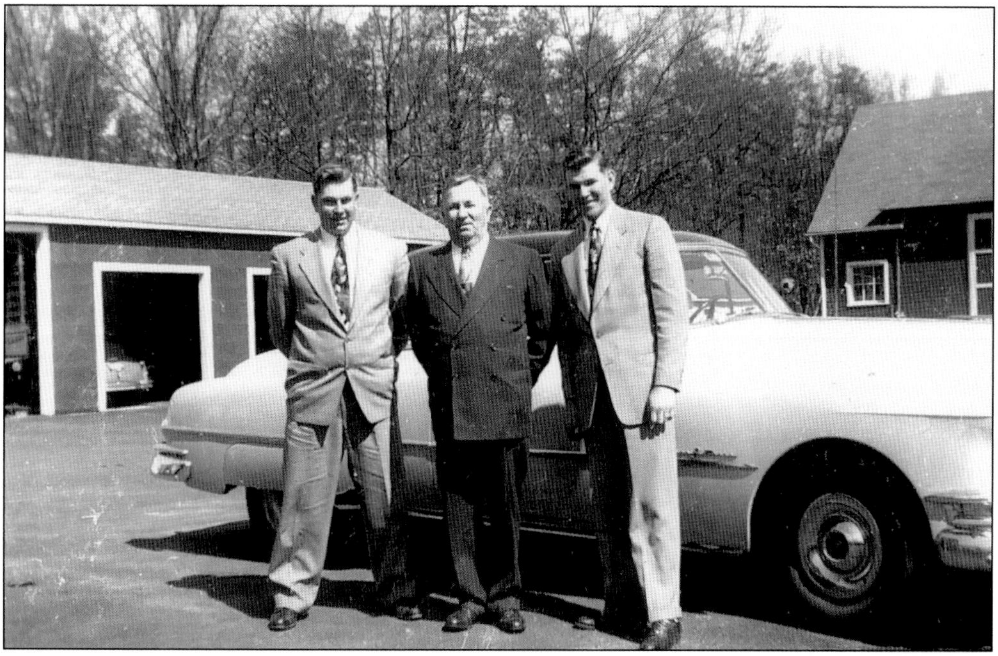

Richard, John, and Edward Stepanik pose for a photograph at the Stepanik's Twin Oaks Road farm in December 1950. (Courtesy Eleanor Stepanik.)

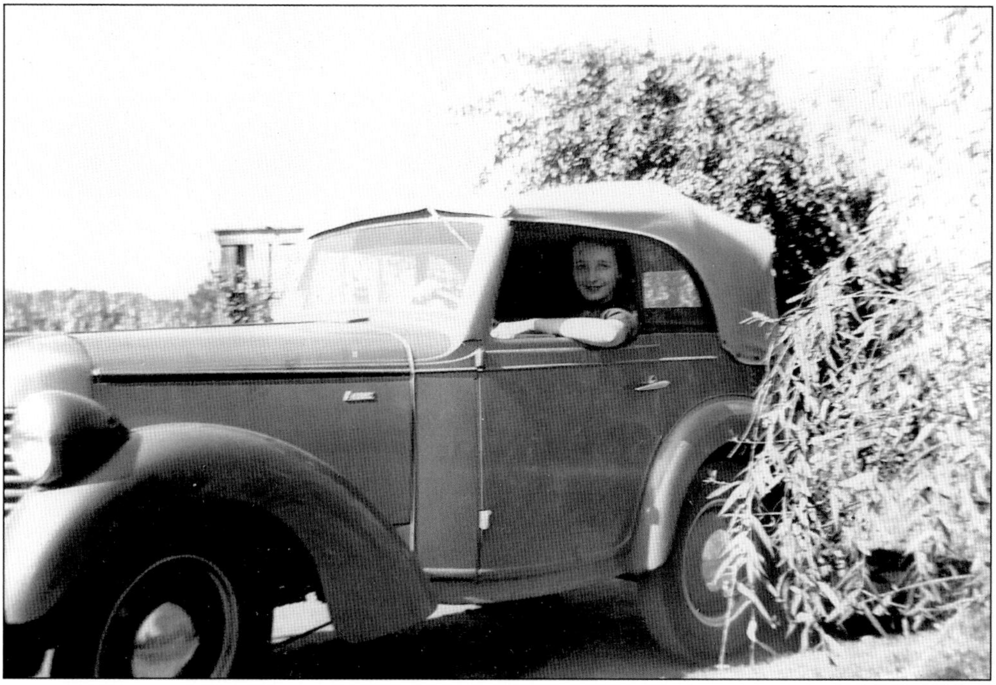

Virginia Catchepaugh is seen in the American Bantam car she drove in the 1955 centennial parade (pages 52–56). (Courtesy Virginia Catchepaugh.)

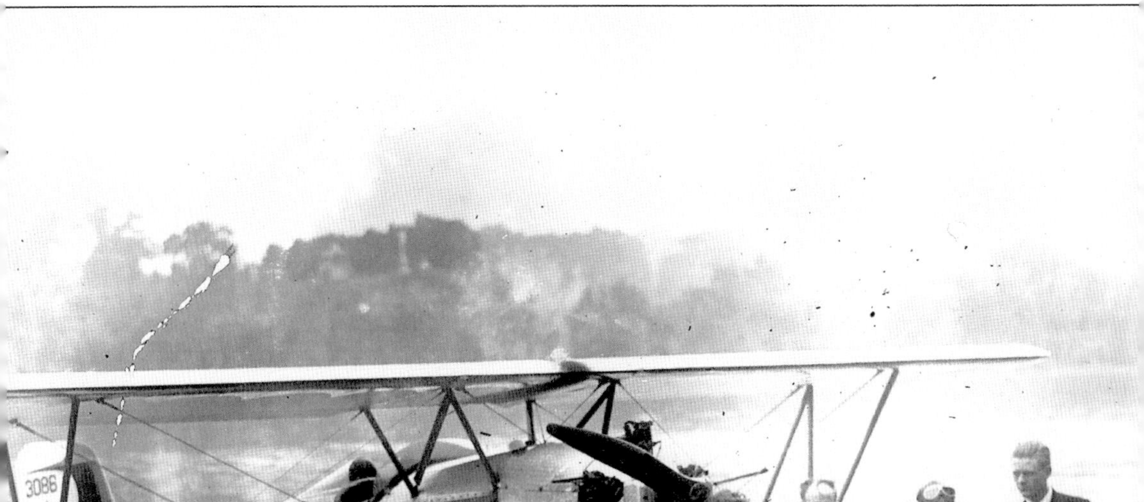

This photograph of a Granville Model A biplane was taken during the summer of 1930 on the shore of the Connecticut River. From left to right are Mark Granville, an unidentified man, Zantford "Granny" Granville, and Charles Lindbergh. The Model A was the first of several planes designed and built by the Granvilles. Advertised as "the fastest and most maneuverable licensed airplane for its horsepower in the United States," the Model A featured a side-by-side cockpit, flaps on the top wing, and a unique horizontal control stick. Eight examples of this model were built in 1929. NR3086 was built in 1930 and sported an experimental engine from automaker Louis Chevrolet. In later years, the Granville Brothers became famous for their "Gee Bee" racers. The Barney Mausoleum in Springfield's Forest Park is faintly visible on the opposite shore at left center. (Author's collection.)

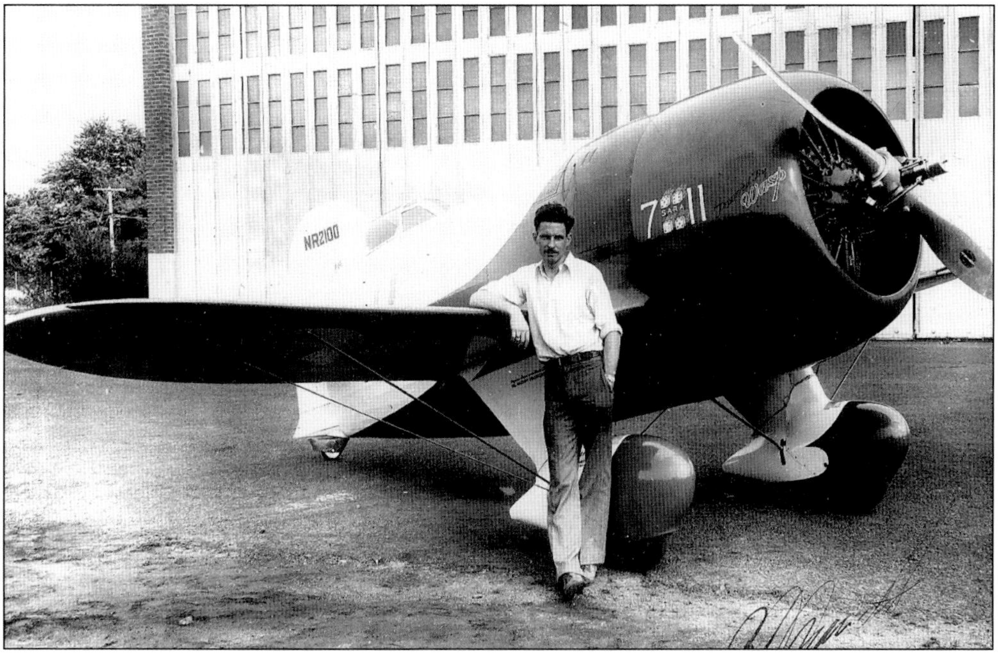

Although based out of Springfield Airport on Liberty Street, the Granville Brothers and their airplanes were a common sight at Bowles field. Here, Zantford Granville stands outside Bowles's Art Deco hangar with the famous Gee Bee R-1 racer, which, with a speed of 253 miles per hour, won the 1932 Thompson trophy with James Doolittle at the controls. (Author's collection.)

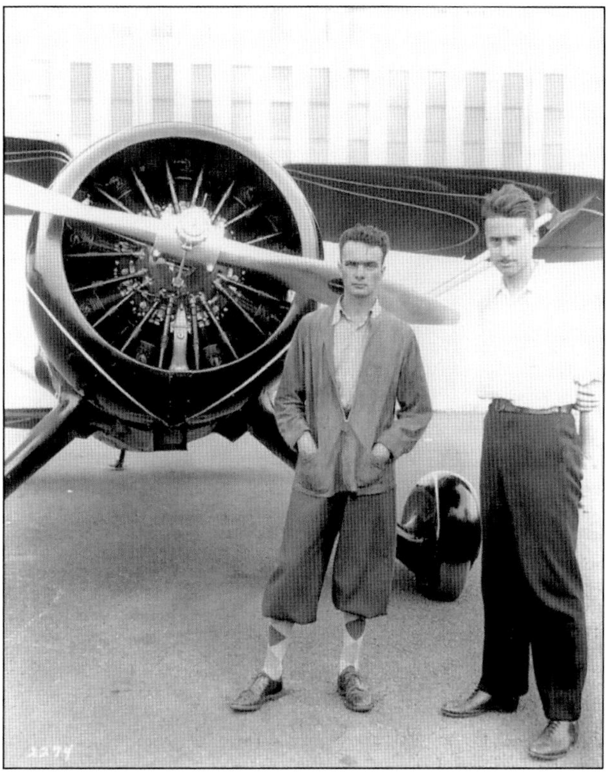

Russell Thaw and Bob Hall pose in front of the Hall Bulldog racer at Bowles field in 1932. Hall had recently resigned from his position as chief engineer and test pilot for the Granville Brothers due to a disagreement over aircraft design with Zantford Granville. Hall then formed Springfield Aircraft and built two aircrafts. Thaw was the chief pilot for New York's Guggenheim family. (Author's collection.)

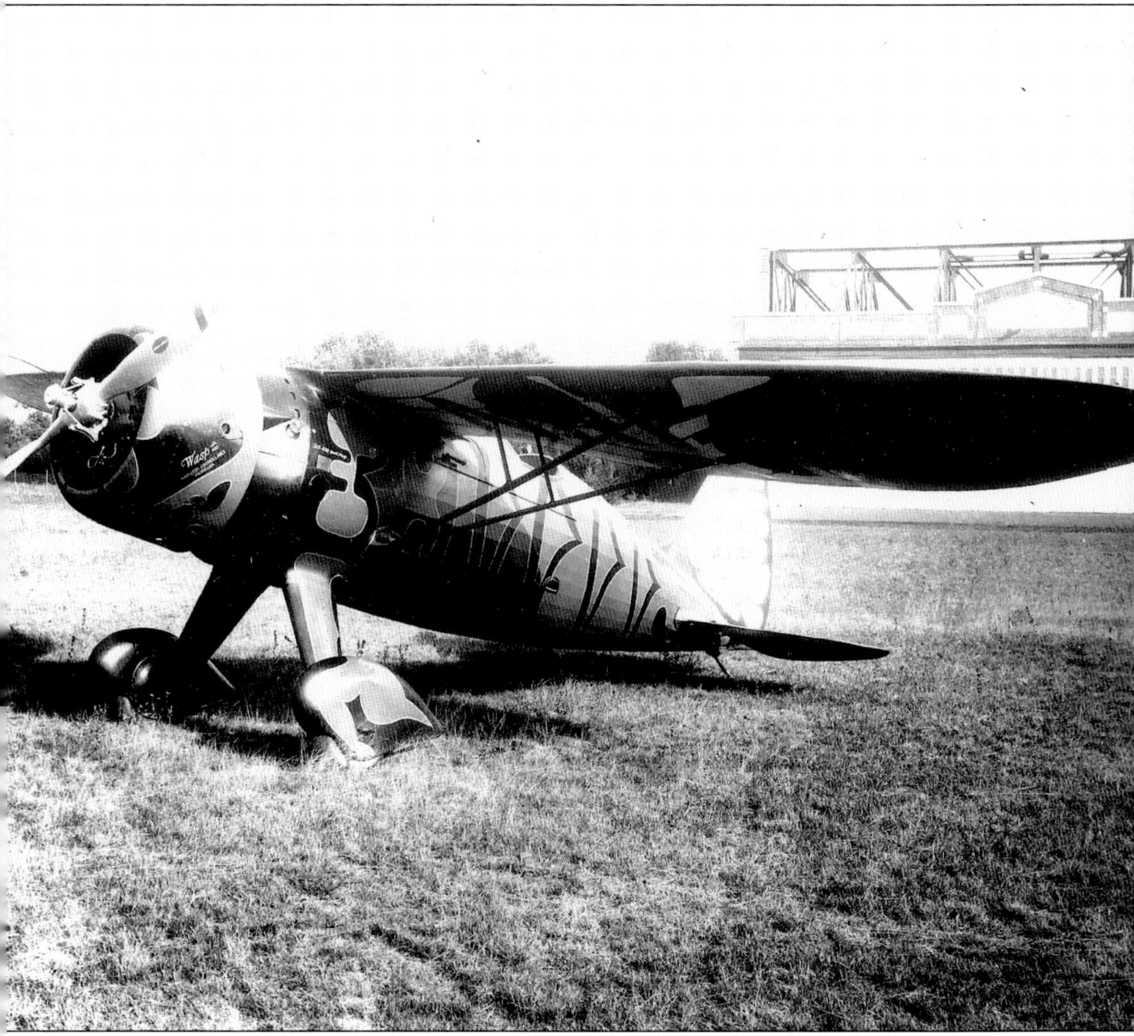

The first aircraft to be built by Bob Hall's new company was the Cicada, registration NR13205, seen here at Bowles field in 1932. The plane was so named due to its tan-and-green, insect-like paint scheme. A two-seater with a staggered side-by-side configuration, the plane was built for Frank Lynch for a transworld flight attempt. In preparation, Lynch entered the craft in the 1932 Bendix Trophy Race in Cleveland but was forced to drop out of the competition due to engine trouble. At the end of the 1932 Cleveland races, Lynch flew the Cicada back to Bowles field for improvements. Later, while taking off on a test flight, the Cicada clipped a hangar and crashed, killing Lynch. (Author's collection.)

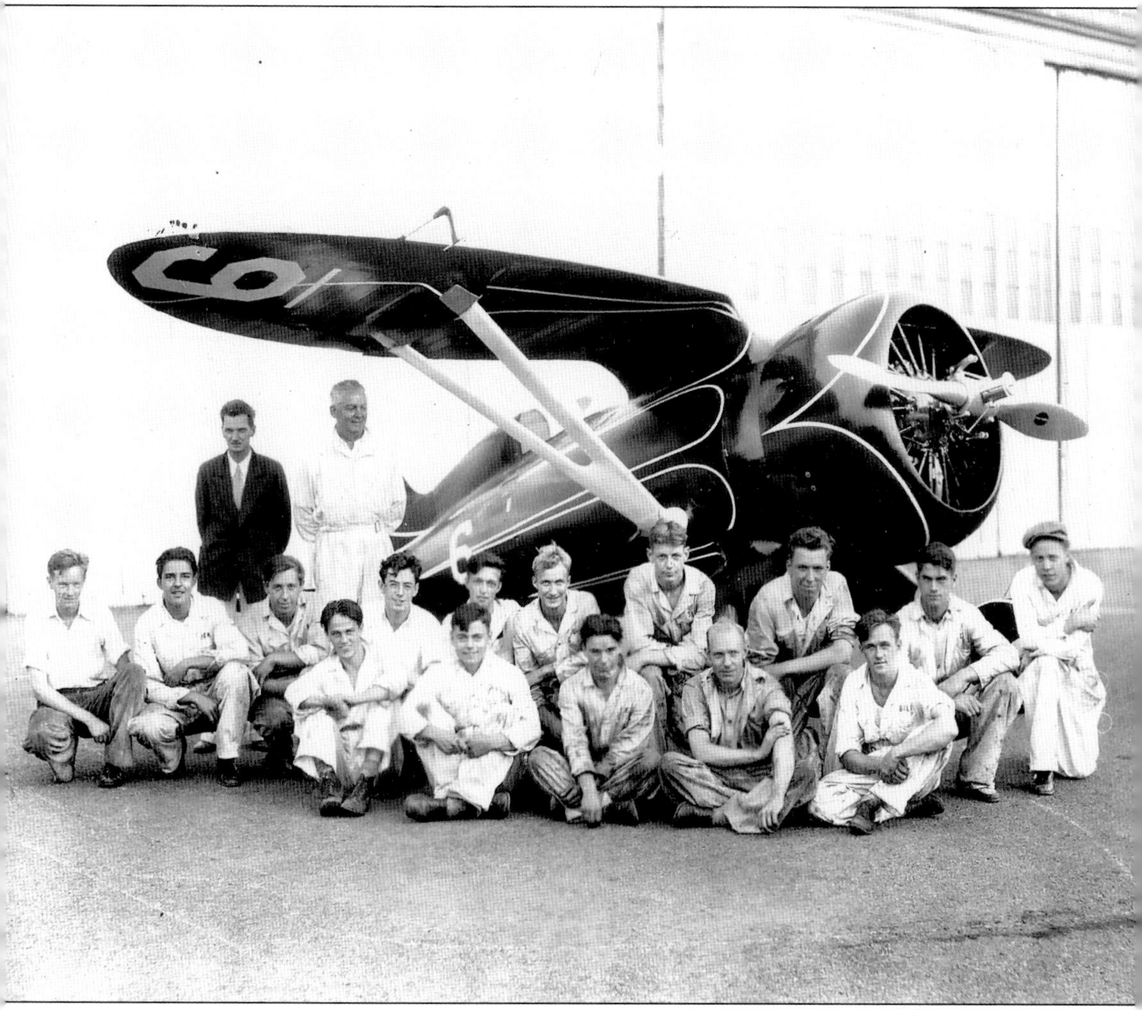

Bob Hall and the builders of the Hall "Bulldog" racer, registration NR2111, pose outside the Bowles field hangar in 1932. Construction of this gull-winged racer was sponsored by Marion Guggenheim for competition in the 1932 National Air Races in Cleveland, Ohio, and named for the Yale University mascot. The contract required Guggenheim family pilot Russell Thaw or his designee to pilot the craft at the nationals. Shortly before the race, Thaw declined, commenting, "The ship is not my idea of a racer." Hall ended up flying the plane himself and, with a speed of 215.5 miles per hour, finished in sixth place. There was speculation that the experimental Hamilton Standard propeller used prevented the 535-horsepower Pratt and Whitney Wasp engine from running at peak performance. Nonetheless, the Bulldog never flew again. Hall was so disappointed with its poor performance that he dismantled it after the race. (Author's collection.)

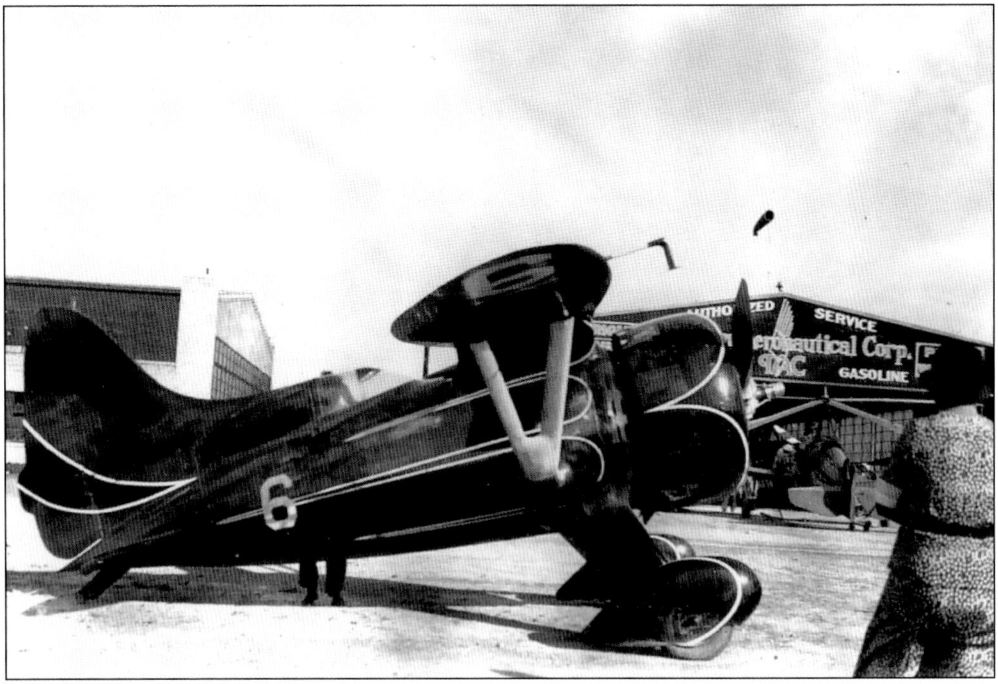

The Hall Bulldog racer is shown at the Cleveland National Air Races in 1932. Johnny Miller's autogyro can be seen outside the hangar in the background. The unusual craft gave a flying demonstration on August 31, 1932, performing rolls and loop-the-loops. (Author's collection.)

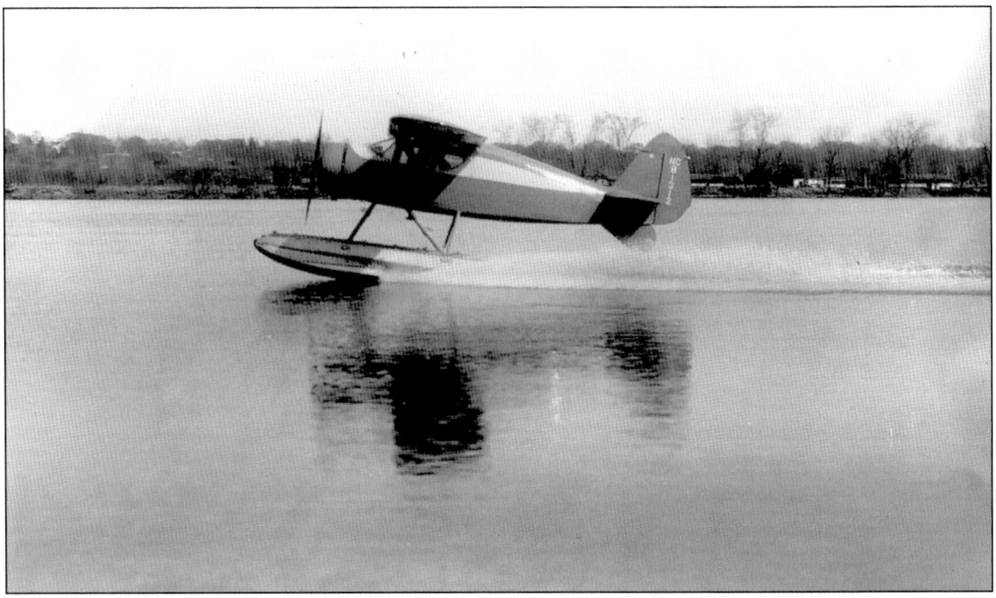

Walter O'Connor's seaplane, seen here in 1947, was a familiar sight to area residents for decades. From his final base at 1000 River Road, at the foot of School Street, O'Connor flew charter trips all over the Northeast. (Courtesy Joan [O'Connor] Martel.)

Nine

The Agawam Police Department

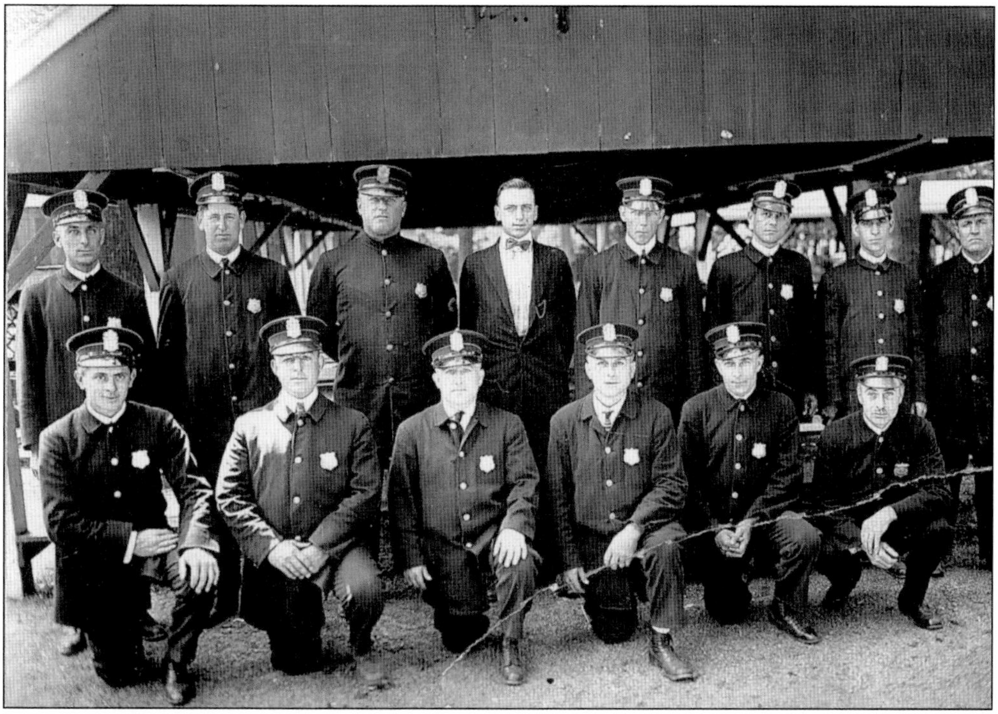

Members of the Agawam Police Department, including Daniel O. Cesan, pose at Riverside Park around the 1920s. Prior to 1927, the police force consisted of one full-time officer on call 24 hours a day and elected constables. (Courtesy Anita [Cesan] Rising.)

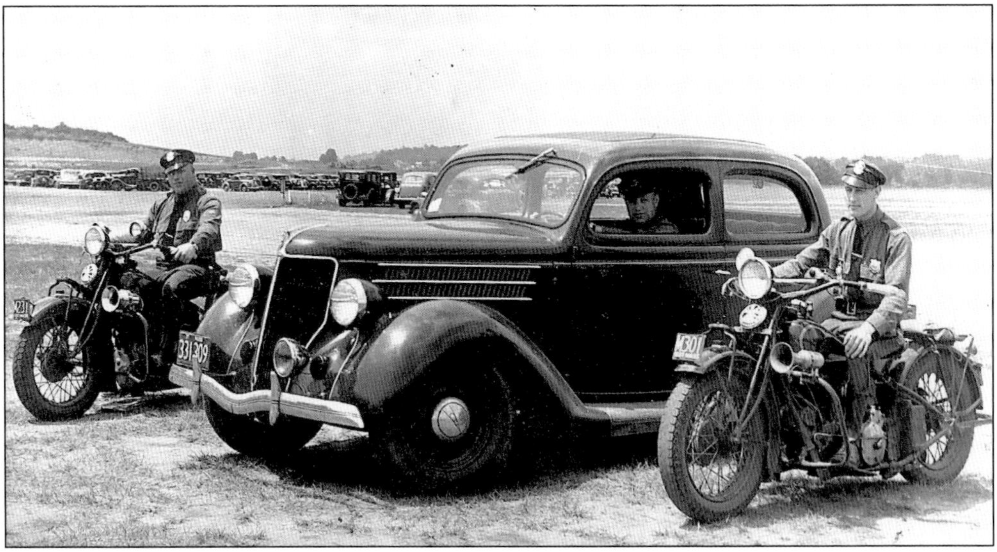

The introduction of horse racing in 1935 at the former Bowles Airport drew thousands of visitors and required a police substation there. Aldege "Dace" Paro, Sgt. Roland C. Reed, Henry "Hank" Madden are seen at Agawam Park (the current Agawam Regional Industrial Park) in 1937. (Courtesy Agawam Police Association.)

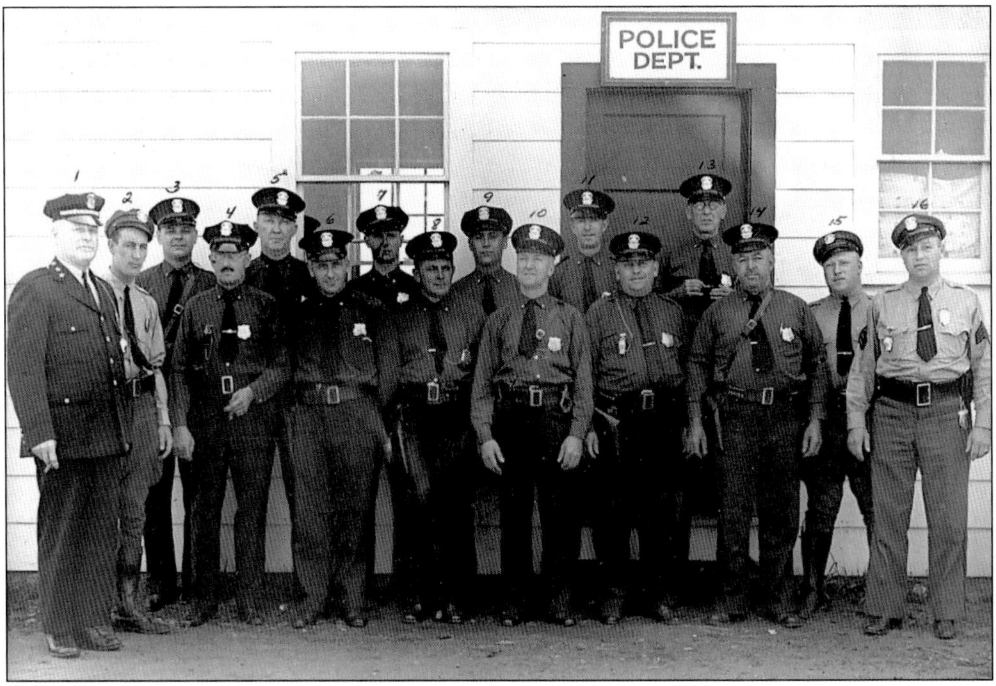

Police force members pose for this photograph at Agawam Park in 1937. From left to right are Chief Perley Hewey, Henry Madden, Edward Bissonette, Clint Wright, Howard Frazier, Dudley Bodurtha, Kenneth Pond, Daniel Cesan, R. Kenneth Grady, Arthur Berthiume, Horace Moratte, Larry Regnier, Michael Mannix, Frank Campbell, Aldege Paro, and Sgt. Roland Reed. Hewey, Madden, Paro, and Reed are the only regular police officers. Others are special officers and constables. (Courtesy Agawam Police Association.)

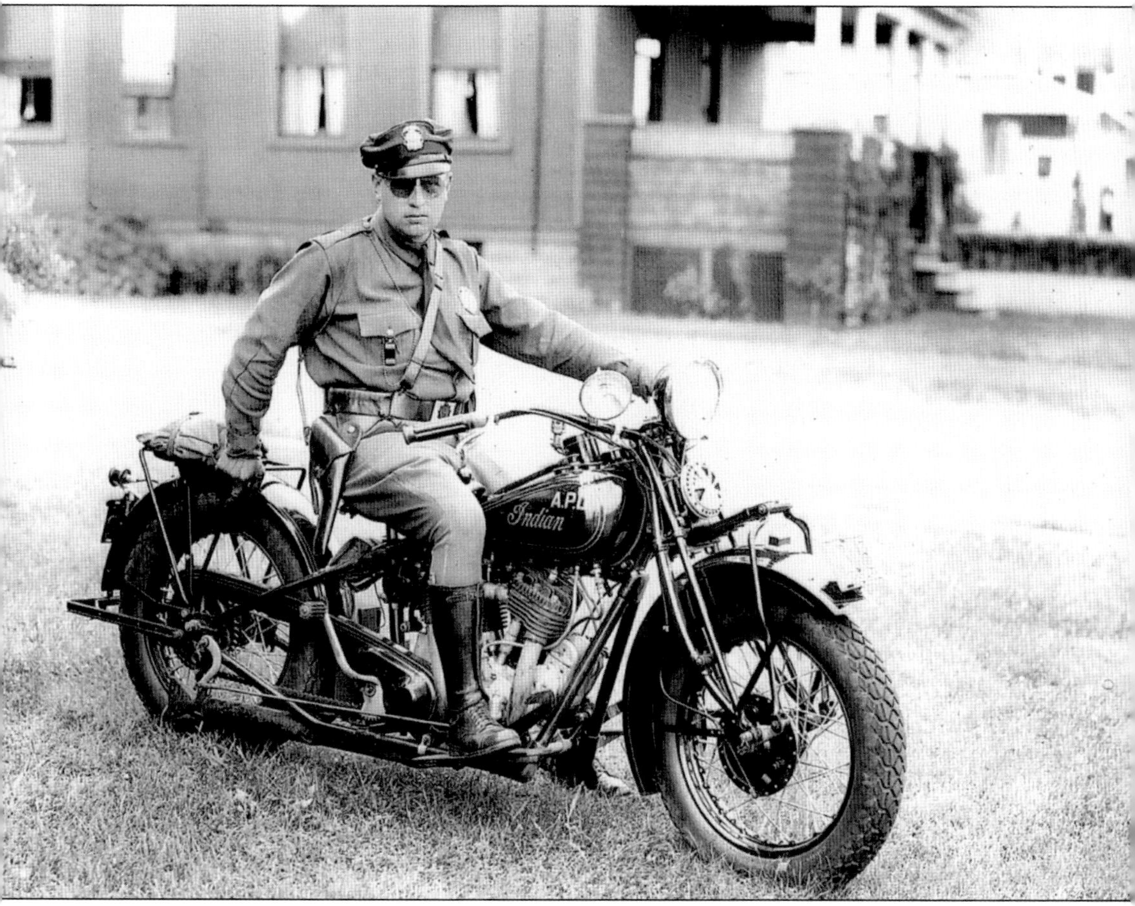

Sgt. Roland Reed is seen outside Chief Perley Hewey's office on Wilson Street c. 1938. In 1931, Reed became the town's first motorcycle patrolman and was paid $950. The house directly behind Sergeant Reed is 11 Wilson Street. Prior to the construction of the new town hall at 36 Main Street in 1942, Chief Hewey's house at 468 Springfield Street, on the corner of Wilson Street, also served as the police station. Chief Hewey, who served in that capacity for over 20 years, had a small office that was accessible by a side door. When Ted Dynia (the author's grandfather) purchased the house in 1950, the holding cell was still extant in the basement, and Chief Hewey's office became Helen Dynia's sewing room. (Courtesy Agawam Police Association.)

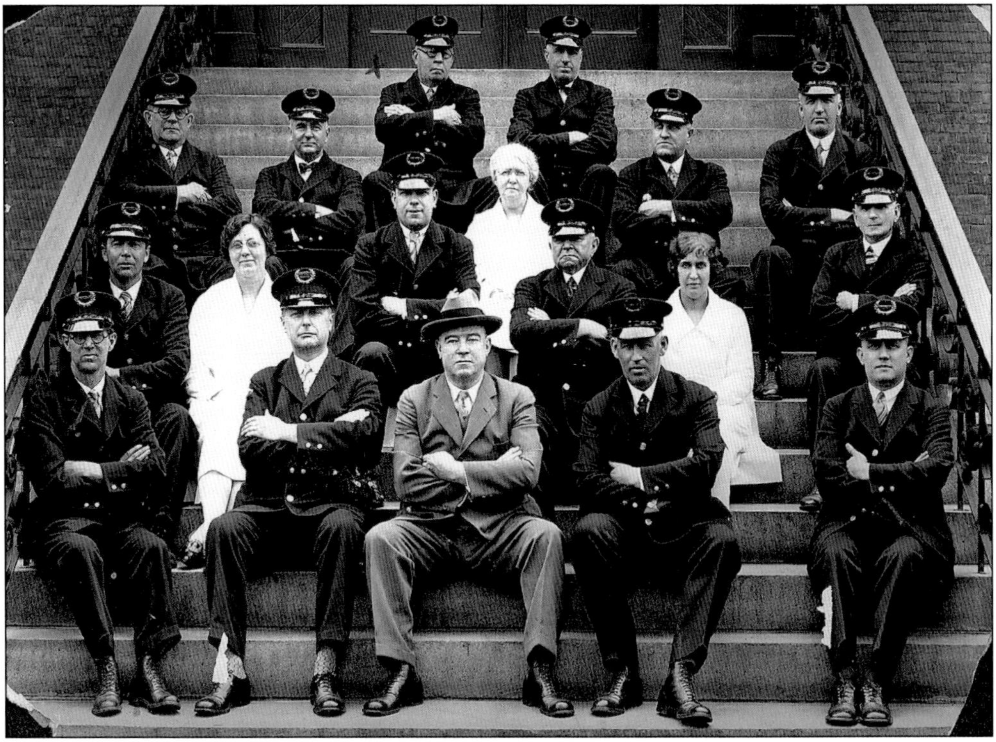

George H. Moore (back row, left) served as the first chief of police in Agawam from 1905 to 1907. He later became a security guard at the Hampden County House of Corrections on York Street in Springfield, where he is seen here, and he served there until his death in 1937. (Courtesy Agawam Police Association.)

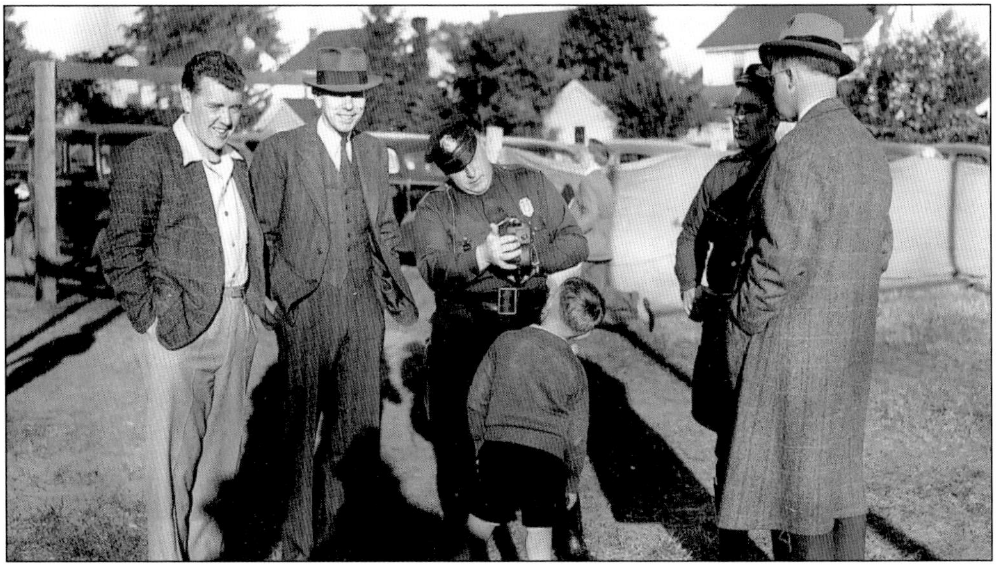

Residents gather at the Thanksgiving Day football game in 1939. Included in the photograph are Fred Dacey, Aldege Paro (looking at camera), an unidentified youth, Henry Madden, and teacher Richard Allen. This photograph was taken next to Agawam High School (now the middle school) on Main Street. (Courtesy Agawam Police Association.)

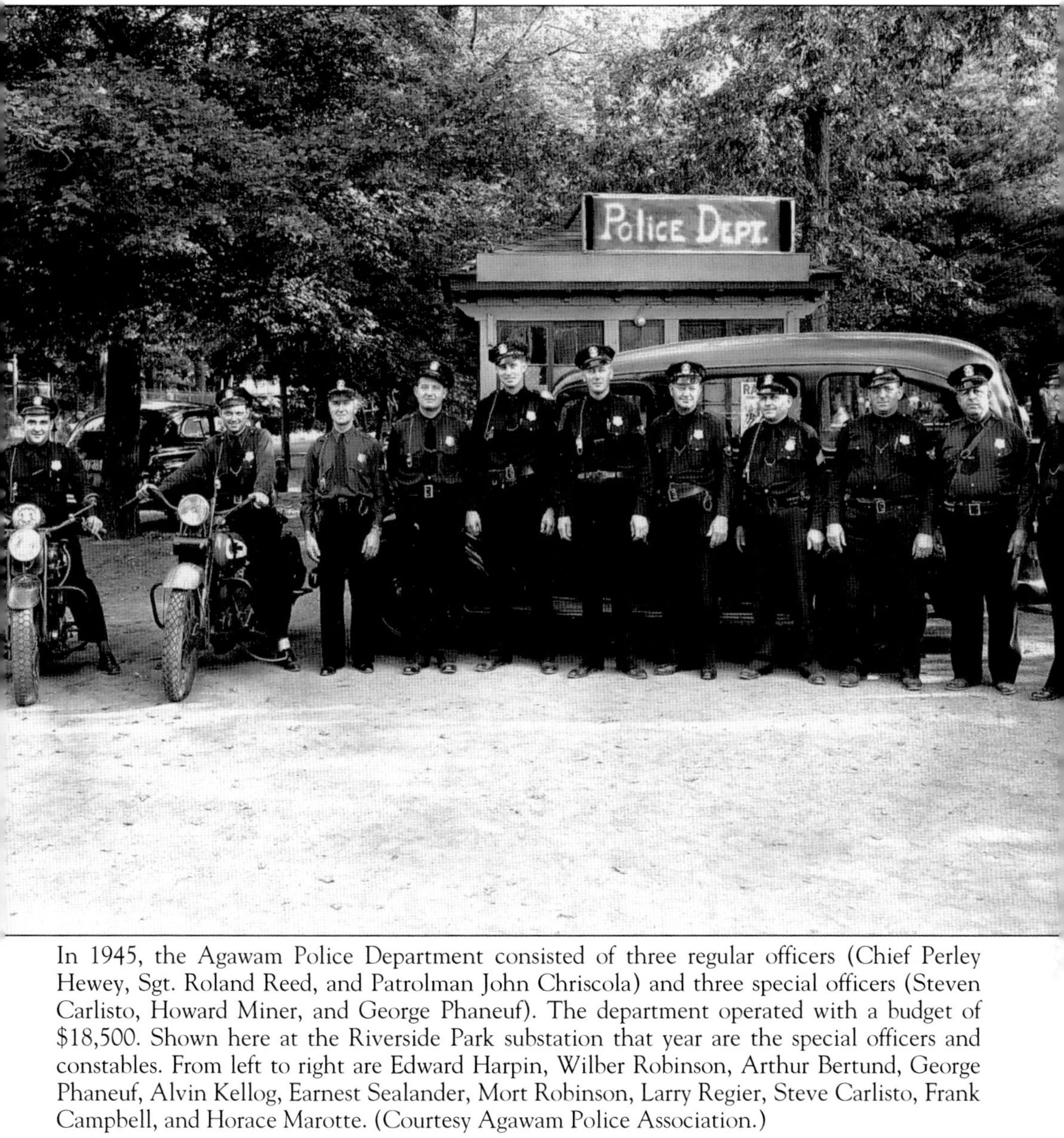

In 1945, the Agawam Police Department consisted of three regular officers (Chief Perley Hewey, Sgt. Roland Reed, and Patrolman John Chriscola) and three special officers (Steven Carlisto, Howard Miner, and George Phaneuf). The department operated with a budget of $18,500. Shown here at the Riverside Park substation that year are the special officers and constables. From left to right are Edward Harpin, Wilber Robinson, Arthur Bertund, George Phaneuf, Alvin Kellog, Earnest Sealander, Mort Robinson, Larry Regier, Steve Carlisto, Frank Campbell, and Horace Marotte. (Courtesy Agawam Police Association.)

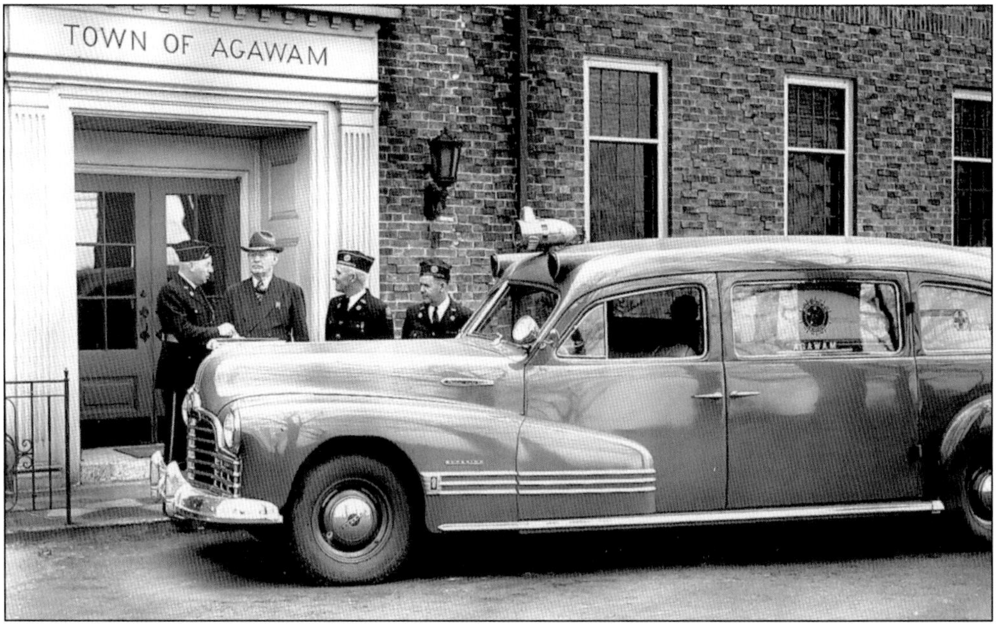

Agawam did not have a true ambulance until a 1947 Packard was donated to the town by the Agawam American Legion post. Accepting the vehicle from two Legion members (far right) are Sgt. Roland Reed (left) and selectman Giles Halladay. (Courtesy Agawam Police Association.)

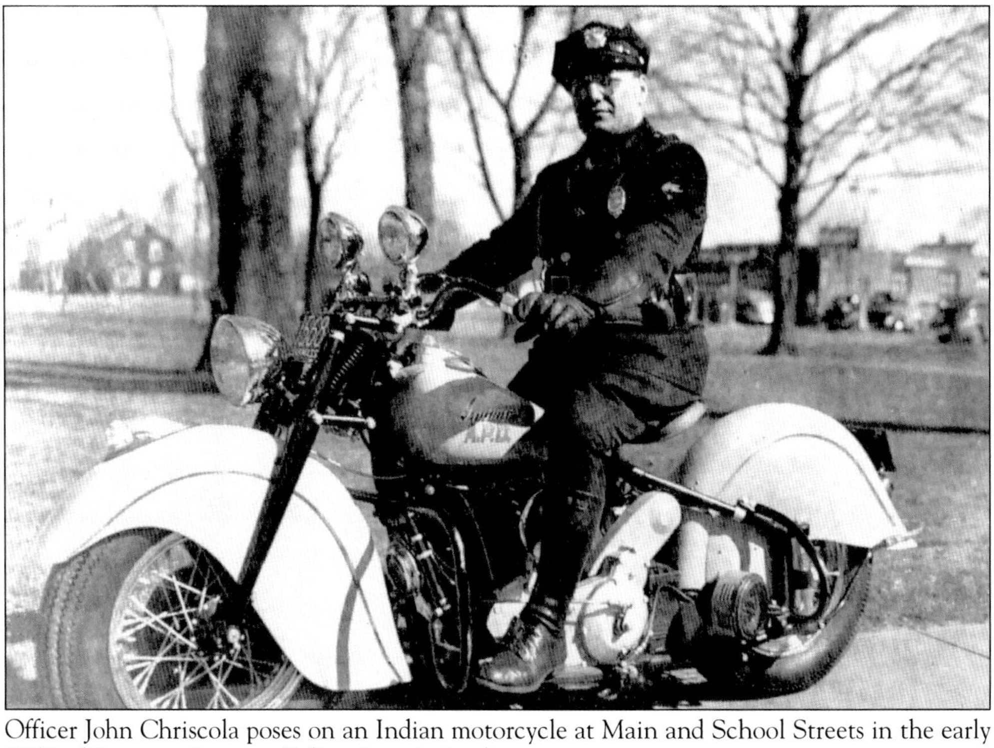

Officer John Chriscola poses on an Indian motorcycle at Main and School Streets in the early 1950s. (Courtesy Agawam Police Association.)

Ten

Around Town

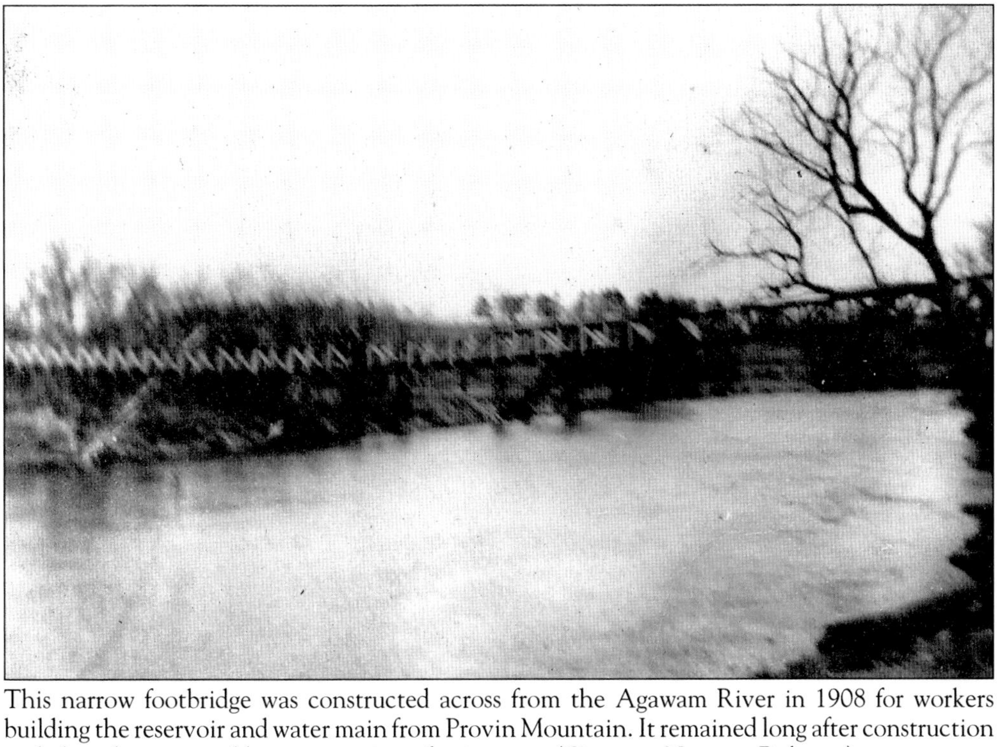

This narrow footbridge was constructed across from the Agawam River in 1908 for workers building the reservoir and water main from Provin Mountain. It remained long after construction ended, and it was used by a generation of swimmers. (Courtesy Norman Roberts.)

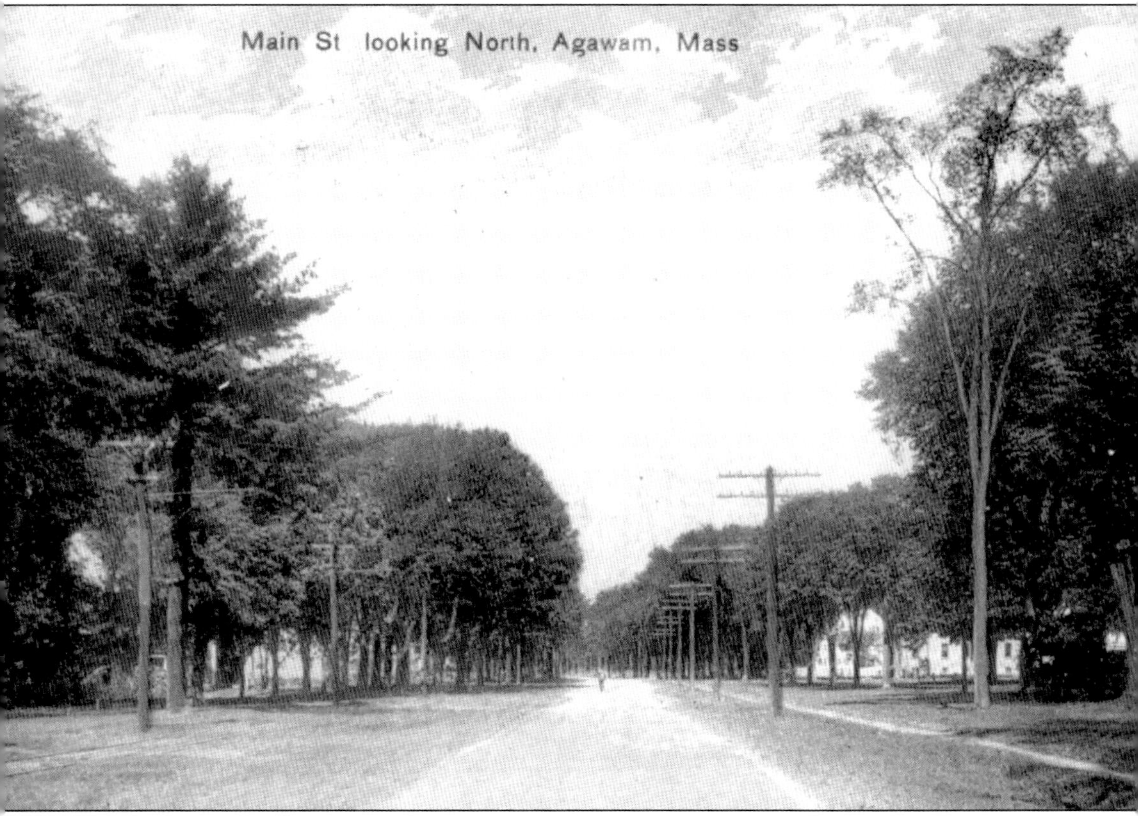

The Agawam Center Historic District was placed on the National Register of Historic Places in June 2001. The town's first historic district includes over 100 structures located from 551 to 1008 Main Street and from 24 to 196 Elm Street. The register nomination states, "[Agawam] Center is significant for its architecture, principally its fine collection of Federal style buildings. It has representative examples of succeeding stylistic periods from Greek Revival through the bungalows of the early 20th century each representing eras of prosperity and growth." The mid-18th-century Bliss Tavern, at 940 Main Street, is the oldest home in the district. This view from the first decade of the 20th century shows Main Street from Elm Street. The Leonard-Hayward House (right) stood at the corner of Main and Monroe Street until it was demolished. (Author's collection.)

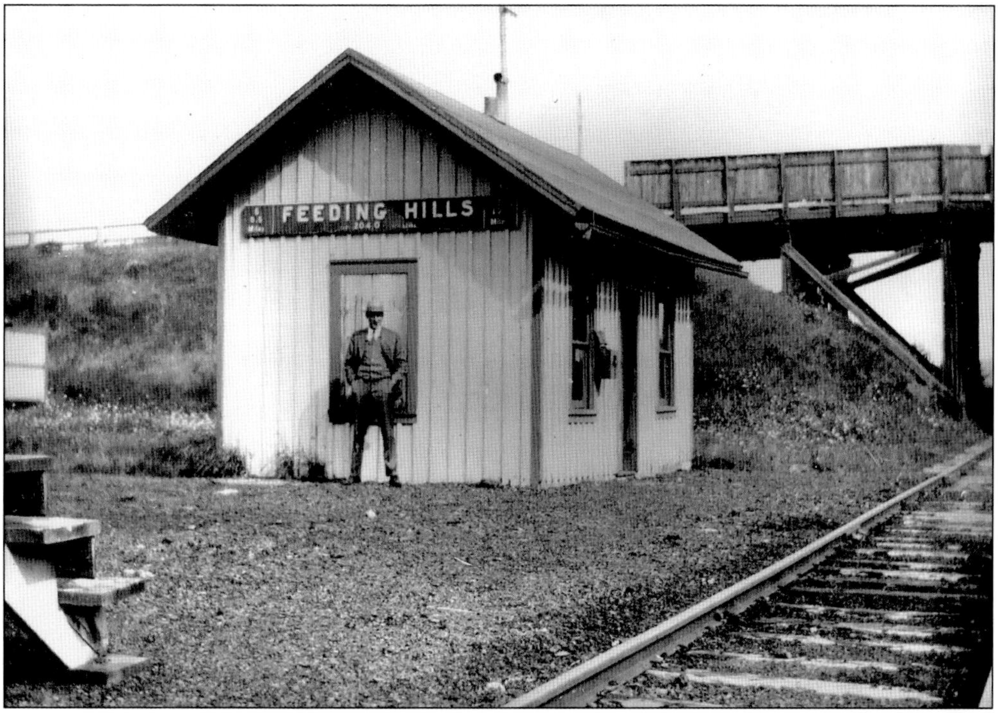

The Central New England Railroad provided rail service to Feeding Hills Center from 1903 to 1938. The Feeding Hills station is shown here on September 7, 1927. The Springfield Street trestle is seen in the background, crossing the tracks approximately where the junior high school driveway now stands. (Author's collection.)

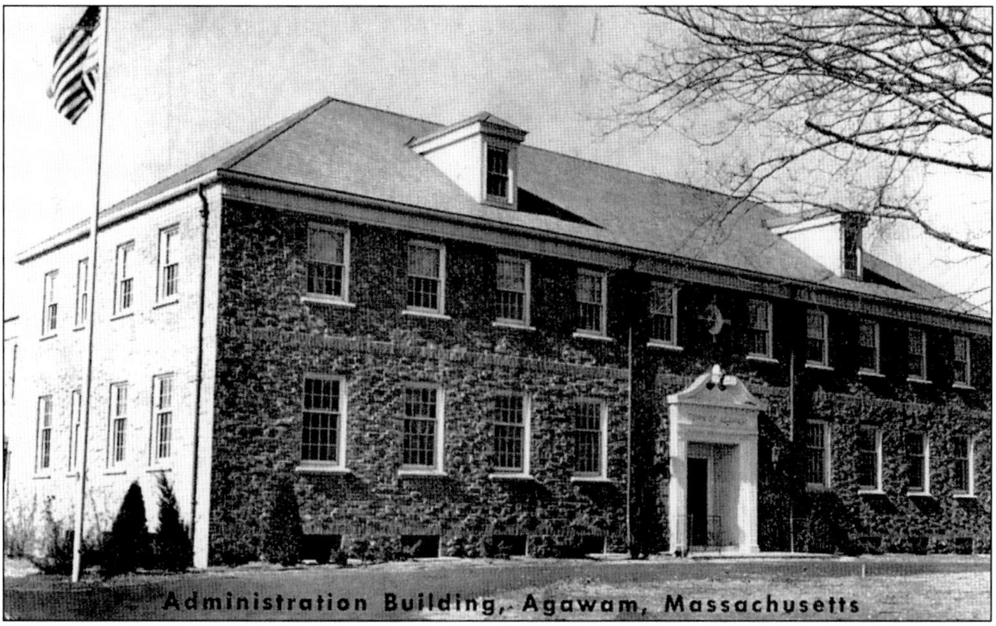

Town offices were consolidated in the new administration building at 36 Main Street, which was dedicated on April 20, 1942. Before this, Agawam Center and Feeding Hills Center each had a town hall building. This building still serves as town hall. (Author's collection.)

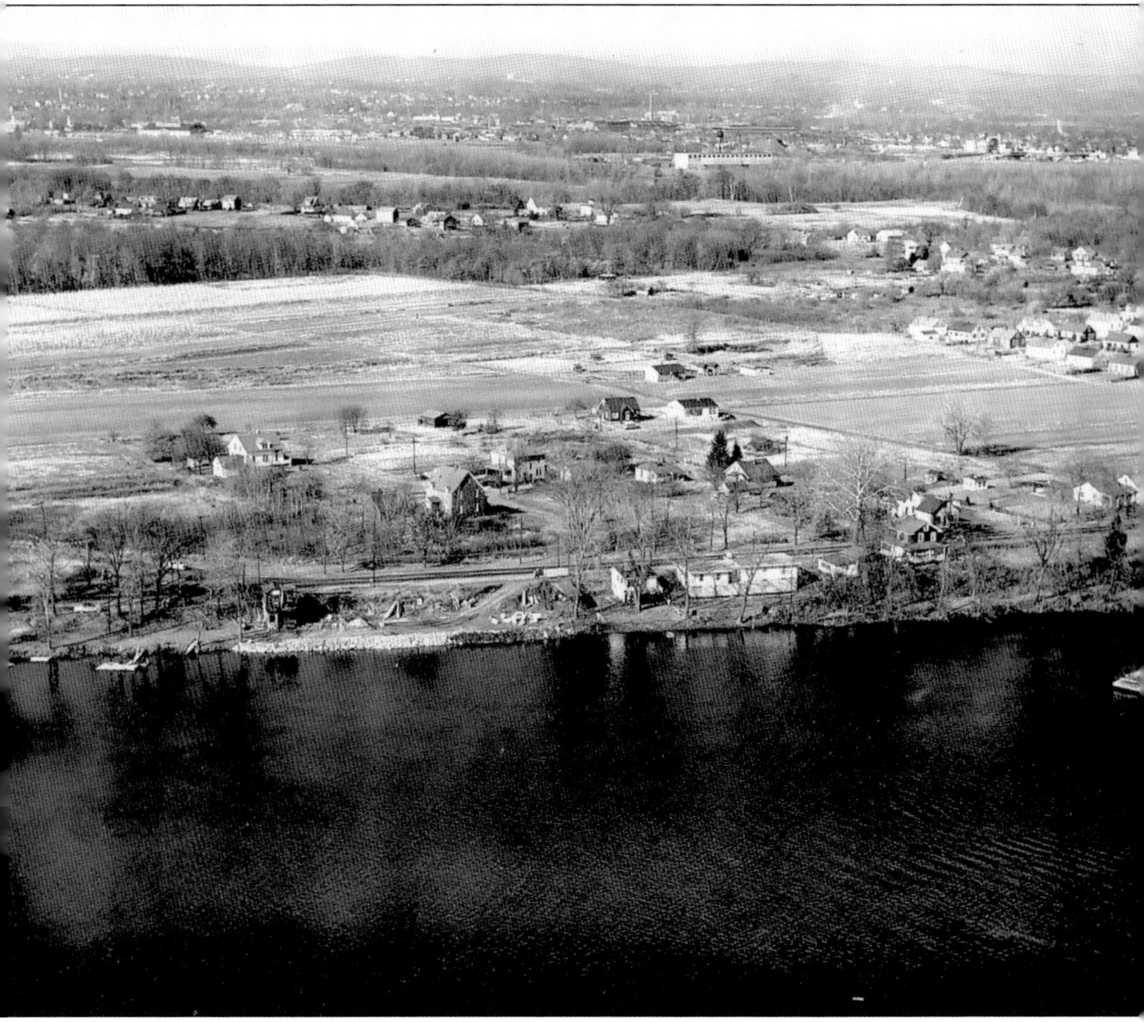

This late-1940s view looking northwest from over the Connecticut River shows Walter O'Connor's seaplane base at the foot of School Street in the lower left, with the Seymour Avenue, Liberty Avenue, and Riverside Avenue neighborhood located in the dead center. The Smith (County Jail) Farm can be seen just beyond this. Alhambra Circle is at the right center. The Gilbert and Barker Complex, at the top center, and the Eastern States Exposition's coliseum and state buildings, at the top left, are just visible. After county government was dissolved in 1998, the town of Agawam purchased the former County Jail Farm in 2002, and the property was permanently restricted by the state to be used for recreational purposes. (Courtesy Joan [O'Connor] Martel.)

Eleven

The Captain Charles Leonard House

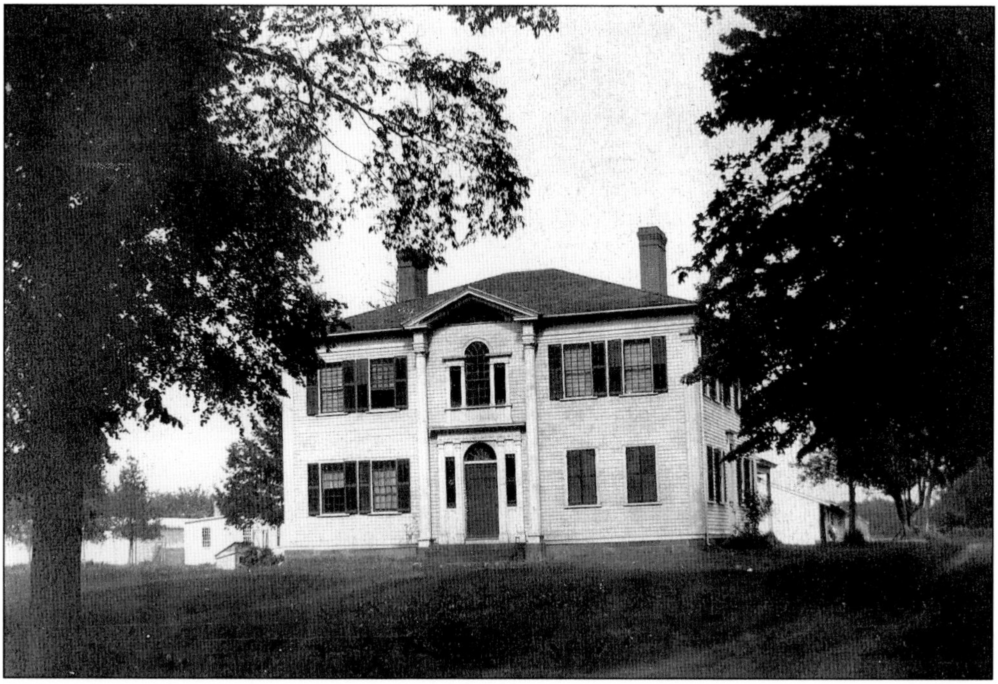

Built in 1805, the Captain Charles Leonard House is recognized as the town's finest Federal-style building. It was featured in the *White Pine Series* in 1925 and was recorded by the Historic American Buildings Survey in 1934. The house is shown here on June 2, 1904. (Courtesy the Board of Trustees of the Captain Charles Leonard House.)

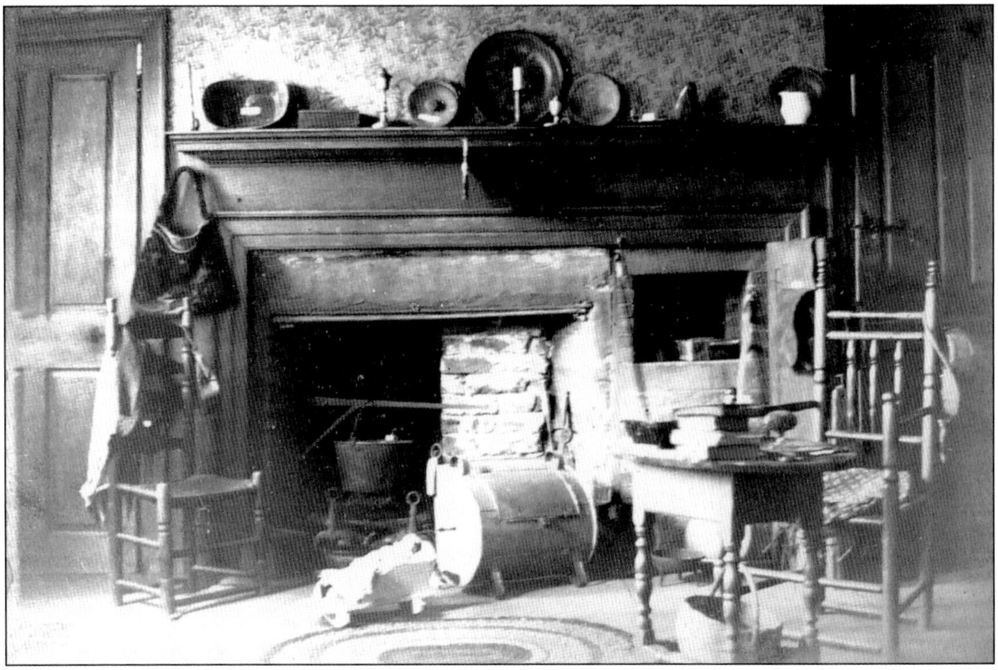

On August 3, 1905, the Fowler House, as it was then known, was on display during the town's 50th anniversary celebration (page 48). Above is the old kitchen. Seen below is the south parlor, which was last renovated in 1975 in time for the nation's bicentennial. The silhouettes on the mantel are still part of the Leonard House collection. (Courtesy the Board of Trustees of the Captain Charles Leonard House.)

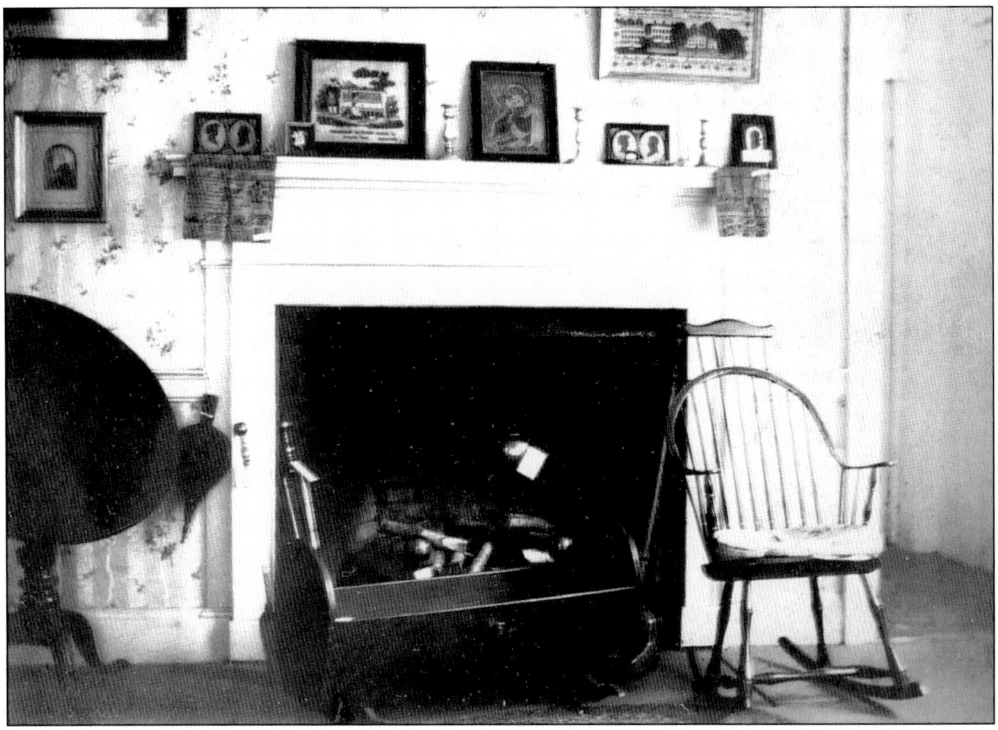

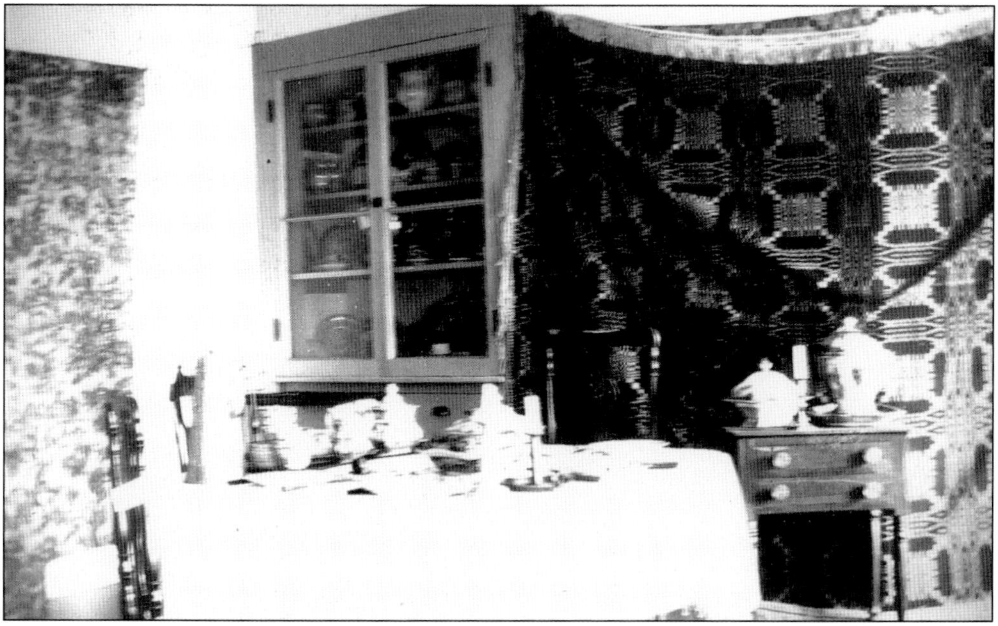

Shown here are more views of the 1905 exhibit. Above is the Fowler House dining table. Pictured below is the north parlor, which was used as a bedroom at that time. Twenty years later, Ernest Newton Bagg wrote in the *White Pine Series*, "In the heart of the old town, on the east side of the wide, elm-arched street, where, on the afternoon of June 30, 1775, General Washington passed . . . stands the fine old Leonard dwelling." The elms are gone, but the Leonard House remains a Main Street landmark. (Courtesy the Board of Trustees of the Captain Charles Leonard House.)

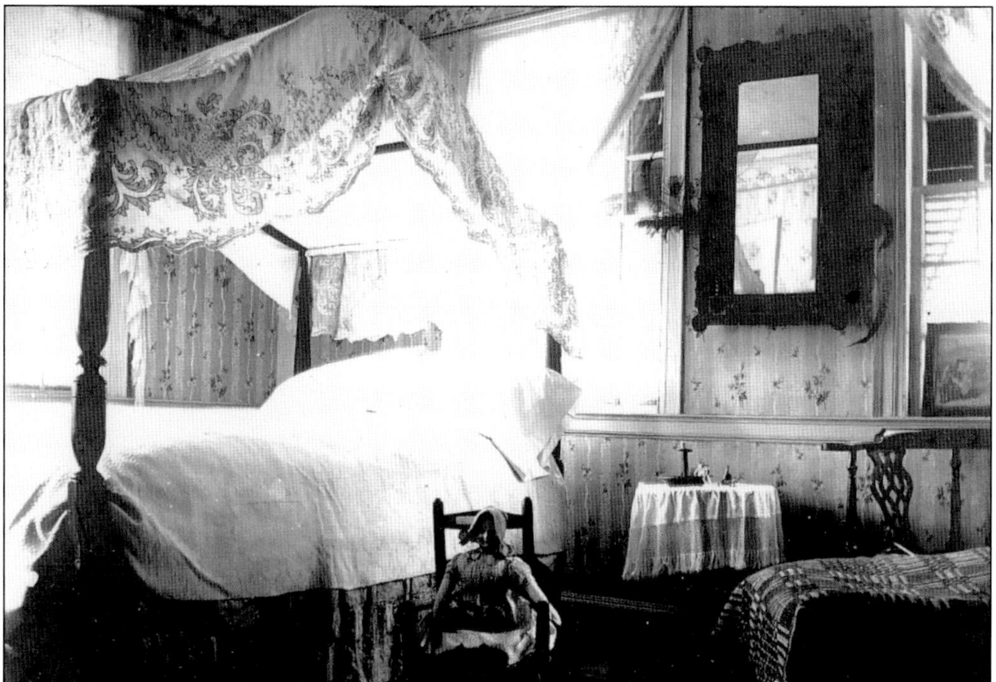

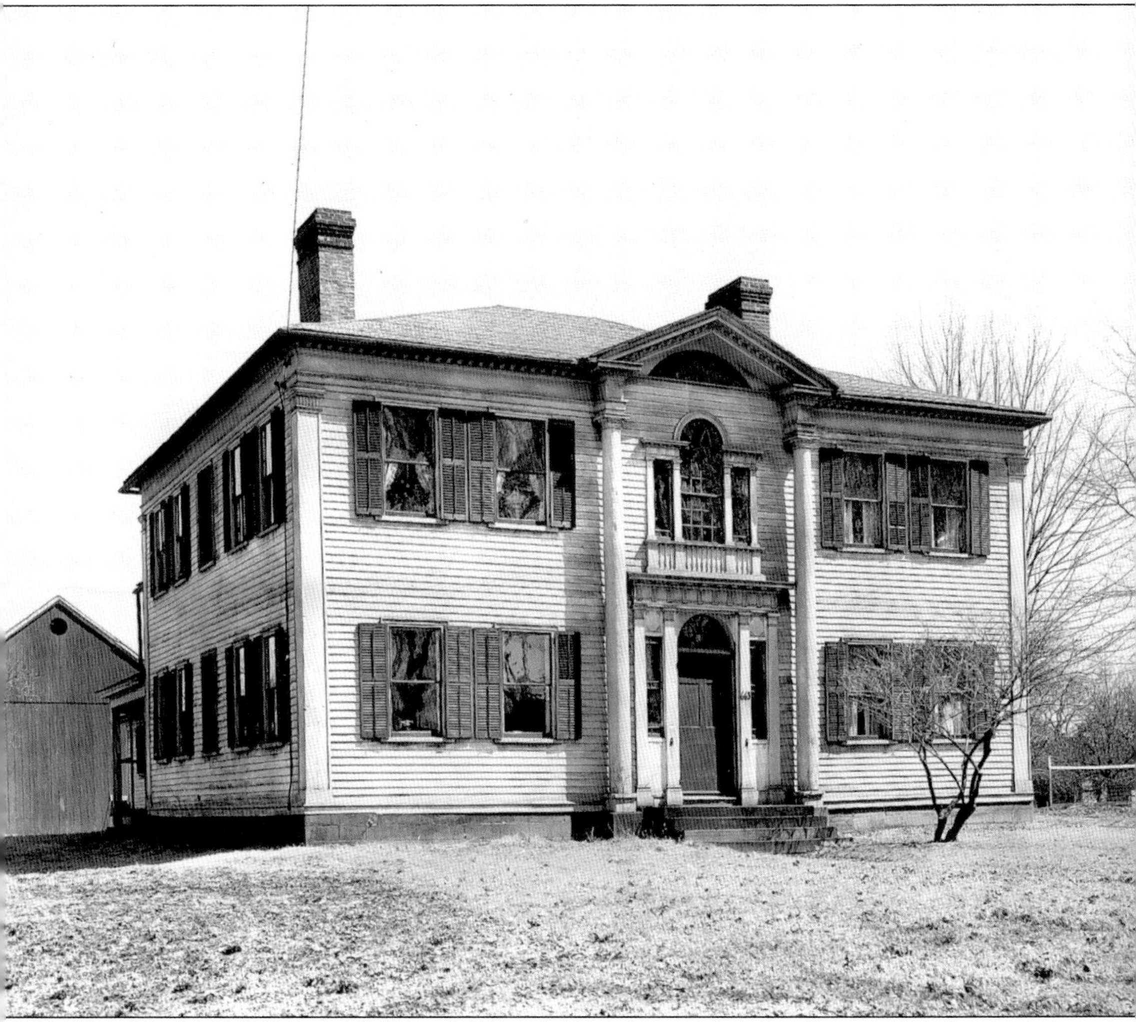

The Historic American Buildings Survey (HABS) began in 1933 as a WPA program for unemployed architects to document America's antique buildings. The Captain Charles Leonard House was one of three homes in Agawam to be chosen for the project. The Lt. William Allen House, at 722–726 Main Street, and the Rufus Colton House, at the corner of Main and Elm Streets, are the others. In April 1934, photographer Arthur C. Haskell snapped three photographs of the Leonard House: the view from the northwest (seen here), the south side door, and the old kitchen. The house was also documented in 14 detailed and measured drawings. At that time, a large tobacco barn was also part of the property, and it was documented as well. In 1938, Minerva Davis purchased the property, had it restored, and created a board of trustees to operate it as a community house. The Captain Charles Leonard House was placed individually on the National Register of Historic Places on March 10, 1975. (Library of Congress; courtesy the Board of Trustees of the Captain Charles Leonard House.)

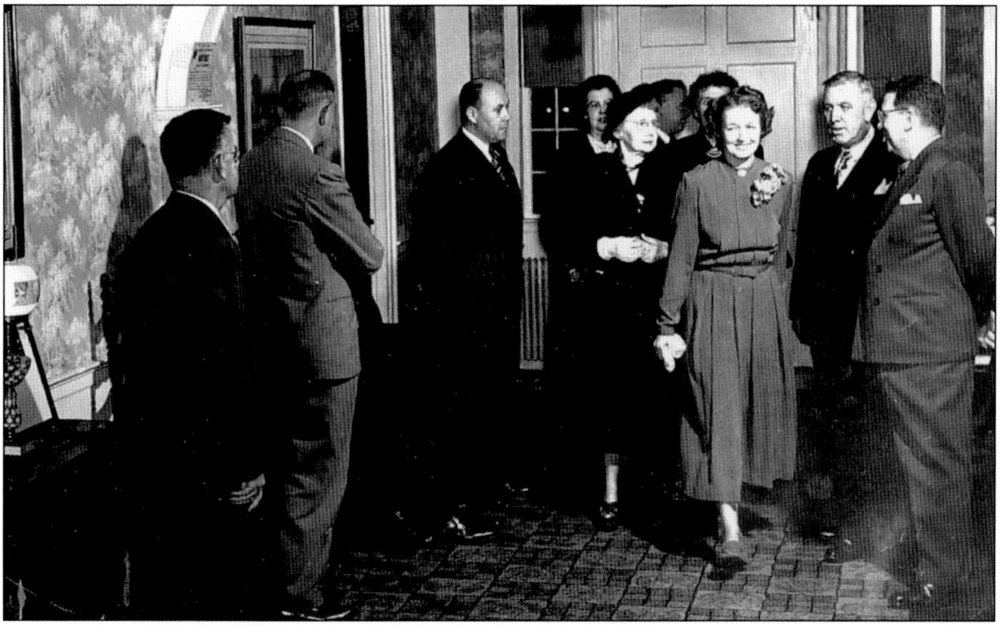

Since its opening in 1939, the Leonard House has been operated by a board of trustees, each of whom serves a lifetime appointment. Pictured third from the left is the president of the board, Wendell Gosse, with other trustees as they welcome guests to the 10th anniversary open house held on October 1, 1949. (Courtesy the Board of Trustees of the Captain Charles Leonard House.)

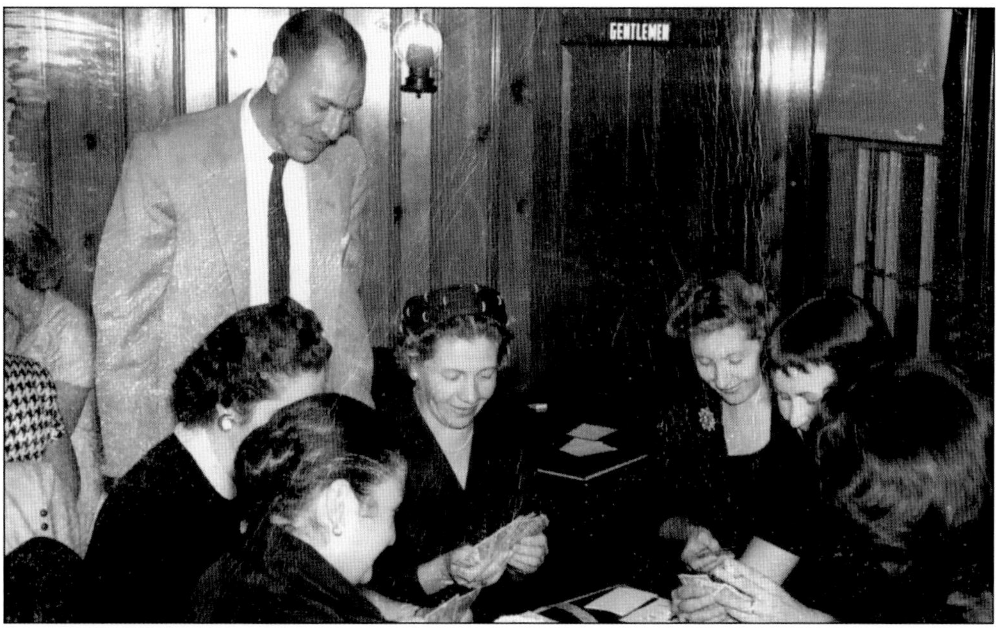

Joseph Della-Giustina stands at a 1953 political fund-raiser in the Pine Room at the Leonard House. When the house was renovated in 1939, the large meeting room was finished with pine paneling in the style of the day. In 1998, the room was redone in a style more in keeping with the Federal era in which the house was built, and it was renamed the Minerva Davis Meeting Room. (Courtesy Jennie and Joseph Della-Giustina.)

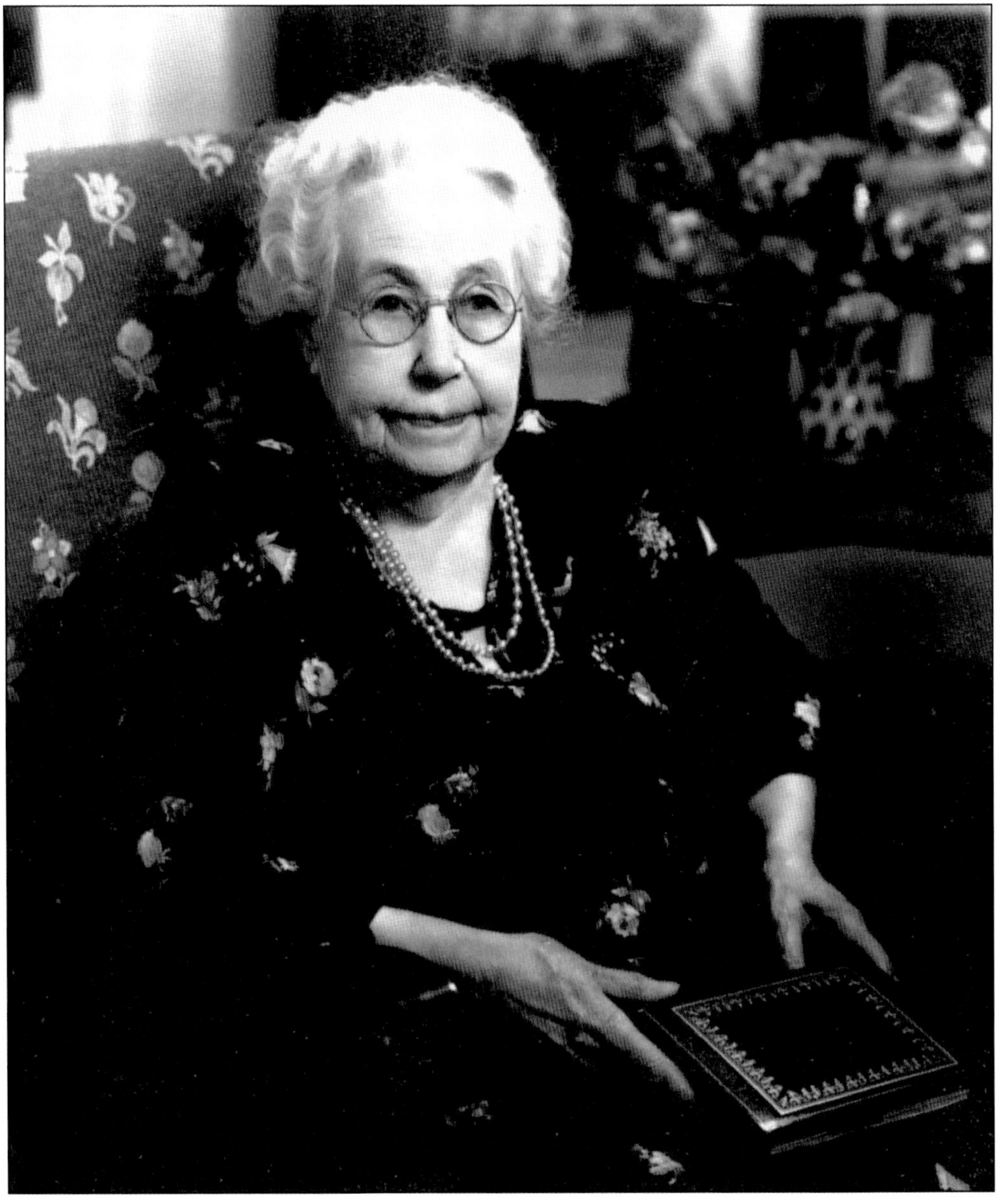

Minerva J. Davis was born in 1861, the daughter of Harvey and Jane Porter, owners of the Agawam Distillery and makers of world-famous Agawam gin. In 1887, she married Charles Palmer Davis, a writer for the *Boston Globe* and *New York Herald Tribune* and creator of *Current Events* magazine. After having lived with her husband in Boston, New York, and Columbus, Ohio, Davis returned to Agawam after her husband's death in 1924. That same year, she presented the town with the Agawam Center Library in memory of her husband. In 1938, she purchased the Captain Charles Leonard House. It is ironic that one of the stipulations that Davis, daughter of a distiller, put in place when her community house was opened was that no alcohol could be served on the premises. Davis was 90 when Agawam photographer Charles DuBois Hodges took this portrait. She died at age 94 in 1956. (Courtesy the Board of Trustees of the Captain Charles Leonard House.)

Twelve

Home Sweet Home

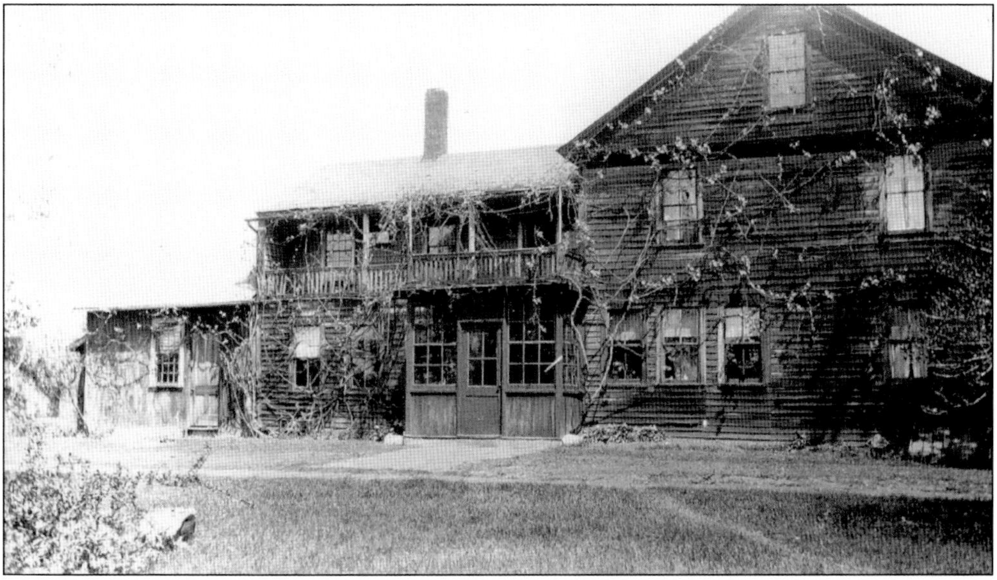

The Charles W. Hull home, at 424 Main Street, was purchased by the Hull family during the Civil War, and it was there that Agawam town historian Edith Hull LaFrancis was born in 1905. Built *c.* 1750, it has long since been demolished. (Agawam Historical Association collection.)

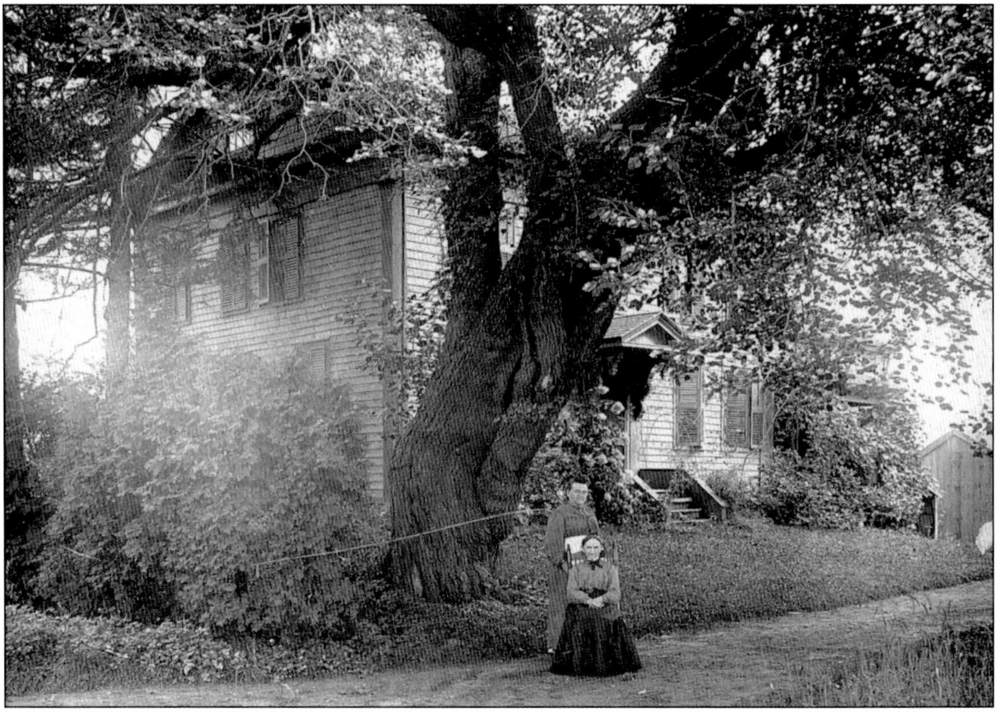

Standing in front of the old Granger home on South Westfield Street is Sarah (Moore) Granger and Larinda (Moore) Halladay. This photograph was taken by the Howes Brothers of Ashfield in 1901. (Courtesy Paul Toelken.)

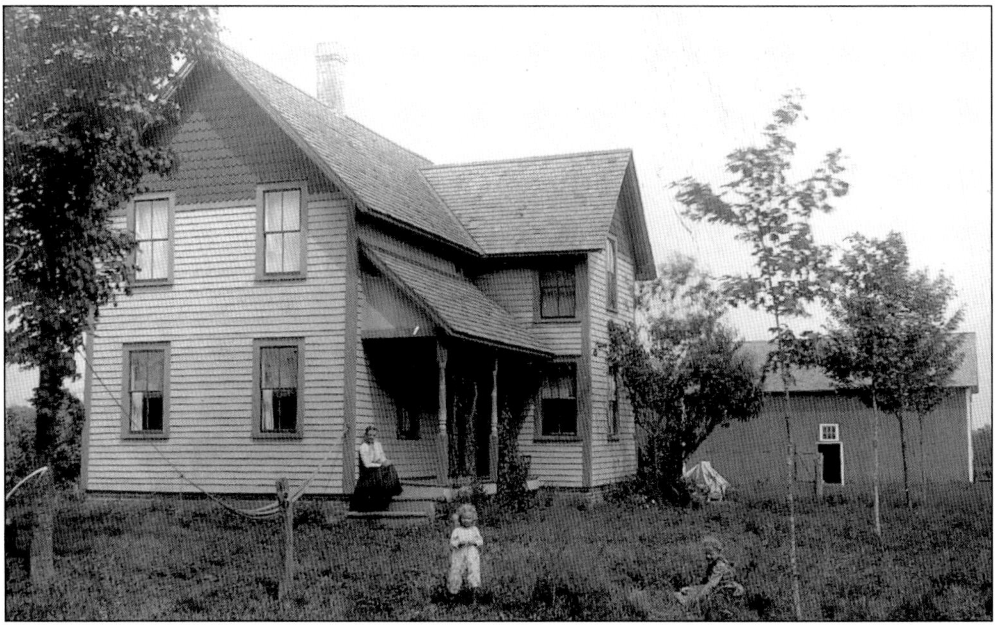

The Howes Brothers also photographed the Granger house, at 160 North Westfield Street, in 1901. Members of the Granger family are, from left to right, Alice (Brown) Granger, Phyllis Granger, and Edith Granger. Having the family pose in front of their house was a Howes Brothers tradition. (Courtesy Paul Toelken.)

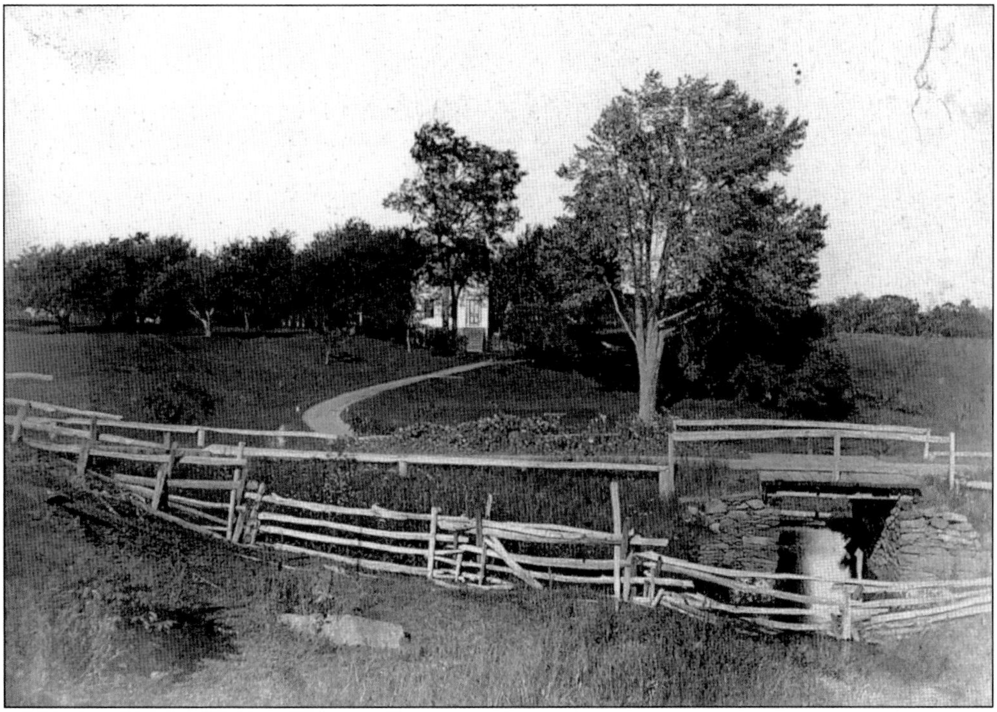

Seen here are two views of the Daniel W. Brown family home on the east side of South West Street. It was torn down *c.* 1972. The Brown family lived there from 1877 until 1899, when Daniel Brown retired. By 1901 (when the Howes Brothers took the photograph below), the Browns had moved. (Above, courtesy Paul Toelken; below, Agawam Historical Association collection.)

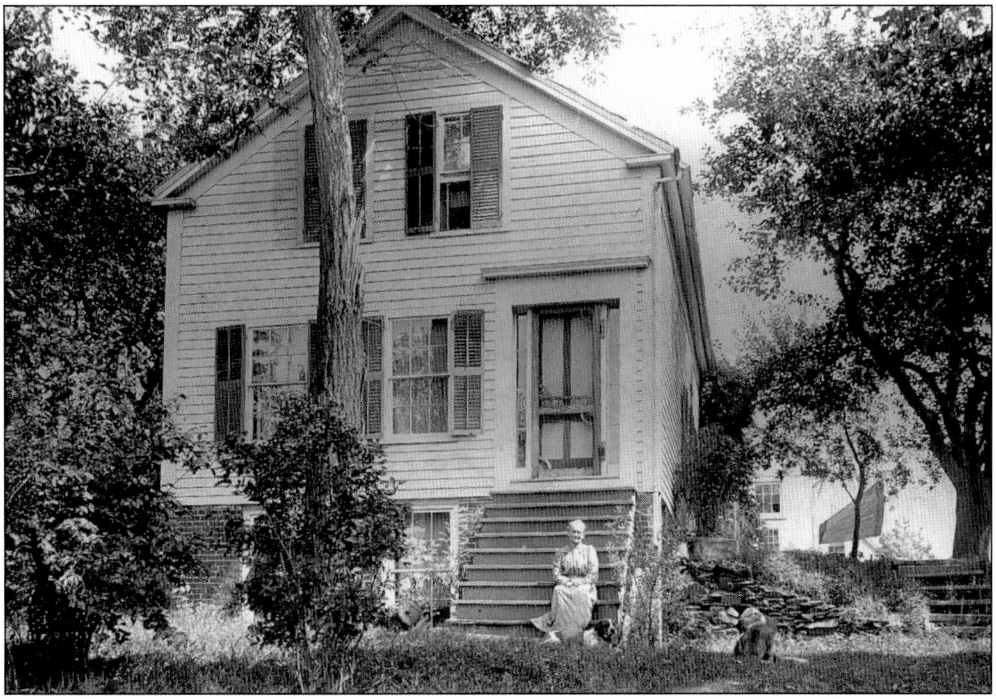

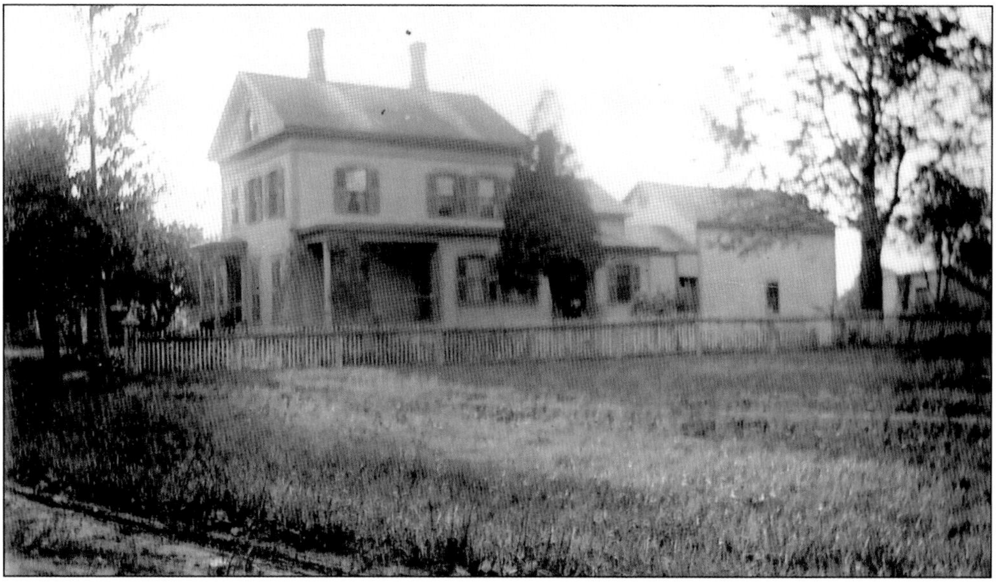

Mrs. Henry Bodurtha took this photograph of the Clark-Billings House, at 32 Elm Street, in 1906. The huge elm for which Elm Street was named is out of view to the left. The connected barn seen here was removed in 1992. The Toelken family lived here for many years. (Courtesy Paul Toelken.)

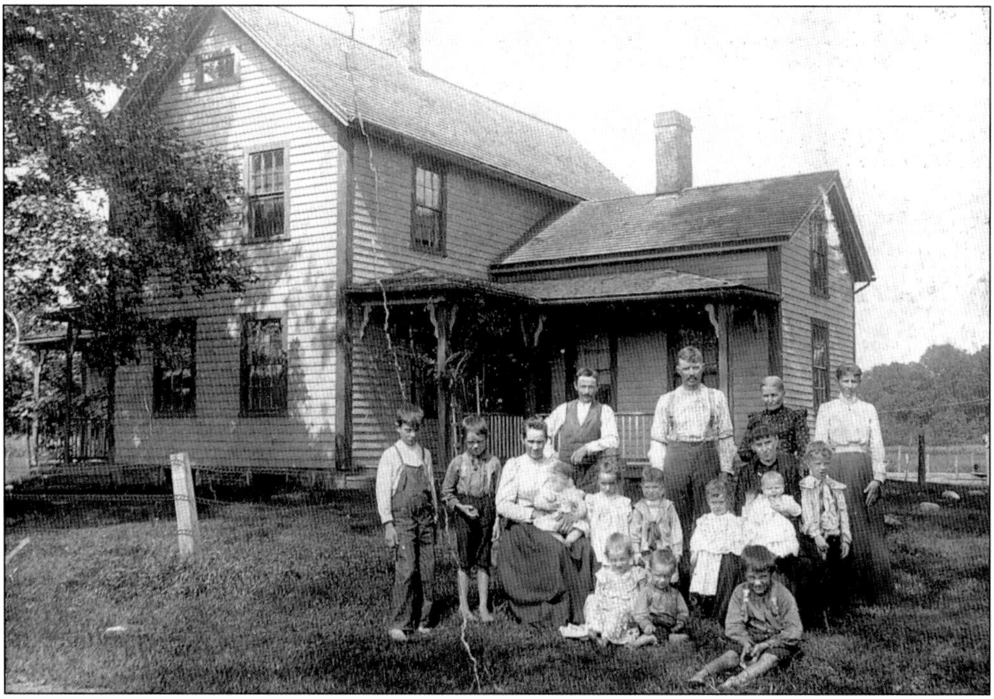

This 1901 Howes Brothers photograph shows the Cesan family at 942 Shoemaker Lane. Rev. James J. Cesan is seen to the left in back row. His wife, Louisa, is seated in front of him. Her mother, Julia Chisholm, is third from the left in the back row. Daniel O. Cesan is seated on the grass in the front. Anita (Cesan) Rising still resides in the family home (pages 14, 26, 60, 89, 99, and 120). (Courtesy Anita [Cesan] Rising.)

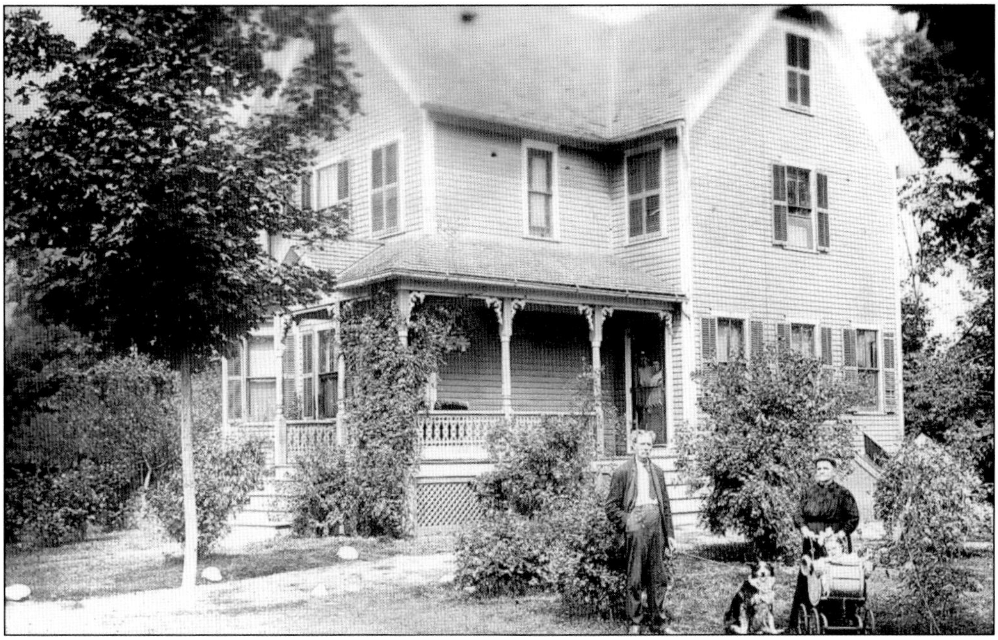

Charles and Mathilda Gosselin pose at the Gosselin home in North Agawam *c.* 1905. (Agawam Historical Association collection.)

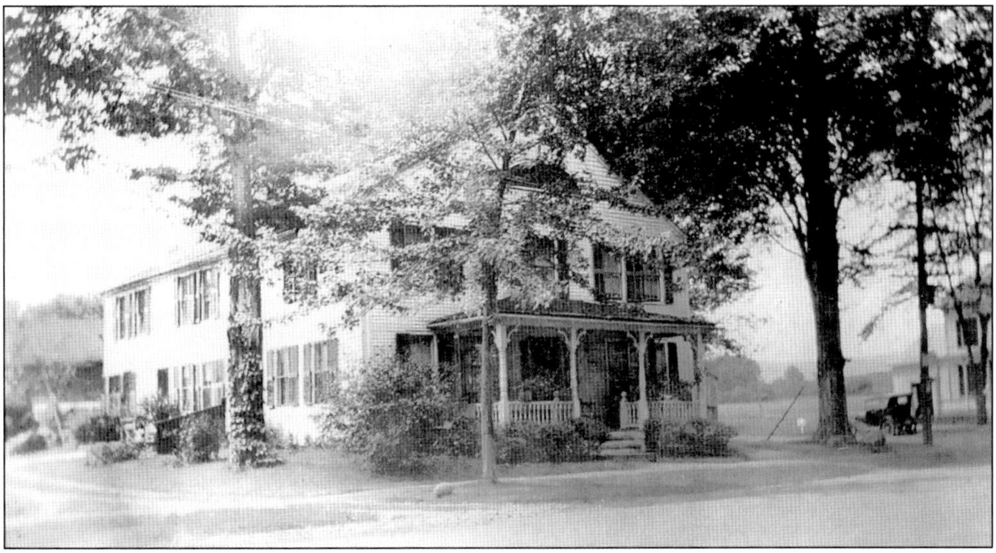

The Hamilton House at Feeding Hills Center is pictured here late in the second decade of the 20th century. A self-service gas station now occupies this location at 2 South Westfield Street. (Agawam Historical Association collection.)

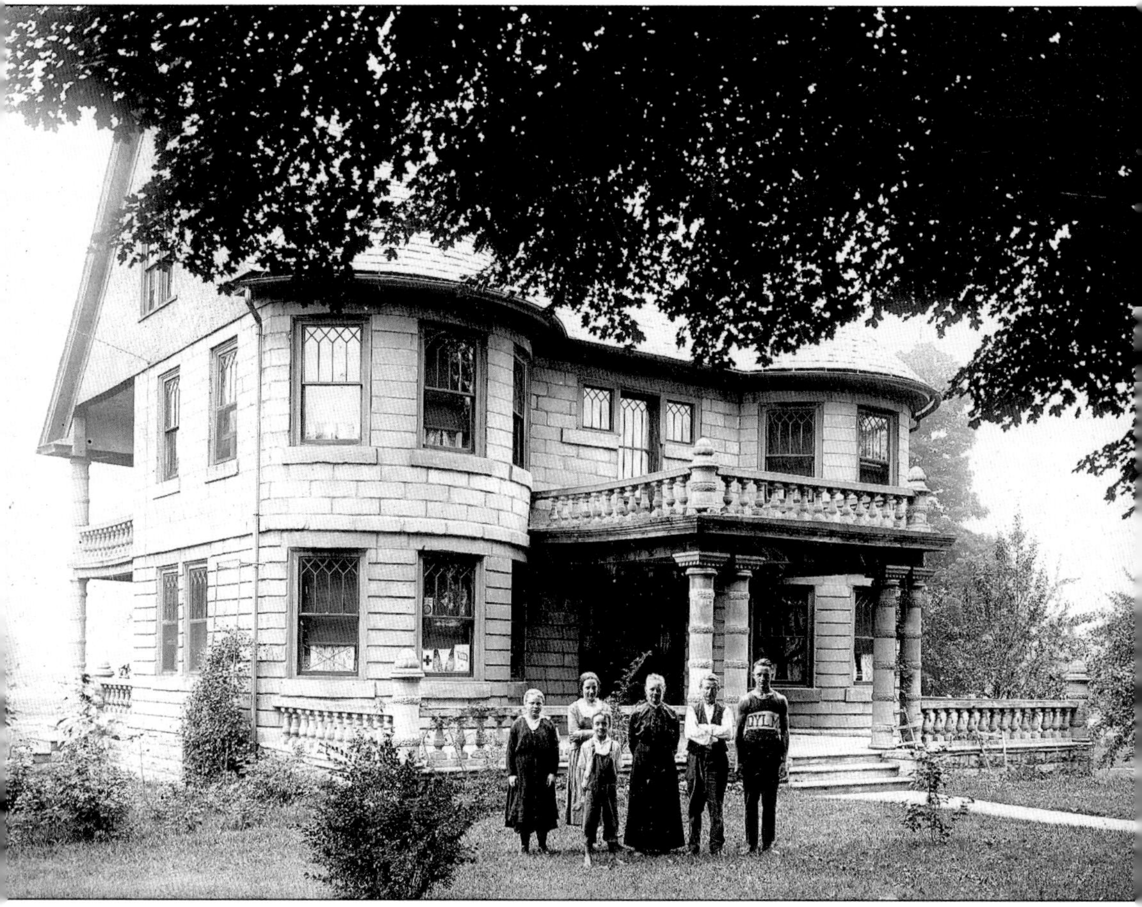

Members of the Cesan family are shown in front of the Michael L. Ahl house, at 954 Main Street, *c.* 1918. Family members are, from left to right, Rebecca Cesan, Emily Cesan, Paul Cesan, Louisa Chisolm Cesan, Rev. James J. Cesan, and David Cesan. The house was built in 1911–1912 by Michael L. Ahl, a prominent local mason, general contractor, and manufacturer of artificial stone, to showcase his work. The house was bought by the Cesan family in 1914. In the 1960s, it was owned by the Dalton family, who operated the Dalton Funeral Home from that location until the 1970s. The house was ordered demolished by Agawam mayor Richard A. Cohen in 2003. (Courtesy Anita [Cesan] Rising.)

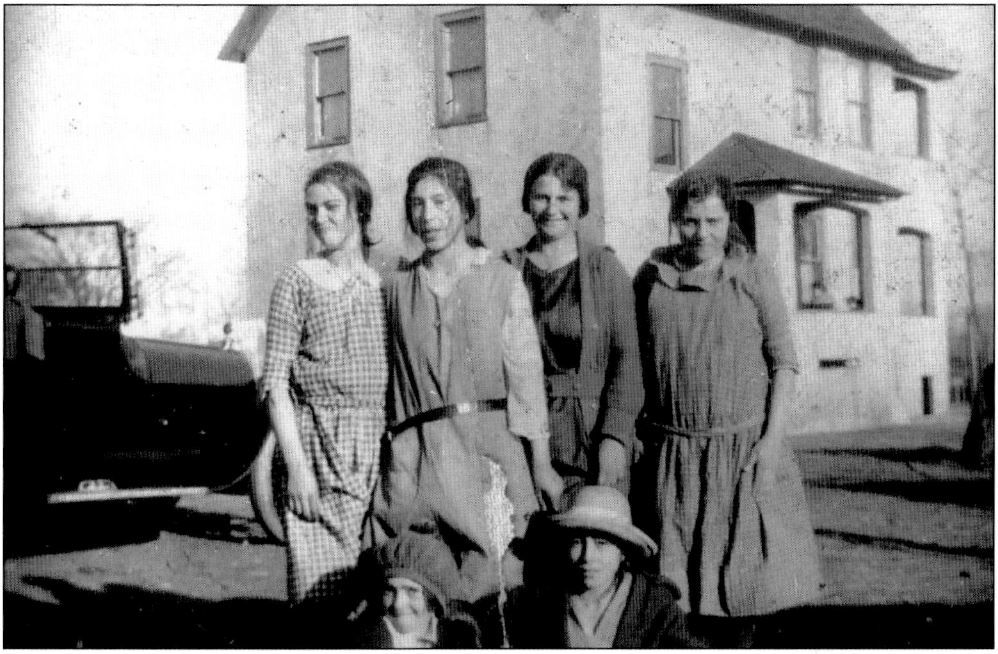

This house at 712 Cooper Street has been home to generations of the Liquori family, and some of them are shown here in the early 1920s. From left to right are the following: (first row) Nancy (Calabrese) Barbero and Nancy (Liquori) Scibelli D'Amato; (second row) Filomena (Calabrese) Albano, Rosie (Calabrese) Raschilla, Mary (Liquori) Surridge, and Mary (Decaro) D'Agostino. (Courtesy Liz Ciurleo.)

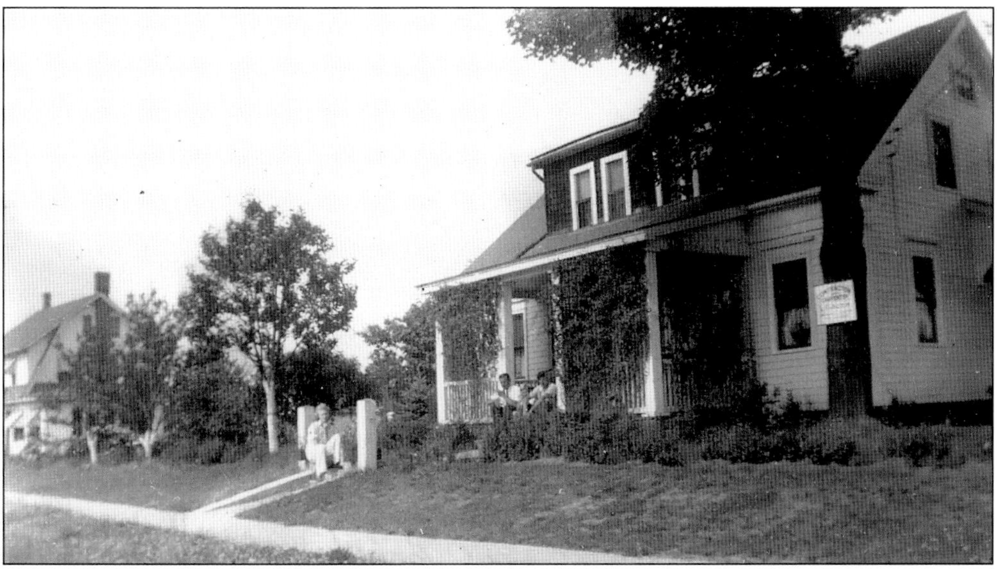

This photograph of Lucas Subotin's home, at 1141 Main Street, was taken on September 10, 1923. The sign on the tree reads, "Contractor and Carpenter L. Subotin." The house on the left is 1129 Main Street. Both homes are still standing. (Courtesy Jennie and Joseph Della-Giustina.)

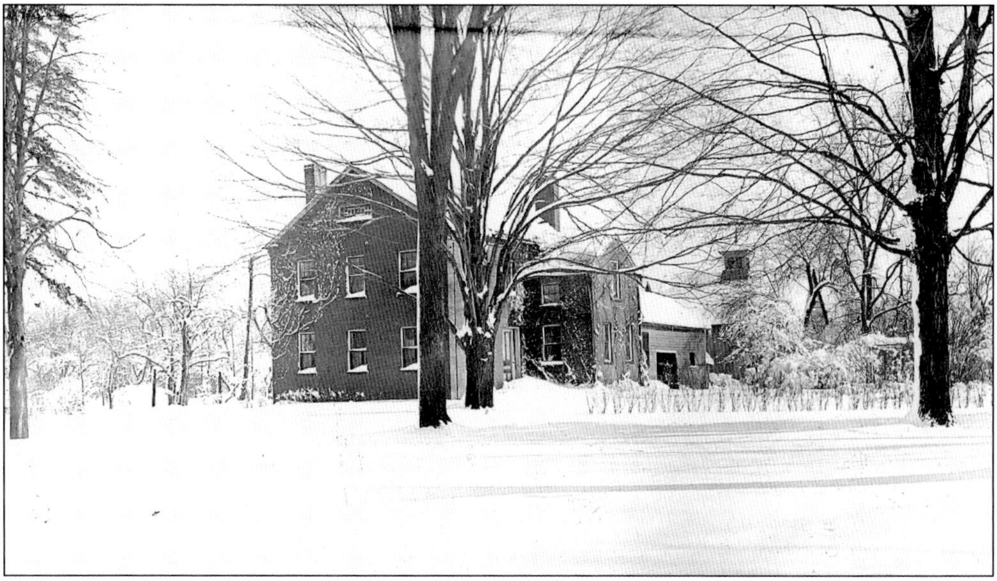

Charles Campbell built this brick house at 769 Main Street in 1841. His grandson Elbert Campbell owned the property when this photograph was taken on February 10, 1932. It was for him that Elbert Road was named when that part of the Campbell Farm was developed by Howard W. Pond. The 1938 hurricane destroyed the large barn seen here, but the house survives. (Agawam Historical Association collection.)

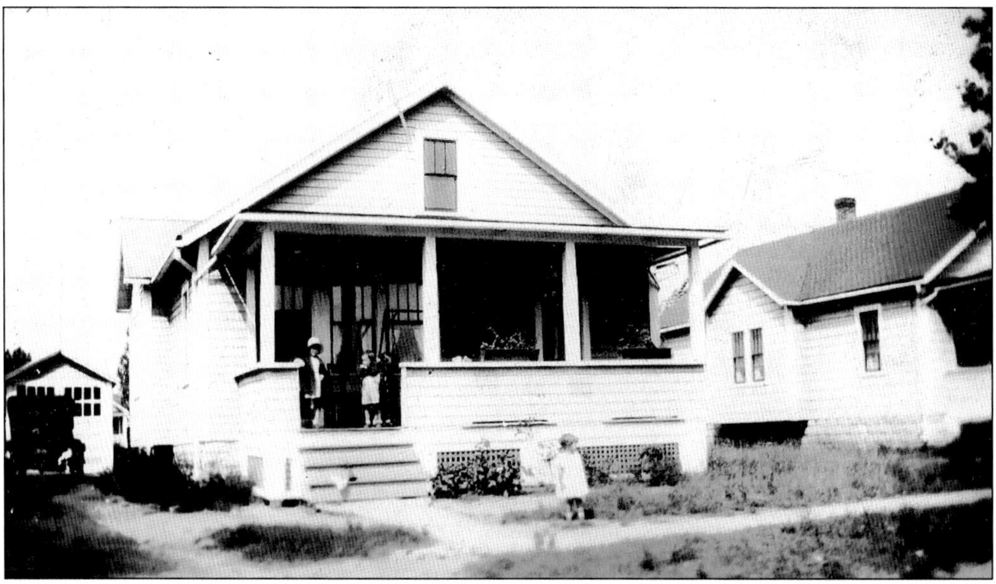

The Haseltine house on Kensington Street is seen here *c.* 1930. Like many neighborhoods, Kensington Street is now a pleasant, tree-shaded road, not the barren place it was when it was first constructed in the Plains section of town. (Courtesy Marian Bradford.)

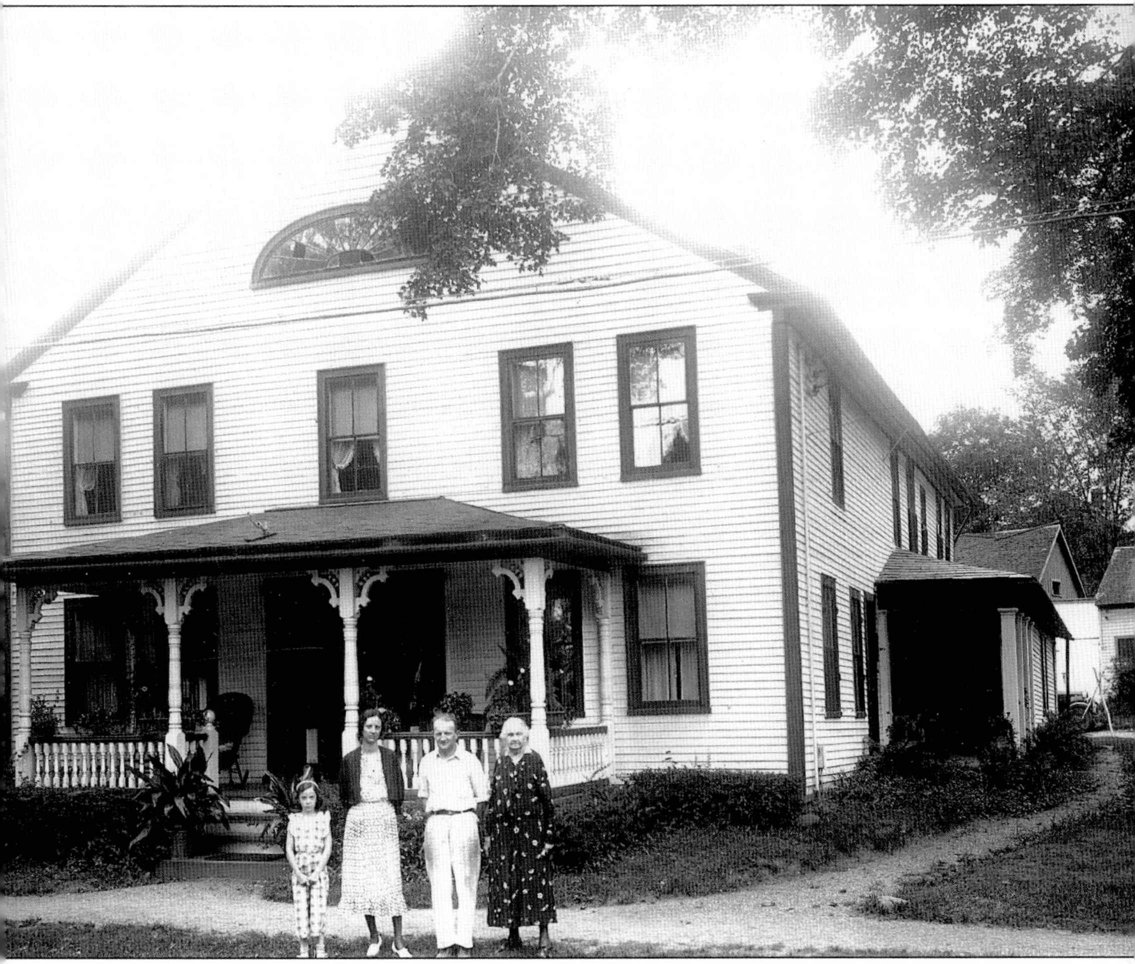

Built in 1750, the Hamilton House (at 2 South West Street) was the first tavern in Feeding Hills Center. In this view, Hamilton family members pose on August 16, 1934. From left to right are Nancy Hamilton, Rose Hamilton, Ray Hamilton, and Grandma Roberts, age 92. This house, rumored to be a stop on the Underground Railroad, was demolished in the 1970s. (Agawam Historical Association collection.)

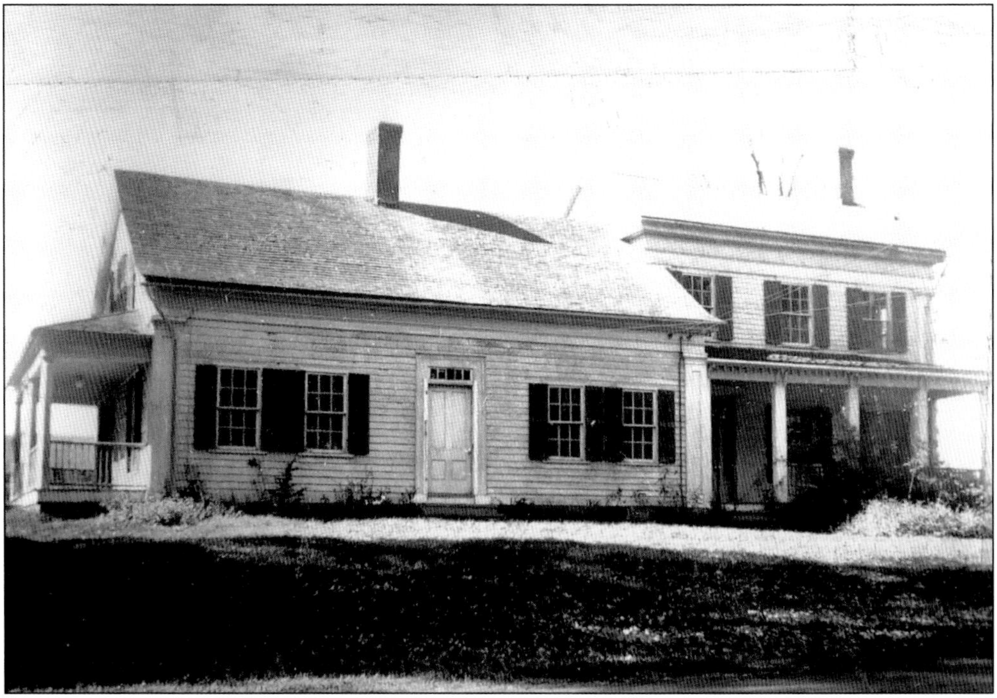

This Federal-style cape, which still stands at 523 North Westfield Street, was built *c.* 1790. The Greek Revival addition was constructed in 1821. The addition was removed in the 1940s, and dormers were added. (Agawam Historical Association collection.)

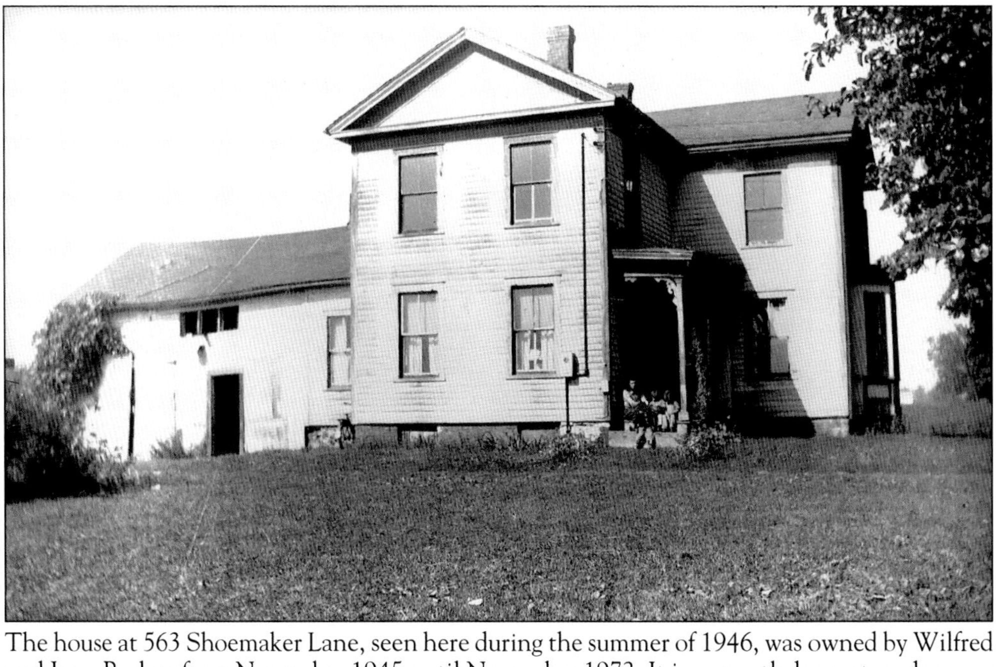

The house at 563 Shoemaker Lane, seen here during the summer of 1946, was owned by Wilfred and Joan Bushey from November 1945 until November 1972. It is currently home to a day-care center. (Courtesy Robyn Kraus-Riccio.)

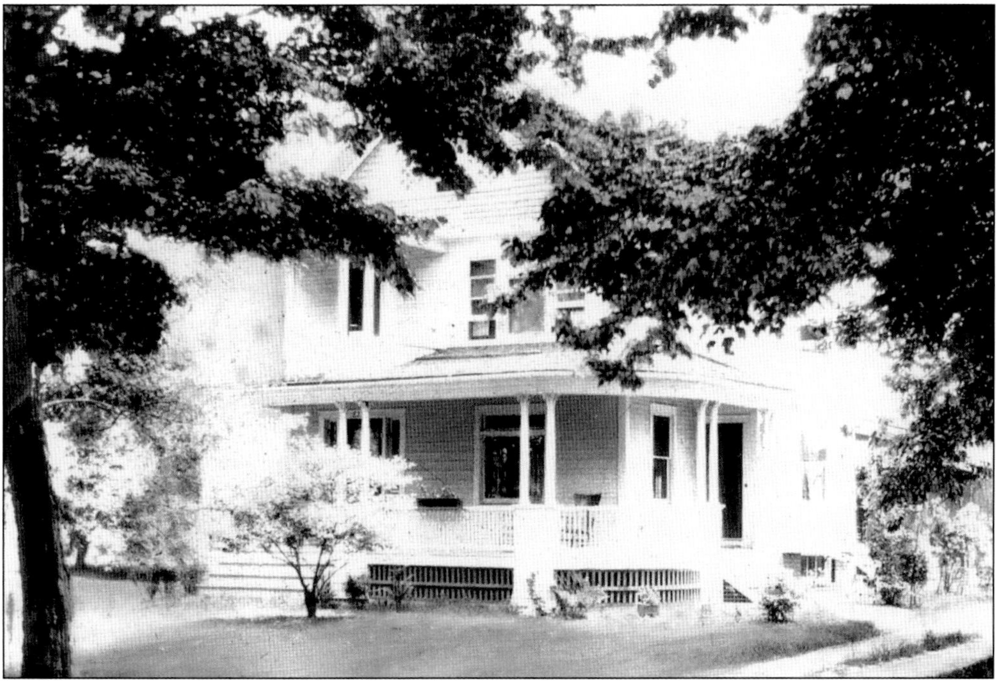

Henry Bodurtha and his family lived in this house at 823 Main Street. It was later purchased by St. John the Evangelist Church for use as a rectory. When land behind the church was purchased for a rectory, this house was demolished to make way for a parking lot. The 817 Main Street home of photographer Charles Dubois Hodges met a similar fate. (Courtesy Jack Bodurtha.)

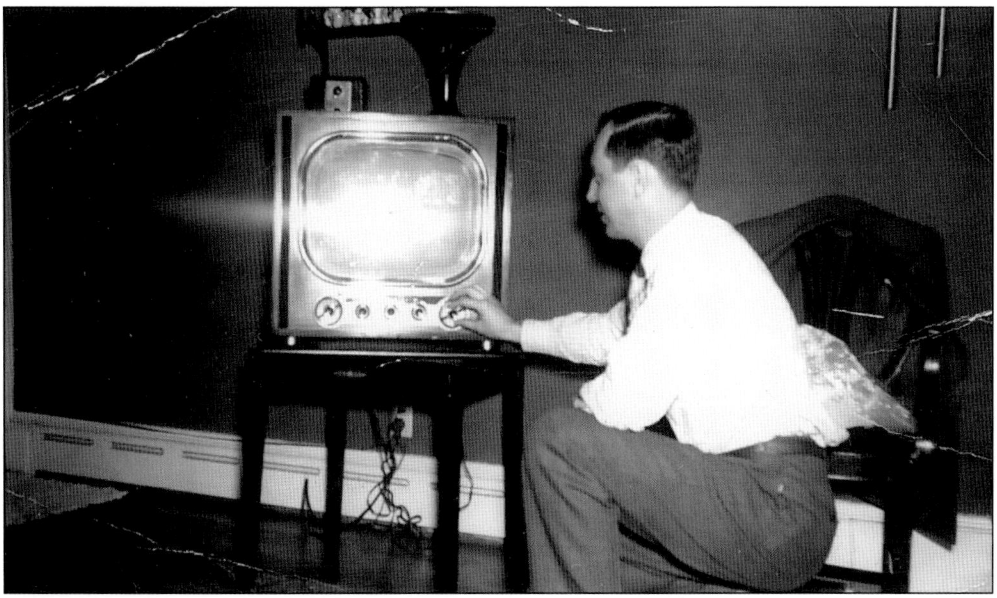

Today, no home is complete without a television, and the bigger, the better. In the days before remote controls (1951), Joseph Della-Giustina adjusts his first television set in the Albert Street home where he still resides. Della-Giustina was very active in town affairs over the years. (Courtesy Jennie and Joseph Della-Giustina.)

The Agawam Historical Association

The Agawam Historical Association was founded on November 15, 1962. It is a nonprofit, tax-exempt organization. Its stated purpose and objectives are to encourage an interest in the collection and preservation of historic materials, documents, and landmarks pertaining to the town of Agawam, Massachusetts; to provide educational opportunities for the dissemination and understanding of facts concerning Agawam's history and the cultivation of civic pride in Agawam's heritage; and to provide facilities for the proper storage, preservation, and public display of historic artifacts and documents.

To that end, the association opened the Agawam Historical & Fire House Museum in May 2002. Memorabilia from Agawam's past is located on the second floor, while the town's 1930 International fire truck and other fire department artifacts are housed on the first floor. The museum is located at 35 Elm Street in the Agawam Center Historic District. Please call 413-789-4631 for more information about exhibits and programs.

The Agawam Historical Association hosts informative and interesting speakers at its four meetings each year, with one fall meeting, a winter meeting, and two spring meetings, one of which incorporates the association's annual meeting.

Membership is open to all, and there is an affordable dues schedule with rates for individuals, families, and seniors. Please send all correspondence and membership inquiries to the Agawam Historical Association, P.O. Box 552, Agawam, Massachusetts, 01001.

As a volunteer organization, the Agawam Historical Association is always interested in anyone willing to donate time, artifacts, or resources. Please contact us at the address above.

The Thomas Smith House

The house pictured on page 8 has been owned by just a handful of families since it was built. Owned for the last half of the 20th century by the Rosenberg family, who purchased it from the family who had owned it for the first half of the 20th century, the Hawthornes, the house managed to slip through time amid all the advancements of the past 250 years. There is no central plumbing, no central heat, and only the most primitive electric service to the main house. Many original features remain.

The Massachusetts Historical Commission (MHC) Preservation Planning Division, described it as "a remarkably intact survival of what probably was a very typical, but largely disappeared regional building form . . . a rare and unusually well-preserved late 18th century, story-and-a-half, gambrel-roofed house." In December 2004, MHC voted the house eligible for inclusion on the National Register of Historic Places.

The house was long thought to have been built by Mathew Noble in 1715. The historical association purchased it from the heirs of longtime member John Rosenberg in June 2002 with plans to preserve the structure. Research undertaken on behalf of the historical association has revealed that the structure was most probably not built by Noble but by local housewright and carpenter Thomas Smith *c.* 1757.

The association has engaged the services of a historic preservation consultant to create a master preservation plan so that the house may someday be opened to the public. Before that time, however, an enormous amount of work must be done to stabilize and prepare the structure. In the same way that proceeds from *Agawam and Feeding Hills* helped to fund the renovation of the Agawam Historical & Fire House Museum, proceeds and royalties from the sale of this book will be used to create an endowment fund for the Thomas Smith House. If you would like more information about the Thomas Smith House or would like to contribute to its preservation in any way, please contact the Agawam Historical Association at P.O. Box 552, Agawam, Massachusetts, 01001. Thank you for your support.

Sources

Agawam Center National Register Historic District Nomination. Bonnie Parsons, Tammy Peters, Pioneer Valley Planning Commission.

Agawam Centennial Picture Album, Centennial Souvenir Booklet, 1955.

Agawam Historical Association. *Registration of Old Homes and Old Buildings in Agawam*, 1962.

Agawam, Massachusetts: Over the Span of a Century, 1855–1955. Centennial souvenir booklet, 1955.

"Agawam's 100th Birthday." *Springfield Sunday Republican*, July 10, 1955.

Archives of the Agawam Historical Association.

Archives of the Agawam Police Association.

Cecchi, David R. *Agawam and Feeding Hills*. Charleston, South Carolina: Arcadia Publishing, 2000.

———. *A History of the Cecchi Family Farm, 1946–1986*. Rhode Island School of Design degree project, 1986.

Chicopee District Telephone Directory. New England Telephone and Telegraph Company, 1959.

Harrison, Shirley, and Clyde Pomeroy. Scrapbooks of articles and photographs from the 1920s through the 1950s.

Hastings, Harry W. *Chowder without Tomato: An Anecdotal Chronicle of Life in a New England Village Seventy Years Ago*. Ann Arbor, Michigan: University Microfilms, 1966.

Granville, J. I. *Farmers Take Flight*. Springfield, Massachusetts: Gee Bee Publishing, 2000.

LaFrancis, Edith. *Agawam, Massachusetts*. Town of Agawam, 1980.

National Archives.

Springfield's Ethnic Heritage: The Italian Community. U.S.A. Bicentennial Committee of Springfield, 1976.

Springfield Suburban Directories. H. A. Manning Company, 1928, 1949.

Whitehead, Russell F. *White Pine Series*, Vol. XI, No. 4, 1925.

www.aerofiles.com.